PRESIDENTIAL TERM LIMITS
IN AMERICAN HISTORY

*Joseph V. Hughes Jr. and Holly O. Hughes Series
on the Presidency and Leadership*

James P. Pfiffner, General Editor

PRESIDENTIAL TERM LIMITS IN AMERICAN HISTORY

POWER, PRINCIPLES & POLITICS

Michael J. Korzi

Texas A&M University Press   *College Station*

This paper meets the requirements
of ANSI/NISO Z39.48-1992
(Permanence of Paper).
Binding materials have been chosen for durability.

Library of Congress Cataloging-in-Publication Data

Korzi, Michael J., 1969–
Presidential term limits in American history : power, principles, and politics /
Michael J. Korzi. — 1st ed.
p. cm. — (Joseph V. Hughes Jr. and Holly O. Hughes series
on the presidency and leadership)
Includes bibliographical references and index.
ISBN-13: 978-1-60344-231-2 (cloth : alk. paper)
ISBN-10: 1-60344-231-6 (cloth : alk. paper)
ISBN-13: 978-1-60344-280-0 (e-book)
ISBN-10: 1-60344-280-4 (e-book)
1. Presidents—Term of office—United States—History.   2. Executive
power—United States—History.   3. Roosevelt, Franklin D. (Franklin Delano),
1882–1945. 4. United States. Constitution. 22nd Amendment.
I. Title.   II. Series: Joseph V. Hughes, Jr. and Holly O. Hughes series
on the presidency and leadership.
JK550.K67   2011
352.23'267—dc22
2010034328

For William & Samuel

CONTENTS

ACKNOWLEDGMENTS

This book got its start a decade ago. Griffin Hathaway, a friend and colleague—not to mention a strong supporter of President Clinton—was trying to divine ways for the president to remain in office beyond the two terms allowed by the Twenty-second Amendment. We discussed some of the possible loopholes and technicalities—all rather fanciful—that would allow Clinton to serve more than two terms, but also debated the efficacy of the Twenty-second Amendment. Increasingly, my thoughts would return to the question of presidential tenure, and within a few years I was starting to delve into the issue. I subsequently discovered that very few scholars had written about the Twenty-second Amendment and that very little work had been done on presidential tenure in general. What had been done was also outdated, much of it having been written in the 1940s and 1950s. At this point my colleague at Towson University, Martha Kumar, suggested that a book-length treatment of the issue was warranted, and encouraged me to pursue the project in earnest. Thanks both to Griff and Martha for helping to push the book along at critical points.

I would like to thank Towson University for its generous support of this project. Much of the research, and some of the writing, was completed during 2006, thanks to a research fellowship in the summer and sabbatical leave in the fall. My colleagues in the political science department at Towson University deserve special notice. Not only are they a congenial bunch, but their high intellectual and scholarly standards are an important source of inspiration and motivation.

It has been a pleasure working with Texas A&M University Press. The series editor, James Pfiffner, was readily accessible and encouraging, particularly during the early stages of the process. Editor-in-chief Mary Lenn Dixon was an excellent guide and great communicator, keeping me apprised of the process and expectations all along the way. The outside reviewers were not only prompt in returning their assessments, but each offered considerable insights that improved the final product. Thanks also to Chris Dodge for an excellent job in editing the manuscript.

It is hard to imagine having a more supportive family. My mother and father never failed to take an interest in my work and were always a source of encouragement. My wife Dawn endured my many hours of researching and writing, with patience, support, and aplomb. Her sacrifices of time and energy undoubtedly hastened the completion of this book. My sons—William and Samuel—to whom the book is dedicated, often took me away from the book and into the worlds of baseball, skateboarding, and bike riding, but I always returned to the project refreshed and reinvigorated, with a sense of balance and perspective.

Portions of the chapters have been published elsewhere and are used with permission: "Theorizing Presidential Tenure: The Difficult Case of FDR's Fourth Term," *Congress and the Presidency* 35, no. 2 (Autumn 2008), courtesy of the Taylor and Francis Group; and "Changing Views of Executive Tenure in Early American History," *White House Studies* 8, no. 3 (2009), courtesy of Nova Science Publishing.

PRESIDENTIAL TERM LIMITS
IN AMERICAN HISTORY

INTRODUCTION

Democracy, Power, and Presidential Tenure

> *Concerns about presidential perpetuation in office are as old as presidentialism itself; they followed naturally from the preoccupation among the founders of America's many republics with maintaining political stability in the absence of monarchy.*
>
> John M. Carey

I n late 2000, soon-to-be-retired President Bill Clinton confessed to what most political observers already knew: that if he were eligible he would have sought a third term as president. Despite losing Democratic control of Congress, jousting with Republicans, and facing an impeachment trial during his two terms in office, Clinton relished the job, had a fair amount of legislative and foreign policy successes, and did not look forward to stepping down. Indeed, polls suggested in 2000 that Clinton would have been competitive for a third term.[1] Clinton, of course, did not seek a third term because he was barred from doing so by the Twenty-second Amendment to the Constitution, ratified in 1951. What is more, there was clearly no emergency situation that might have prompted calls for repeal of the amendment and the retention of Clinton as president.

But the example of Clinton—a term-limited executive pining for a term extension—is not unique in recent years. In late 2001, the Republican mayor of New York, Rudy Giuliani, considered possible means to extend his tenure as mayor beyond the designated two terms. In the face of a resistant state legislature, Giuliani dropped his pursuit of tenure extension. Although Giuliani had the pretext of crisis—the attacks of September 11, 2001—which has long been an argument *against* term limits, his drive to extend his second term was unsuccessful, in part because of the opposition of Democrats in the New York state legislature.[2] Yet, only seven years later, Giuliani's successor as New York mayor, Michael Bloomberg, would convince the New York City Council to pass legislation allowing him to seek a third term in 2009. Bloomberg had begun exploring the idea of a third term early in 2008, but stepped up efforts in the wake of the financial turmoil of September 2008, which, like September 11th did for Giuliani, "gave him an opportunity to argue that his leadership was needed."[3] While Giuliani's argument was unsuccessful, Bloomberg did indeed win a third term, if not by as comfortable a margin as he expected.[4]

Were his popularity not so compromised during his second term, surely George W. Bush (or at least his supporters) would have considered the possibility of a third term and a repeal of the Twenty-second Amendment. After all, there had been a brief—albeit unsuccessful—third-term drive for Ronald Reagan in 1986. And although it is early in his first term, President Barack Obama possesses two key qualities that could augur well for his future: his personal appeal and his age. Only forty-seven years old at the time of his inauguration, Obama would be only fifty-five at the end of a second term. In his victory speech on election night in 2008, Obama already strongly suggested the need for a second term: "The road ahead will be long. Our climb will be steep. We may not get there in one year or even in one term, but America, I have never been more hopeful than I am tonight that we will get there."[5] It is not hard to imagine some of Obama's supporters considering steps to allow him to seek a third term.[6]

Nevertheless, to this point Americans seem to be comfortable, especially at the presidential level, in limiting their executives to two terms.[7] Other countries, however, have recently at least second-guessed, if not reformed, their executive term-limit provisions. Although Russian President Vladimir Putin eventually "swor[e] off amending the constitution to allow himself a third term," for many months there was much speculation that he and his supporters would work to extend his tenure beyond the two terms permitted by the Russian Constitution.[8] In Nigeria, in 2006, a serious attempt was made to amend the constitution to allow sitting president Olusegun Obasanjo to run for a third term. Despite considerable lobbying by Obasanjo himself, opposition lawmakers ultimately marshaled enough support to kill a measure that would have allowed Obasanjo to pursue a third term.[9] In some cases, however, quests for tenure extensions have been successful. In Chad and Uganda, constitutions have recently been amended to allow sitting presidents (Deby and Museveni, respectively) to seek third terms. In 2006 both were reelected to third terms.[10]

Latin America affords several examples of presidents and their supporters amending constitutions in recent years to allow for reelection of the president. As John Carey notes, "Longstanding prohibitions on immediate reelection were overturned in Peru (1993), Argentina (1994), Brazil (1996), and Venezuela (1999)." In the case of Venezuela, Hugo Chavez was elected in 1998 to a presidential term of five years with no chance for reelection. In 1999, Chavez and his supporters effected a change in the constitution—allowing a president two six-year terms—and he was since reelected in 2000 and 2006.[11] Chavez and his supporters tried—and failed—in 2007 to amend the constitution yet again to allow his continued service beyond his current term. Undeterred, they succeeded in a February 2009 referendum to eradicate term limits entirely for the presidency. Chavez subsequently said of the next election (which he would have been barred from participating in prior to the reform) that "[u]nless God decides otherwise, unless the people decide otherwise, this soldier is already a candidate."[12]

Scope of the Inquiry

Presidentialism as it evolved in the United States witnessed key debates at the Constitutional Convention over the tenure of the office of the presidency, during the ratification debates, and episodically ever since. But the debate over *executive*—not specifically *presidential*—tenure is much older than 1787, with strong roots in the seventeenth-century English reaction toward monarchy, particularly that of John Locke in his *Two Treatises of Government.* Not only did Locke reject hereditary monarchy (and hence life tenure for the executive), but he argued for legislative supremacy, that is, executive subordination to the legislature. As Locke put it, the executive "may be at pleasure changed and displaced" by the legislature—quite a departure from life tenure.[13] But while Locke was an opponent of monarchy and strong executive authority, he also sought to limit legislators and the legislative branch.[14] Our early political traditions, as we will see in chapter 2, accord well with these Lockean principles. Colonists often had little control over their royal governors—as they were agents of the English king—so they allied themselves, not surprisingly, with their colonial legislatures. Moreover, when the newly independent states developed gubernatorial offices, they were decidedly limited in terms of power and, importantly, tenure. Nevertheless, like Locke, early Americans were also wary of their legislatures, and sought to limit their power as well, which included limiting the terms of their legislators.

Despite the breadth and reach of the topic of executive tenure, the scope of this book is clearly drawn. While it does not avoid discussion of gubernatorial term limits, nor the examples of executives in other countries,[15] nor the philosophical underpinnings of the tenure debate, the focus here is specifically on the American *presidency* and the deeply conflicted American experience with presidential tenure. Although term limits on *legislative* bodies have some relevance, limiting the terms of a single-member office—which thereby immediately effects a turnover in the office—is substantially different from limiting terms in a multi-member body. In the absence of term limits, the latter will nonetheless experience natural turnover (through resignations, loss of election, and so forth) in its membership; moreover, no one member of a multi-member body is equipped to wield the authority of an executive officer. Thus, the book focuses much of its energy on the American founding and the constitutional debate over *presidential* tenure, the establishment of the "two-term tradition," challenges to that tradition, and the passage of the Twenty-second Amendment to the Constitution. While the book is organized chronologically, it is also tied together theoretically by the democratic tensions or dilemmas that are inherent in questions of executive tenure. Indeed, the presidential tenure debate reflects deep and recurring conflicts—as well as evolving views—in the American belief system over the scope and definition of democracy and, particularly, its proper relationship to leadership. Although clearly a philosophical struggle, the tenure debate also illustrates the not-inconsiderable role of political advantage in the shifting contours of the debate. And however much these questions are first and foremost *American* questions, they not only speak to contemporary American debates over democracy and leadership but to broader debates about leadership in democracies in general. Given the recent trends on the international scene, the American experience may have much to contribute to broad, contemporary debates about executive tenure and leadership in democracies.

It should be noted at the outset that although this book is intended as a theoretical and developmental history—wherein all viewpoints receive their due—I count myself as a somewhat reluctant supporter of the current two-term constitutional limit. Although I refrain from editorializing during the main sections of the book, it will doubtless at times be clear—for instance, in the discussions of Jefferson's decision to step down in 1809 and FDR's pursuit of third and fourth terms—where my loyalties reside. In the concluding chapter, I spend some time explaining and developing my support of the current two-term limitation.

Before developing the major theoretical perspectives of the book, it is important to first define some of the key terms and parameters of the study. It should be clear by now that executive tenure is the focus of the book. However, what is meant by "tenure" and what does it entail? Simply put, tenure is that amount of time that an executive is able to stay in office. As such, there are two critical points of emphasis: 1) the length of term and 2) the rules of reeligibility. In the United States, the question of executive tenure has been fairly straightforward in law, if not theory. The Constitution provided for a four-year term and unlimited reeligibility. This was changed with the Twenty-second Amendment in 1951, which retained the four-year term but allowed reeligibility only once. Presently U.S. presidents are prohibited from seeking a third term, and no president may serve longer than ten years.[16]

Yet this seeming elegance masks a number of nuances and interconnections that require more explanation and elaboration. First, there is nothing sacred about a four-year term, and, in fact, at the time of the Constitutional Convention and since, many have questioned the wisdom of four years. Indeed, the delegates to the Constitutional Convention started off with *seven* years as the desired term length, while the term lengths for state governors at that time ranged from one to three years, with most having a term of one year. Thus, while the four-year term has been entrenched from the beginning, it has not been so without serious opposition and debate. Similarly, reeligibility seems a simple and straightforward concept on its face. However, there are substantial variations among term-limit provisions in American history and throughout the world. The Twenty-second Amendment provides a definite term limit on presidents—two terms with no reeligibility—and this is probably the most straightforward term-limit model. When congressional Republicans won majority control of the House and Senate in the 1994 elections, they were pledged (via the Contract with America) to term limits that would allow members of the House and Senate to serve a total of twelve years (six terms for House members and two terms for senators).[17] After serving their twelve years in a given chamber, members would be prohibited thereafter from serving in that chamber. While the term-limits provisions did not pass, a number of Republicans made pledges to their constituents to only serve a certain number of terms and thereafter "return back to the people," as it were. The key to this type of term limit is a prohibition on serving in the office *ever again* after a certain number of terms. Additionally, this model need not even provide for more than one term. One of the most long-standing reform models for presidential tenure in American history has been a six-year term with no possibility of reelection.

But these examples of term limits only scratch the surface of the many different variations. At the time of the founding of the United States, it was common for governors in the states to be subject to what was then termed "rotation." As we will see in chapter 2, rotation provisions generally required governors, after serving a certain number of terms, to be ineligible to run again until the passage of a specified number of years. The governors would thereby have to "rotate" back into the citizenry for some time before being eligible again for service. But the key point here is that they would not be barred forever thereafter from seeking the office again. Unless there is a change in the Constitution, neither Bill Clinton nor George W. Bush will be able to seek a third term, *ever*. Under provisions of rotation, there is a prohibition of some sort on *consecutive* terms, but generally speaking not the total number of terms. The variety of term limitation can be seen at the state level, with some states allowing their governors unlimited reeligibility, others one or two terms and then no reelection, and still others some form of rotation.[18]

Understanding the variety in tenure restrictions is critical to making informed recommendations for possible reforms today in the United States and elsewhere. What ties all of this variety together, however, is that there are clear rules for length of service in the presidential or executive office. It should be noted that this differs substantially from tenure in a monarchy or authoritarian regime, where the executive's term is indefinite, based upon life span and political fortunes rather than an established time frame. Indeed, the American concern with limiting or restraining the tenure of executives stems directly from the assault on the English monarchy that began in England in the seventeenth century and intensified in America during the Revolution and the constitutional period.

Having defined the subject matter, a final comment on the scope of the inquiry is warranted. While presidential tenure will be our main focus, it will at times be necessary to address and examine other key aspects of the presidency, particularly the election of presidents and presidential powers. What one quickly discovers in examining the issue of executive tenure is the texture and interconnectedness of the issue. While length of term and reeligibility are obviously and inextricably linked aspects of the tenure question, most debates over tenure in American history have also prominently featured discussions of the proper method for electing the executive, the extent of the executive's powers, whether the executive would be assisted by a "council" of some sort, and who would be qualified to serve. The founders of the United States grappled mightily with the interrelationships between method of election, length of term, and reeligibility. And the congressional debate in 1947 over the Twenty-second Amendment brought into sharp relief the connections between presidential powers—which most agreed at the time had grown substantially since the founding—and tenure, with proponents of the amendment contending that it was too dangerous to allow one individual to occupy the presidency longer than eight years, given the growth of presidential power.

DEMOCRACY, POWER, AND THE PROPER PARAMETERS OF LEADERSHIP

The presidential tenure question, while obviously practical, is also fundamentally theoretical. It emerged from debates over the proper scope of executive leadership and especially attempts to make executive offices accountable to the people. Naturally, given the American colonists' experiences with monarchy, the newly independent American states sought to avoid its trappings and thereby set up gubernatorial offices that were not only elected positions—whether directly by the people or by state legislatures—but restrained by short terms and in most cases limits on the amount of terms a governor could serve. Most American states in the aftermath of the Revolution saw democracy and executive power to be in conflict, and thus they erred on the side of making governors strongly accountable to the people while severely limiting their power.

In debates over tenure at the Constitutional Convention, and thereafter in the ratifying conventions, Americans discovered that the issue was not so simple. Rather, there was considerable variety in theories of presidential tenure, with divergent views of democracy, power, and leadership offered. To be sure, many still clung to the longstanding concerns about executive power—and long tenure—undermining democracy, and this perspective finds adherents throughout the sweep of American history. Yet others developed alternative understandings of the relationships between democracy, power, and presidential tenure. Some saw that it was not a matter of having *either* a weak executive tied strongly to the people *or* a strong executive with little restraint or connection to the people, but that there could be a balance.

At the heart of the matter is the ostensible tension between power and democracy. In the classic *Whig* view, executive power is inherently at odds with democracy and must thereby be restrained. In this view, the English monarchy had been unaccountable to the people and un- restrained in tenure, and its power had been awesome and abusive. In response, executives were to be substantially stripped of their powers and made accountable to the people through election, short terms, and term limits. To give power or long tenure to an executive was to invite tyranny. This view dominated the colonial and Revolutionary periods but came under assault at the Constitutional Convention. The *consti- tutional* view that was developed at the Convention did not posit such a strict antinomy between democracy and power. In fact, as Alexander Hamilton would elaborate in *The Federalist,* democracy—especially in the form of short terms and term limits—might hinder the legitimate and necessary exercise of executive power. For Hamilton, a longer term, and hence distance from the people, was often essential to proper leadership. An additional concern for Hamilton was that term limits would deprive the nation of skilled and experienced leadership in a time of crisis. It was thereby necessary to balance the interests of power and democracy. In the framers' minds, a four-year term with unlimited reeligibility— in conjunction with "independent" electors—satisfied this balancing act.[19]

Although this constitutional view would be dominant throughout the nineteenth century, it would face continued opposition from the Whig view—particularly in the form of the two-term tradition established by Jefferson—as well as increasing challenges from what can be termed the *plebiscitary* model.[20] This model would bud in the nineteenth century—as the presidency not only grew in power but became more fully democra- tized—and would flower in the twentieth century. The plebiscitary model is best expressed in the "stewardship" theory of the presidency articulated by Theodore Roosevelt in the early twentieth century.[21] Here a president would be strongly linked to public opinion *and* would be the powerful center of the political system. Rather than balancing democracy and power, the plebiscitary model marries them, envisioning a president who draws power from the people and acts on their behalf. The plebiscitary model is Hamiltonian in the sense that the presidency is a powerful office, and especially necessary in times of crisis, but it avoids Hamilton's cynical view of the people and the need to check their influence on the presidency. Moreover, the plebiscitary model envisions a much stronger role for the president in the legislative process. This model of leadership would in many ways reach its fulfillment in the presidency of Theodore Roosevelt's cousin, Franklin Roosevelt.

We will see throughout American history that the terms of the tenure debate often follow these theoretical models. Despite the twentieth-century dominance of the plebiscitary model of executive leadership, the Whig and constitutional models would maintain an important presence in debates over presidential tenure. Indeed, the debates over the Twenty-second Amendment would reveal a strong residual of Whig philosophy in the Republican Party and in the promotion of the two-term limit as constitutional rule.

PLAN OF THE BOOK

The narrative begins in chapter 2 with coverage of the origins of the executive tenure question, first examining pre-constitutional views of executive tenure. Here the focus is on colonial governorships and especially the state governorships created in the wake of the American Revolution. The dominant view of executive tenure in these years—the Whig view—is developed and explicated. This view would find a strong challenge at the Constitutional Convention with the creation of the American presidency, a powerful office with a long term—for the time period—and no limits on reeligibility. This constitutional view is also explained and developed. A discussion of several additional ideal-typical models of executive leadership and their provisions on tenure—including the plebiscitary model—rounds out the chapter.

Chapter 3 examines the development and consolidation of the two-term tradition in the United States, while also noting the several unsuccessful challenges to the tradition in the nineteenth and early twentieth centuries. The chapter covers the modification of the constitutional view through the informal two-term tradition, reflecting something of a concession to the continuing power of the Whig view. Declining to seek a third term in 1808, Jefferson founded the two-term tradition, advancing a clear Whig rationale for a decision that would be followed by his immediate successors Madison and Monroe, and later Jackson. By the 1830s, the two-term tradition would be fully in place, with the Whig Party pushing even further in the direction of presidential restraint through advocacy of a one-term presidency. Despite this general antipathy toward more than two terms, there would be challenges to the tradition even before FDR's shattering of it in 1940. This chapter looks briefly at the campaigns of Ulysses Grant and Theodore Roosevelt for third terms, as well as the debate surrounding Calvin Coolidge's decline of a third-term pursuit in 1928.[22]

These challenges were but a prelude to the 1940 election, the subject of chapter 4, when Franklin Roosevelt not only challenged but successfully defied the two-term tradition. Held in the midst of a growing war in Europe, the 1940 election would bring to the fore questions of presidential tenure that had largely laid dormant since the Constitutional Convention. Most important was the question of "crisis leadership," a key aspect of the debate over tenure since the beginning. Much like Hamilton had argued in *The Federalist,* supporters of Roosevelt argued that it would be folly to deny the country the experienced hand of a leader during an emergency or time of crisis. Critics worried that the war was just an excuse for Roosevelt to continue in the presidential office and that it represented just another example of a troubling trend toward escalating presidential power. FDR would win the election, of course, and successfully lead the United States through World War II, offering a powerful example of the wisdom of long presidential tenure and unlimited reeligibility.

Chapter 5 examines a rather neglected chapter in the annals of American history: FDR's pursuit of a fourth term. While it is often treated as an afterthought—FDR had already shattered the two-term tradition in 1940—this election is important, especially for our purposes, because it arguably illustrates well the concerns of the Whig view with long presidential tenure. As FDR's third term advances the case for long presidential tenure, so does his fourth term point in the other direction. Diagnosed with alarmingly high blood pressure and congestive heart failure in early 1944, FDR and his supporters nonetheless pushed on for the fourth term. Not only was FDR forced to severely curtail his work schedule in 1944 and early 1945 due to his illness (he died during the second week of April 1945), he played little role in the selection of vice presidential nominee Truman and did almost next to nothing to inform Truman of the administration's policies—foreign or domestic—after he had won the election. The poor decision making and insularity of the Roosevelt administration in 1944 and 1945 raise important questions about the wisdom of long presidential tenure.

The elections of 1940 and 1944 were the inspiration for the Twenty-second Amendment to the Constitution, the focus of chapter 6. Passed by Congress in 1947 and ratified by the requisite number of states in 1951, the amendment has had a peculiar history. On the one hand, it was and still is controversial, often considered to be predominantly, if not exclusively, the result of partisan pique, payback for Roosevelt's stunning success at election time. Moreover, its critics see in it considerable recklessness, as it may deny Americans a trusted and experienced leader—like Roosevelt—in time of crisis. On the other hand, the amendment is little remarked upon and little studied. Even at the time of its passage, the amendment was scarcely covered in the newspapers, even in the "paper of record," the *New York Times*. What is more, despite some serious concerns by scholars and observers at the time, the amendment was accepted with almost no public resistance and has quickly become one of the settled facts of the U.S. presidency. This chapter follows the amendment from its passage to the current day, offering a reassessment of sorts. It shows that the Republican proponents of the amendment, whatever the virtues of their position, were undoubtedly tapping into a strong theoretical strain in their party's—and America's—heritage, namely, the Whig view of executive power. While partisans throughout American history have shifted their tenure beliefs based upon political calculation, the amendment should at the very least be understood to partially reflect longstanding American principles and values.

Chapter 7, the final chapter, begins with a brief look at the legacy of the Twenty-second Amendment, focusing especially on one of the central criticisms of the amendment's opponents: that it would produce "lame duck" second-term presidents. The evidence, as we will see, is not unambiguous, but generally the lame duck status of a president seems not to have a substantial impact on the power of a president. But, as the lame duck criticism does not exhaust the ostensible problems with the Twenty-second Amendment, the merits of various reform proposals are considered. Arguments for repealing the Twenty-second Amendment and allowing unlimited reeligibility, especially with the backdrop of international uncertainty and the consequent need for experienced and strong presidential leadership, are addressed. Also discussed are two possibilities for reform: changing to one non-renewable term of six years or allowing rotation in the presidency (that is, reeligibility after vacating the office for one or two terms). Despite the considerable attractiveness of the idea of rotation, the chapter concludes that the status quo, a constitutional prohibition on more than two terms, whether consecutive or not, is ultimately the best way to balance the competing interests of democracy and of presidential power and ambition.

EXECUTIVE TENURE IN

EARLY AMERICAN HISTORY

*If we judge from the experience of all other countries, and
even our own, we may conclude that, as the President of
the United States may be reelected, so he will.*

George Mason, Virginia Ratifying Convention, 1788

D ebates over executive tenure in general revolve around concerns
over power and democracy and the perceived relationship of
tenure to these values. Prior to the debate at the Constitutional Convention in 1787, it was standard to assume that long tenure
in an executive office without "rotation" or term limits was inconsistent
with democratic ideals. This *Whig* view of the executive emerged from
the English struggle between Parliament and the monarchy during the
seventeenth century and is perhaps best articulated in John Locke's *Two
Treatises of Government*.[1] Although I will cover later in the chapter some
nuances of Locke's theory of executive power, his legacy to American
political thinkers and politicians is primarily his wariness of executive
authority. For our purposes here, this Whig view embraces limited tenure
in office for executives.

Jefferson perfectly embodied this traditional, or Whig, view. In a well-
known letter to James Madison, Jefferson commented on the lack of
presidential term limits in the proposed constitution. He observed that
"[e]xperience concurs with reason in concluding that the first magistrate
will always be re-elected if the constitution permits it."[2] Jefferson saw it as
a question of a long-serving president consolidating power and wielding it
in corrupt ways, against the interests of democracy and the people. From
the Whig perspective, long executive tenure was practically synonymous
with monarchy, which was, of course, synonymous with tyranny and

abuse of power. The Whig perspective also viewed leadership in a more collective sense and thereby encouraged multiple centers of leadership, and especially sought to avoid the temptation of "indispensable" leadership. Short terms and term limits, including the idea of rotation—which will be discussed more fully later—sought to address these concerns.

What the delegates to the Convention discovered was that there would be no neat dichotomy: that short terms and limits did not necessarily mean a democratic and less powerful (or even viable) executive, nor did a long-serving, reeligible executive naturally connote an anti-democratic tyrant. Alexander Hamilton best encapsulated the new view in *The Federalist*. He saw the possibility of a long-serving president nobly wielding power in times of crisis, arguing against "banishing men from stations in which, in certain emergencies of the state, their presence might be of great moment to the public interest or safety."[3] And he and other delegates also saw democratic claims as the *justification* for unlimited reelection of a president. In this view, the people could be trusted to elect good leaders (even if for numerous terms) who would keep the people's interests, not their own, in mind—sometimes even by acting against the immediate desires of the public.[4]

Guided by this conceptual focus on power and democracy, this chapter examines the tenure debate from the colonial through the constitutional periods. It addresses colonial as well as state gubernatorial tenure restrictions and pays particular attention to the debates surrounding presidential tenure at the Constitutional Convention. The chapter concludes with a two-dimensional theoretical table to help focus the connections between power, democracy, and executive tenure historically and contemporarily.

HISTORICAL ROOTS: THE COLONIAL GOVERNORS

While an evolutionary study of theoretical views of executive tenure in early American history is relatively uncharted ground, there is an extensive literature on the political ideas of the Revolutionary and Founding generations.[5] Moreover, a number of works are devoted, at least in part, to examining American views of executive power, including their views on executive tenure.[6] Although what follows is heavy on interpretation of primary documents, this extensive scholarship on the Revolutionary and constitutional periods and the American presidency guides and shapes the analysis.

When creating the office of the presidency under the Constitution, the founders looked to the state governors for guidelines on powers, length of term, reeligibility, and so forth. But, state gubernatorial offices were not invented out of whole cloth in the wake of independence; however much they departed from the colonial tradition, the offices were nevertheless rooted in the mores and structures of colonial governorships. And there was substantial variety among these colonial governorships, some of them offering distinct models for the independent state governorships created in the 1770s and 1780s.

Most of the variety in colonial governorships came from the different types of colonies: royal, charter, and proprietary. While all of the governors in the colonies in theory served at the pleasure of the king, the reality was quite different, depending on the type of colony and the point in time. As a general rule, the governors of the proprietary and charter colonies were more accountable to the people and the legislatures of those colonies, in some cases being directly elected for short terms with ineligibility after a certain number of terms. Furthermore, colonial governors were often more accountable to the people—and hence less "royal"—in the early period of colonial development, namely the seventeenth century. Over time, English kings would increasingly exert control over not just the royal colonies but the charter and proprietary colonies as well. As Greene put it in his classic volume:

> In 1763 the royal government was the predominant type in the English colonies which were later to become the United States of America. Of the twelve colonial governments, eight belonged to the class of royal or provincial governments, and two were proprietary governments, and two were chartered colonies with elective governors. This condition was, however, the result of very gradual development, inasmuch as the policy of direct control by the crown was finally adopted only after a long period, during which it was the rule to intrust the government, as well as the soil of the colonies, to proprietors or colonizing companies. . . . *So, too, the form and the powers of the colonial executive were not fixed from the start, but were adopted after various experiments with other forms, and were the result of a gradual limitation of powers at first vague and undefined.*[7]

The "popular" nature of the colonial governorship can be most clearly seen in the early constitutions and provisional governments of the New England colonies, such as Massachusetts, Rhode Island, and Connecticut.

For instance, in a 1632 "Agreement on the Legislature" in the Massachusetts colony, John Winthrop "was chosen to the place of Governor (by the general consent of the whole Court, manefested by erection of hands) for this yeare next ensueing, & till a newe be chosen."[8] Here we have a very early example of an executive being chosen by the "people"—to be sure an elite group of them—and serving for merely one year. The founding-era mantra, often voiced by the Anti-Federalists, that "when annual elections end, tyranny begins" thus had a long pedigree and not just in relation to legislators but also to executives. A later codification of Massachusetts law in 1641, "The Massachusetts Body of Liberties," would reaffirm yearly elections: "It is the constant libertie of the freemen of this plantation to choose yearly at the Court of Election out of the freemen all the General officers of this Jurisdiction. . . . By General officers we meane, our Governor, Deputie Governor, Assistants, Treasurer, Generall of our warres."[9]

And this was not limited to Massachusetts. In "Organization of the Government of Rhode Island," a 1642 document, we find that "Mr. Will'm Coddington is chosen Governour for one whole yeare, or till a new be chosen."[10] Similarly, Connecticut decreed in 1639 that the governor would be chosen "for the yeare ensueing and vntil another be chosen, and noe other Magestrate to be chosen for more then one yeare." Furthermore, the document "[o]rdered, sentenced, and decreed that noe prson be chosen Gouernor aboue once in two years."[11] Here in the early establishment of New England colonies, then, we see a distinct trend toward holding executives—not just legislators—accountable to the people of the colony, especially by limiting their tenure. Over time, kings would exert more and more control over these executives.

In most of the other colonies outside of New England, democratic accountability for the executive was absent. For example, New York's governorship is described thusly in a 1683 "Charter of Liberties and Privileges": THAT The Supreme Legislative Authority under his Majesty and Royall Highness James Duke of Yorke Albany &c Lord proprietor of the said province shall forever be and reside in a Governour, Councell, and the people mett in General Assembly."[12] While the General Assembly would be elected, the governorship was established "at the pleasure of his

Royall Highness his heires or Successours."[13] Similarly, in Pennsylvania, there were clearly defined governors, such as William Penn, who would maintain the governorship until their death or when it was passed on to their heirs. In more strictly "proprietary" colonies, such as Virginia and Georgia, it was the custom for these colonies to appoint governors via a council residing in England.[14] In general, though, the difference between "royal" and "proprietary" governors was that "in the one the governor received his authority from a quasi-feudal dignitary or body of proprietors, while in the other he received his authority from the crown."[15]

It is important to note that even in colonies such as Virginia, a proprietary colony with a governorship responsible to an English council, democratic forms did spring up from time to time. For instance, after 1652, Virginia was "left largely to itself, having for a few years an elective government. In this period the governor and council were chosen by the assembly, which had become the real source of authority within the colony."[16] This experiment, however, would be short-lived, and outside control of the governorship would be reasserted. Similarly, even though most colonial governors were appointed either by the king or a proprietary council, this did not mean that someone from outside of the colony always would be chosen. For instance, "in New Jersey, the first governor appointed, after the 'personal union' of that province with the government of New York had been broken, was Lewis Morris, a representative colonist."[17] Although not widespread, these types of actions belie the notion that "appointive" governors were necessarily insulated and removed from their colonists. What is more, the open-ended tenure of the provincial governors did not necessarily translate into long-serving governors. Indeed, a governor's position was dependent on matters such as partisan politics in England, conflicts between the Crown and the colonies, and the death of the king, at whose pleasure the appointive governors served.[18] While some governors served until death, many did not, and it was not unusual for the average term of governors in a given colony to be well below ten years.[19]

In general, then, the colonies had two major forms of governor: elective and appointive, with the latter being far more prominent. Nevertheless, when the colonies declared independence in 1776, they did have experiences to draw upon with elective governorships, particularly the prominent elective governorship of Massachusetts, which was undoubtedly a model for the new state constitutions crafted in the wake of the

Revolution. Additionally, the colonists had had considerable experience in all of the colonies with legislatures and legislators accountable to the people through popular election, relatively short terms of service, and, often, term limits.

<h2 style="text-align:center">INDEPENDENCE AND THE CREATION OF STATE GOVERNORSHIPS</h2>

Given that the American Revolution was fueled by Whiggish opposition to monarchical authority, and strongly influenced by Locke's idea of legislative supremacy,[20] the new state constitutions[21] "deprived the executive of its political independence and nearly every power that smacked of royal prerogative."[22] Most importantly for our purposes, state governors' tenure in office—and the method of their selection, always closely linked to tenure—would be similarly restrictive. Nearly all of the states prior to the Constitutional Convention established executive offices that were short in term, some of them being term limited, and many states also provided for legislative selection of the governor as well as an executive council[23] to further restrain governors. Thach put it well in characterizing state constitution-building in the wake of the Revolution: "Short terms, strict limitations on reeligibility, and election by the legislature were the outstanding characteristics of the chief magistracy."[24]

New Hampshire's constitution of January 1776, even prior to independence, set the tone for the next decade of state constitutional development. After the departure of New Hampshire's governor, John Wentworth, it was necessary "for the preservation of peace and good order" to establish a new government. This government would consist of a House of Representatives—the colonial legislature of New Hampshire—and a "Council" to be chosen by the House of Representatives. The Council would then select from among its number a president, and the Council and its president would serve for one year. Although the powers of the government were underdeveloped and in fact mixed—the Council, while executive in some ways, also formed the second branch of the legislature—the colonists of New Hampshire were clear in the view of executive power: it was to be constrained through legislative selection and short terms.

Not long after New Hampshire, in March 1776, South Carolina followed with a similar constitutional declaration. After listing a litany of offenses by the English parliament and king against the colonies, a "legislative council" was discussed—a small body of thirteen to be chosen from the "general assembly." A "president and commander-in-chief" would then be chosen "by ballot from among themselves [assembly and council], or from the people at large." All of the members of the government would serve two-year terms; there is no mention of limitations on reelection. The president was also to be restricted by a "privy council." As with New Hampshire, South Carolina's government mixed executive and legislative functions far more than would the U.S. Constitution a decade later. Despite this mixing of powers, the executive was nonetheless restrained, being elected most likely by the assembly and legislative council and serving for merely the duration of the legislative session—two years. While the governor was given a veto power, a rarity among the states (only New York and Massachusetts would also give governors a veto power), it would be deleted from the constitution two years later in 1778.[25]

The Virginia constitution, which followed in June 1776, was much more refined and philosophical and was particularly careful to distinguish between separate branches of government with different and distinct powers. The extensive document begins with an exposition of the rights of citizens—the famed "Virginia Declaration of Rights" that would form the model for Jefferson's Declaration of Independence—among which is that state officials "should, at fixed periods, be reduced to a private station, return into that body from which they were originally taken." This discussion is then followed by a critique of the British government, particularly King George—this critique also serving as a model for Jefferson—and then finally the different departments of government are explained. The "Governor, or chief magistrate, shall be chosen annually by joint ballot of both Houses . . . [and] shall not continue in that office longer than three years successively, nor be eligible, until the expiration of four years after he shall have been out of that office." The governor also would administer the office with the "advice of a Council of State."

Here with Virginia's early constitution we have a key embodiment of Whig thought in the early period of the Revolution. Not only was the document, at least parts of it, a critical influence on the Declaration of Independence, but, like Massachusetts, Virginia was a leading colony in terms of political ideas and especially political leaders. In the creation of the executive office we see ideas that would strongly influence other states' constitutions and also continue to sustain the Anti-Federalists—a number of whom were prominent Virginians —in their opposition to the presidency under the Constitution of 1787.

Of special note are that the governor would be selected annually by the legislature, not by the people at large, thereby keeping the governor subordinate to the legislature, and the governor would step down after three successive terms and also could not seek the office again for four years after having vacated it. This last provision is a perfect embodiment of the concept of "rotation" that would be an important part of other states' constitutions and the subject of debate especially at the time of ratification in 1787–1788. Rotation, as the Virginia formulation evidences, is a more subtle term-limit provision. It generally does not bar the officeholder from future service; rather, it requires officeholders to take a break and return to the people for a period of time, allowing for a possible return to office after being sufficiently reacquainted with the public and their concerns.

By the end of 1776, many of the former colonies would adopt state constitutions with similar provisions. New Jersey's constitution, following in July 1776, did not provide for rotation but did similarly provide for a governor for one year to be elected by the "Council and Assembly," the two branches of the legislature. The governor would also be assisted by a "privy council."[26] Delaware's constitution of September 1776 provided for legislative selection of the governor ("president or chief magistrate"); it also provided for a three-year term for the governor, slightly out of line with the others. Still, the governor was subject to rotation: he should not be "eligible until the expiration of three years after he shall have been out of that office." The governor also had a privy council, chosen by the legislature, to give advice to the governor "to be laid before the general assembly when called for by them."

These state constitutions, in seeking to restrain executives and empower legislatures, undoubtedly embodied the Whig view of executive authority. Pennsylvania's constitution of September 1776, however, took the Whig view to a new level. As Gordon Wood has written, "a[ll] American Whig writing in the spring of 1776 was filled with a spirit of adventure, but it was in Pennsylvania that the sense of excitement and experimentation attained its greatest intensity." The Pennsylvania constitution of 1776, not surprisingly, was the "most radical constitution of the Revolutionary era."[27] The constitution proved to be quite interesting on several accounts, particularly the unicameral nature of its legislature and, more importantly for our purposes, the institution of a virtually plural executive in its "executive council." While most other states provided for "councils," they were usually either upper chambers of the legislature, which often had some executive functions, or a type of "privy council" giving advice to the governor. In the case of Pennsylvania's executive council, it would wield executive authority along with the "president" or governor. For example, the "president, and in his absence the vice-president, with the council, five of whom shall be a quorum, shall have power to appoint and commissionate judges" and other public officials. This is not merely a governor being advised by a council but is very much a plural executive, wherein executive action often does not occur by the doings of one individual.

The members of the council, however, were not to be selected by the legislature; they were elected directly by the "freemen" of Pennsylvania for three-year terms. There were to be twelve "counsellors" chosen in a staggered manner (that is, like the U.S. Senate), so that while there would be elections annually, only a third of the council's seats would be contested in any given election. The "president" of the council would be chosen annually by "joint ballot of the general assembly and council, of the members of the council." The governor would be selected, then, to an important degree by the legislature, but from a pool of candidates, the "counsellors" already selected by the people. Additionally, "[a]ny person having served as a counselor for three successive years, shall be incapable of holding that office for four years afterwards." Rotation would assure, according to the Pennsylvania constitution, that "more men will be trained to the public business . . . and moreover the danger of establishing an inconvenient aristocracy will be effectually prevented." With Pennsylvania, we see the most dramatic departure from the median colonial governorship model. While many of the former colonies would provide for extensive checks on governors, such as legislative selection, one-year terms, rotation, privy councils, and so forth, in Pennsylvania, "the governor was actually totally eliminated, and replaced by an Executive Council."[28]

Maryland's constitution of November 1776 would be much more in line with the other states. A governor would be chosen "by joint ballot of both Houses" annually. There would be a five-person "Council to the Governor" to provide "advice and consent" on a number of matters and "whose proceedings shall be always entered on record." Moreover, the governor "shall not continue in that office longer than three years successively, nor be eligible as Governor, until the expiration of four years after he shall have been out of that office." North Carolina's constitution of December 1776 also followed the general contours of the other states, excluding Pennsylvania. The legislature "shall by ballot elect a Governor for one year, who shall not be eligible to that office longer than three years, in six successive years." There would also be a "Council of State" composed of seven members, elected by the legislature, "who shall advise the Governor in the execution of his office." Georgia's February 1777 constitution would also break no new ground, providing for legislative selection of the governor annually, to be ineligible for the office "more than one year out of three." Additionally, an executive council was created to advise the governor, also to be chosen by the legislature on an annual basis.

Yet, "as powerfully as . . . [the] anti-executive bias worked in 1776, it quickly began to wane."[29] In particular, New York's constitution of April 1777 would be remarkable in how much it veered from the others *toward* strong executive power and thus away from the Whig model. As Donald Roper has put it, "the desire for a eunuch-type executive" at this time was "understandable, but the exigencies of the moment, with the state a battleground and its heart occupied by the enemy, caused second thought." New York, therefore, created "the first strong governor in the country."[30] A "wise and descreet freeholder of this State shall be, by ballot, elected governor, by the freeholders of this State . . . [and] the governor shall continue in office three years." Not only was the governor selected directly by the people, but the term—three years—was considerably longer than the norm of one year in the other states, with the exceptions of Delaware (three-year term) and South Carolina (two-year term). What is more, neither term limits nor rotation were applied to the office (nor even to legislators). Just as importantly, the New York governing structure did not contain a council that would significantly restrain the governor. A "council," composed of a select number of senators, would aid the governor with appointments, but this would be a far cry from the "executive councils" of other states. The New York governor's powers were also robust, including a modified veto power (exercised in conjunction with state judges) and the powers of commander-in-chief, convening and proroguing the assembly,[31] and granting reprieves and pardons. New York's governor would undoubtedly be the model of most influence on the Convention of 1787.

Vermont's constitution of July 1777 reverted more to the weak executive format. "The Supreme Executive Council of this State, shall consist of a Governor, Lieutenant-Governor, and twelve persons," although they were to be elected popularly rather than by the legislature. Voters would cast ballots for governor and lieutenant-governor and would cast votes for twelve "Councillors," the top twelve assuming the seats. Governors and councilors would be elected yearly as well. The major powers of the governor would be exercised in conjunction with the Council, seven of whom would constitute a quorum. Although there were no term limits and the governor was popularly elected, the one-year term and the Council certainly restrained the executive.

Finally, the Massachusetts constitution of March 1780 would round out the flurry of constitution writing taking place in the wake of independence. (Oddly, Connecticut and Rhode Island did not engage in constitution drafting during this period. Connecticut would not establish its first official constitution—as opposed to its colonial charter—until 1818, and Rhode Island would wait until 1842.) The Massachusetts constitution strongly embraced the idea of separation of powers, and thus it was an important influence on the framers in 1787. It is probably worth mentioning that John Adams played a considerable role in the drafting of the Massachusetts constitution. Adams's admiration of the British system and his concern for the independence of the executive from the legislature[32] are notable in this constitution and obviously somewhat at odds with the Whig view of executive power and leadership. The Massachusetts constitution of 1780 would affirm a popularly elected executive, in keeping with Massachusetts tradition, to be elected yearly with no provision for term limitation. Like New York's governor, the Massachusetts governor would have substantial powers, such as adjourning and proroguing the assembly, vetoing legislation, and granting pardons. However, unlike in New York, most powers would be exercised in conjunction with a "Council," consisting of the lieutenant-governor and "[n]ine counsellors . . . chosen from among the persons returned for Counsellors and Senators . . . by joint ballot of the Senators and Representatives," five of the Council constituting a quorum.[33] At any rate, the Massachusetts constitution in the 1780s "came to represent much of what reformers in other states [now] desired for their own constitutions—a strengthening of the governor at the expense of the legislature, particularly the lower house."[34]

The trends in the states are clear, as Table 1 shows. Most governors were selected by the state legislative bodies and served short terms, often with term limitations of one sort or another, and were further constrained by a council of some type. What is more, they often had few powers of

TABLE 1

SUMMARY OF STATE CONSTITUTIONS
ON EXECUTIVE TENURE AND PROVISIONS

STATE	TERM (YRS)	LIMIT	SELECTION	COUNCIL
New Hampshire	One	None	Legislative	Yes
South Carolina	Two	None	Optional[a]	Yes
Virginia	One	Rotation (3/4)[b]	Legislative	Yes
New Jersey	One	None	Legislative	Yes
Delaware	Three	Rotation (3/3)	Legislative	Yes
Pennsylvania	One	Rotation (3/4)	Legislative	Yes
Maryland	One	Rotation (3/4)	Legislative	Yes
North Carolina	One	Rotation (3/3)	Legislative	Yes
Georgia	One	Rotation (1/2)[c]	Legislative	Yes
New York	Three	None	Popular	No
Vermont	One	None	Popular	Yes
Massachusetts	One	None	Popular	Yes

[a] South Carolina's constitution provided for either legislative or popular election.

[b] Virginia provided for three years of service followed by four years ineligible.

[c] Georgia's rule was that a governor could not serve more than one year out of three.

which to boast. Surely there were outliers, such as Pennsylvania and New York and Massachusetts, but in general the executive offices forged in the wake of independence were weak ones restrained structurally and in terms of power. Generally speaking, one can observe here the emergence of a simple theoretical dichotomy: (executive) power is in opposition to democracy. This is what we have termed the Whig view of executive power. If executives are not held strictly accountable to the people or the people's agents—legislatures—they will amass great power, which they will in short order abuse. Limiting the actual powers of executives is not enough: they need to be frequently elected and either denied reelection or rotated back into the general population regularly. When their terms are too long or they are afforded unlimited opportunities for reelection, or both, they may easily oppress and tyrannize the people. What the framers would discover during the course of their debates at the Constitutional Convention was that the relationship between power and democracy was not so simple.

Before the Constitutional Convention is discussed, however, a brief mention of the Articles of Confederation, adopted in 1781, is warranted. As some trivia buffs take care to note, John Hanson was truly the first president of the United States, for he was first to hold the title "president" (of the Congress) under the Articles of Confederation. There is a trivial point of truth to this: the Articles did provide that the Congress could "appoint one of their number to preside, provided that no person be allowed to serve in the office of president more than one year in any term of three years."[35] But this was certainly not an independent executive office; it was not even on par with the restrained state governors and certainly paled in comparison to the much more independent and powerful presidency created in 1787. What is more, this president was restricted to a one-year term and could only serve one term within any given three years. Coupled with the fact that this "president" oversaw a Congress—a legislature—with very limited powers, the "office" has deservedly been given little attention by presidency scholars. It is worth stressing that the Articles were without question consistent with the anti-executive Whig ethos of the Revolutionary period—indeed, so much so that the executive department of government was basically eviscerated, even more so than in the Pennsylvania model. Even the legislators were limited considerably: members were to be elected annually by state legislatures, could be recalled by their states when desired, and could not serve "more than three years in any term of six years."[36]

CONTESTING REPUBLICANISM: THE CONSTITUTIONAL DEBATE OVER TENURE

Although the Whig view was embodied in these state constitutions and at the federal level with the Articles of Confederation, by the mid 1780s, this view was being seriously reconsidered. Historian Gordon Wood has notably pointed out the complexity of the situation in the 1780s. To be sure, "the problems of war and reconstruction . . . [created] a time of financial confusion and social flux."[37] And the state legislatures and the national government were partly to blame for the problems of the time. The former were considered too powerful, and at times tyrannical, especially with regard to the rights of property, and they were viewed as also partly responsible for the economic downturn of the 1780s.[38] The national government, on the other hand, was seen as feckless and incapable of forging unity among the states. Hamilton, for instance, in *Federalist* #6, articulated the various problems stemming from the "dissensions between the States themselves, and from domestic factions and convulsions" within the states.[39] A major concern was the ability (or willingness) of the states to repay their debts (and thereby assure the commercial development of the new nation), as well as the states' likelihood to come together in the face of "foreign arms and influence."[40]

Yet, Wood points out, despite the political and economic tensions of the 1780s, "[o]n the surface at least the American states appeared remarkably stable and prosperous. . . . Both the Confederation government and the governments of the separate states had done much to stabilize the finances and the economy of the country. The states had already moved to assume payment of the public debt, and the Confederation debt could not be considered serious. Despite a temporary depression in the middle eighties the commercial outlook was not bleak."[41] And still many prominent American leaders—such as Washington, Madison, and Hamilton—became more and more disillusioned with the Whig philosophy of governance that had so influenced and guided them during the Revolutionary fervor. In a certain sense the high expectations embodied in Revolutionary political sentiments proved their own undoing: "because the Revolution . . . represented in fact a utopian effort to reform the character of American society and to establish truly free governments, men in the 1780s could actually believe that it was failing."[42]

By the time of the Constitutional Convention, many Americans had worries about not only the Articles of Confederation but also the structure and power of the state governments. There was great concern that the national government did not possess requisite unity and power. Additionally, a key theme was that legislatures (and even the people themselves) were not always to be trusted; the obverse of this was that executive power had been substantially lacking at both the national and the state levels.[43] There nevertheless remained considerable resistance to strong executives, and thus the Convention delegates spent ample time grappling with the tensions between power (giving the presidency requisite strength) and democracy (making the office sufficiently accountable to the people). The neat and tidy opposition between power and democracy that had guided most states in their constitution building turned out to be a chimera. No longer was it universally accepted Republican practice to bolster legislatures and restrain executives. Democracy was not necessarily at odds with firm executive leadership; indeed, in the view of some convention delegates, democracy would be only salvageable through "independent" executive leadership.[44]

Because of the contested nature of executive power and its relationship to democracy, the debate over presidential tenure at the Convention is fascinating in its texture and also its extended nature. Reeligibility and length of term—the key components of presidential tenure—were intertwined almost inextricably with the method of selection. Presidential tenure was, of course, also related to the powers of the presidency and its interactions with other branches (for example, impeachment), but most important is the method of selecting the president. The debate was tortuous[45]—and somewhat torturous as well—because the delegates, in an impressive display of deliberation, debated many different alternatives and changed their minds frequently, not settling on the final plan until very late in the Convention.

As most students of the U.S. Constitution are aware, two differing plans—the Virginia and New Jersey plans—structured the debate at the Convention. What is interesting about these two divergent plans, however, is that they were virtually indistinguishable when it came to presidential tenure and selecting the president. The Virginia plan resolved that "a National Executive be instituted; to be chosen by the National Legislature for the term of _____ years . . . and to be ineligible a second time."[46] The New Jersey plan resolved that "the U. States in [Congress] be authorized to elect a federal Executive to consist of _____ persons, to continue in office for the term of _____ years, . . . to be ineligible a second time, & removeable by [Congress] on application by a majority of the Executives of the several States."[47] While neither plan offered a length for the term, both were in agreement that the legislature should select the president and that the president should be ineligible to serve beyond one term. It is important to note that the New Jersey plan, in line with more radical post-independence sentiment, did not even endorse a single executive.

Despite no settled number of years for the length of term, early on in the convention (by the middle of June), a seven-year term would be agreed to, and thus the following would be the working model (derived largely from Virginia's plan), that "a National Executive be instituted to consist of a single person, to be chosen by the [National] Legislature for the term of seven years, with power to carry into execution the national laws, to appoint to offices in cases not otherwise provided for—to be ineligible a second time."[48] It would be a month before major debate would center on presidential selection—and thus presidential tenure again. Delegate Charles Pinckney was surprised, though, as he "did not expect this question would again be brought forward; An Election by the people being liable to the most obvious and striking objections."[49]

Gouvernour Morris, however, was particularly opposed to legislative selection: "If the people should elect, they will never fail to prefer some man of distinguished character, or services; some man, if he might so speak, of continental reputation.—If the Legislature elect, it will be the work of intrigue, or cabal, and of faction."[50] Most importantly, Morris and others pointed out, the president could not be independent of the legislature if appointed by it, and "if not independent, usurpation and tyranny on the part of the Legislature will be the consequence."[51] Here we see an obvious expression of the growing distrust of legislatures between 1776 and 1787.

Delegates would not muster support to abandon legislative selection, but the bar against reeligibility would be lifted at this point in the Convention. Morris again would support the revision: ineligibility "tended to destroy the great motive to good behavior, the hope of being rewarded by a re-appointment."[52] However, this would raise many concerns from other members, some like James McClurg suggesting that the president should serve during "good behavior" so as not to be dependent on the legislature for reappointment but still be able to hold office for a long period of time, if performing duties serviceably. Madison would second the concern: an executive who is reeligible would be "tempted to cultivate the Legislature, by an undue complaisance, and thus render the Legislature the virtual expositor, as well [sic] the maker of the laws."[53] George Mason, however, saw this "good behavior" provision as "a softer name only for an Executive for life . . . [and] it would be an easy step to hereditary Monarchy."[54]

Upon reconsideration of the reeligibility provision two days later, the delegates would thoroughly debate the issue and thereby show the strong links between length of term, reeligibility, and method of selection. Morris framed some of the tensions succinctly: he "saw no alternative for making the Executive independent of the Legislature but either to give him his office for life, or make him eligible by the people."[55] James Wilson, a strong supporter of popular election of the president, offered that it "seemed to be the unanimous sense that the Executive should not be appointed by the Legislature, unless he be rendered in-eligible a [second] time: he [Wilson] perceived with pleasure that the idea was gaining ground, of an election mediately or immediately by the people."[56] And indeed, by the end of this day of deliberations, the Convention had agreed to "electors" chosen by state legislatures selecting the president for a term of six—instead of seven—years, with the possibility for reeligibility. Yet only five days later the convention would reinstate legislative selection, which would open the debate yet again about length of term and reeligibility, with some members suggesting terms as long as twenty years to keep presidents independent of the legislature.[57] Elbridge Gerry summed up the exasperation of the delegates: "We seem to be entirely at a loss on this head."[58]

The next several days would feature extensive deliberations on the method of selection as well as presidential tenure. Little new ground would be covered, as delegates mainly rehashed the arguments over legislative selection, popular election, and reeligibility. However, it should be noted that the idea of rotation ("no person be eligible for more than 6 years in any twelve years"[59]), not simply full ineligibility, was seriously addressed and debated.[60] By July 26, the Convention had returned to the original formulation: legislative selection, a seven-year term, and ineligibility for reelection.[61] The status quo would remain until late in the Convention—early September—when a committee charged with ironing out details (the Committee of Eleven) would propose yet again an electoral college election, a four-year term, and reeligibility.

By this time, many members were convinced that legislative selection was problematic (because the president could not thereby be truly independent of the legislature), but there were still considerable worries about the new plan, particularly the provision, later changed, that if no candidate received a majority of electoral votes, the Senate would choose from the top five candidates. Delegate Pinckney nicely framed the objections to the plan: "1. that it threw the whole appointment in fact into the hands of the Senate. 2. The Electors will be strangers to the several candidates and of course unable to decide on their comparative merits. 3. It makes the Executive reeligible which will endanger the public liberty. 4. It makes the same body of men which will in fact elect the President his Judges in case of an impeachment."[62] Alexander Hamilton offered important observations at this juncture, previewing arguments he would make in *The Federalist*: "He [Hamilton] liked the new modification, on the whole, better than that in the printed Report [legislative selection, seven-year term, ineligibility]. In this the President was a Monster elected for seven years, and ineligible afterwards; having great powers, in appointments to office, & continually tempted by this constitutional disqualification to abuse them in order to subvert the Government. Although he should be made re-eligible, still if appointed by the Legislature, he would be tempted to make use of corrupt influence to be continued in office. It seemed particularly desireable therefore that some other mode of election should be devised."[63] Hamilton went on to support a plurality rule for counting electoral votes, namely, rather than allowing the Senate to make the selection, whoever had the most votes, whether a majority or not, would become president. It would be delegate Hugh Williamson, however, who would propose the critical compromise: "better than an eventual choice by the Senate, that this choice should be made by the Legislature, voting *by States* and not *per capita*."[64]

With this compromise, then, late in the Convention the delegates approved what would become the election and tenure provisions for the presidency. James Wilson predicted during the Convention that the issue of constituting the executive (election and tenure) "has greatly divided the House, and will also divide people out of doors."[65] He was partially correct. As Richard Ellis has pointed out, during the ratification process, "the most frequently criticized part of the convention's plan for presidential selection was the absence of a bar on reeligibility."[66] However, the *election* of the president would not engender significant opposition. As Hamilton put it in *Federalist* #68: "The mode of appointment of the Chief Magistrate of the United States is almost the only part of the system, of any consequence, which has escaped without severe censure, or which has received the slightest mark of approbation from its opponents. . . . I venture somewhat further, and hesitate not to affirm, that if the manner of it be not perfect, it is at least excellent."[67]

Although this optimism on Hamilton's part seems fanciful from the perspective of the twenty-first century (especially after the 2000 election), it points to the compromise nature of the electoral college and undoubtedly how most observers could see what they wanted in it.[68]

With the four-year term and especially reeligibility, however, there would be no such flexibility of interpretation, and battle lines would be drawn during the ratification process. Although the major opponents of the Constitution, the Anti-Federalists, were a disparate group theoretically, they were generally what might be termed "populist" in their political sympathies, favoring legislative authority for its close connection to the people, and likewise seeking to restrain executive power, given its historical relationship with royalty and, from their perspective, tyranny. Many of these men were comfortable with the tenure restraints on executive power prominent in the colonial era and at the state level in the pre-constitutional period; they, in other words, continued to embrace the Whig view of executive authority. Thus, these critics were scandalized by the length of term and especially the lack of term limits on the presidency.[69] For instance, "Cato," a prominent critic of the Constitution who many believe was New York's governor, George Clinton, quoted Montesquieu in making his case: "[I]*n all magistracies, the greatness of the power must be compensated by the brevity of the duration; and that a longer time than a year, would be dangerous.*" Under this Constitution, in Cato's opinion, "if the president is possessed of ambition, he has power and time sufficient to ruin his country."[70] "Federal Farmer,"[71] while admiring the notion of a "single executive," was quite opposed to the idea of reelection, describing it as "very exceptionable": "The convention, it seems first agreed that the president should be chosen for seven years, and never after to be eligible. Whether seven years is a period too long or not, is rather a matter of opinion; but clear it is, that this mode is infinitely preferable to the one finally adopted. When a man shall get the chair, who may be re-elected, from time to time, for life, his greatest object will be to keep it; to gain friends and votes, at any rate."[72] On the other hand, "[w]hen a man constitutionally retires from office, he retires without pain; he is sensible [that] he retires because the laws direct it, and not from the success of his rivals nor with that public disapprobation which being left out, when eligible, implies."[73] But, it was probably George Mason, a member of the Convention involved intimately in the deliberations—and who declined to sign the final product—who made some of the most searching criticisms at the time of ratification.

Mason was deeply committed to the idea of rotation and saw its absence as a great problem: "If we judge from the experience of all other countries, and even our own, we may conclude that, as the President of the United States may be reelected, so he will."[74] And reflecting not merely paranoia but very real concerns at the time, Mason averred that "[t]his President will be elected time after time: he will be continued in office for life. If we wish to change him, the great powers in Europe will not allow us."[75] Mason would clearly have preferred rotation: "I should be contented that he might be elected for eight years; but I would wish him capable of holding the office only eight years out of twelve or sixteen years."[76] Mason additionally criticized the close relationship between the president and the Senate. The Senate as a "council" of sorts to the president was problematic because the Senate would try the president in cases of impeachment. "In its present form," according to Mason, "the guilty try themselves. The President is tried by his counsellors."[77]

Several state ratifying conventions produced statements or commentary on the Constitution accompanying their ratification, and all were critical of the presidential tenure provisions of the Constitution. Virginia, New York, North Carolina, and Rhode Island each included statements specifically directed at presidential tenure. Virginia suggested amendments to the Constitution, the thirteenth of which was that "no person shall be capable of being President of the United States for more than eight years in any term of sixteen years."[78] Much like what would become our Twenty-second Amendment, New York proposed an amendment that "no Person shall be eligible to the Office of President of the United States a third time."[79] North Carolina, like Virginia, proposed that "no person shall be capable of being president of the United States for more than eight years in any term of sixteen years." North Carolina not only proposed this amendment but provided, in an earlier statement of general principles, the theoretical underpinning of term limits: members of the legislative and executive branches "may be restrained from oppression by feeling and participating in the public burthens, [so] they should at fixed periods be reduced to a private station, return[ed] into the mass of the people."[80] Rhode Island, while not advocating the adoption of any amendments dealing with presidential tenure, nonetheless offered (in terms almost identical to North Carolina) that legislators and executives "should at fixed periods be reduced to a private station."[81]

These Anti-Federalist arguments for term limits or at least rotation, which would resonate across American history, can be distilled to the following key points. First, an ambitious president, if reeligible, would naturally curry favor with various interests and especially wealthy elites to retain office; thus he would be beholden to private or partial interests rather than the public interest. And even if a president were cultivating a broader public for reelection, the constant politicking would discourage proper leadership and still would force presidents to offer favors and make promises that would distract from the duties of statesmanship. Second, as the temptations of office and power were so great—especially a singular office such as the presidency—the longer a person stayed in the office, the more likely were abuses and usurpations of power. Whatever stability and experience may be gained by a long-serving president would be offset by serious potential for abuse of power. Third, if a president did not, after some short time, have to return to the people, he would be less likely to act in their interest and would become too distant from them. A long-serving president would not have to feel the impact of the laws and precedents that he helped to establish. Finally, as Anti-Federalists generally favored change over stability, they worried that a long-serving president would deprive the political system of a needed infusion of new ideas and leadership at regular intervals. This would be an idea developed more fully by Thomas Jefferson, as covered in the next chapter. At any rate, what we see most clearly in these criticisms is an abiding belief in the Whig antinomy between power and democracy: an executive with too much power is a threat to democracy and hence must be restrained, especially through the democratic vehicle of term limits or rotation.

In the face of these and similar criticisms of presidential tenure, Alexander Hamilton published *Federalist* #71 and #72, providing in many ways the definitive words on presidential tenure. However, these ideas built upon those developed in his *Federalist* #70. It is important then to first briefly discuss the central idea of this paper—"energy in the executive." Hamilton noted at the outset that there were those who believed "that a vigorous Executive is inconsistent with the genius of republican government." This is, of course, what the Whig view held. Hamilton, however, disagreed: "Energy in the Executive is a leading character in the definition of good government. It is essential to the protection of the community against foreign attacks; it is not less essential to the steady administration of the laws; to the protection of property against those irregular and high-handed combinations which sometimes interrupt the ordinary course of justice; to the security of liberty against the enterprises and assaults of ambition, of faction, and of anarchy."[82] Hamilton further explained that the "ingredients which constitute energy in the Executive are, first, unity; secondly, duration; thirdly, an adequate provision for its support; fourthly, competent powers."[83] By establishing a unitary executive[84] and arming the office with substantial powers, the new Constitution would have an important force for action and decisiveness. By providing a relatively long term (four years) and the possibility for continuous reelection, the framers courted accusations of monarchy, in that presidents might be reelected for life, but also assured a steadiness and continuity of administration. Yet, although the president was not to be chosen by the Congress, the electoral college nevertheless put the people, if indirectly, in charge of presidential selection and thereby tethered the presidency to the will of the public, at least in a broad and extended sense.

Herein lies the uniqueness of the framers' presidency, given the dominant Whig conceptual language of the time. Hamilton and the Federalists were undoubtedly creating a "republican" executive. The new president would be elected by, and held accountable to, the people. But the people would not have *immediate* control over the president—they would not vote directly for the president, nor would presidents come up for election very frequently (remember that most governors served terms half or even a quarter of the presidential term of four years). As Hamilton put it: "The republican principle demands that the deliberate sense of the community should govern the conduct of those to whom they intrust the management of their affairs; but it does not require an unqualified complaisance to every sudden breeze of passion, or to every transient impulse which the people may receive from the arts of men, who flatter their prejudices to betray their interests."[85] Presidents, then, would have some independence from Congress and also from public opinion, but a president could only get so far away from the public and, particularly in a broad sense, would seek to act in the public interest. Moreover, this president would be buffeted by two competing branches of government, one of them (the Congress) possessing serious weapons to curtail and restrain executive power. Therefore, neither was this executive all-powerful and virtually unaccountable—the English king and royal governors—nor was the executive denuded of power and subject to close control by the people and their legislature—the median state governor. The constitutional president was somewhere in between these and thus was a conceptual challenge to many critics, and even supporters, of the Constitution, especially those beholden to the Whig view of the executive.

The tenure restrictions on the new office would play an important role in forging this energetic executive. In *Federalist* #71, Hamilton offered strong arguments for the four-year term, and in #72 he defended reeligibility. For Hamilton, the four-year term played a crucial role in providing independence for the president from both Congress and the people:

> It may perhaps be asked, how the shortness of the duration in office can affect the independence of the Executive on the legislature, unless the one were possessed of the power of appointing or displacing the other. One answer to this inquiry may be drawn from the principle already remarked—that is, from the slender interest a man is apt to take in a short-lived advantage, and the little inducement it affords him to expose himself, on account of it, to any considerable inconvenience or hazard. Another answer, perhaps more obvious, though not more con-

clusive, will result from the consideration of the influence of the legislative body over the people; which might be employed to prevent the reelection of a man who, by an upright resistance to any sinister project of that body, should have made himself obnoxious to its resentment.[86]

A longer term would invest the president more fully in the office and give him a stronger interest in protecting the office (especially from legislative usurpations). Moreover, the length of the term would allow a president to resist the designs of the legislature or the people. But elections would still be meaningful devices for holding the president accountable: "as he approached the moment when the public were, by a new election, to signify their sense of his conduct, his confidence, and with it his firmness, would decline."[87] Although Hamilton acknowledged that a four-year term might not fully address the problem of legislative dominance, he concluded that it would "contribute to the firmness of the Executive in a sufficient degree to render it a very valuable ingredient in the composition . . . [and] it is not enough to justify any alarm for the public liberty."[88]

In *Federalist* #72, Hamilton linked term length with reeligibility: "With a positive duration of considerable extent, I connect the circumstance of reeligibility."[89] While duration provided for firmness and stability, reeligibility allowed the people to continue a president in office "in order to prolong the utility of his talents and virtues, and to secure to the government the advantage of permanency in a wise system of administration."[90] From Hamilton's perspective, term limits offered many disadvantages and really only two ostensible advantages: "1st, greater independence in the magistrate; 2nd, greater security to the people."[91] And these advantages "are at best speculative and equivocal, and are overbalanced by disadvantages far more certain and decisive."[92] The disadvantages are as follows. First is the "diminution of the inducements to good behavior," which means that presidents would not pursue great works and bold policies because their time in the office would be curtailed. Second is that beyond failing to produce good behavior, term limits would encourage *bad* behavior because presidents, as their terms run out, would be free to pursue whatever policies they chose, without the punishment of elections. They may thereby give in to "the temptation to sordid views, to peculation, and, in some instances, to usurpation." Third is "depriving the community of the advantage of the experience gained by the Chief Magistrate in the exercise of his office." A fourth related disadvantage is "banishing men from stations in which, in certain emergencies of the State, their presence might be of the greatest moment to the public interest or safety." The final ill effect of term limits is the disruption of "stability in administration"; in other words, the forced transfer of power would be the enemy of continuity of administration. Ultimately, in Hamilton's view, term limits were "an excess of refinement" that brought little advantage and the potential for great disadvantages.[93] As we will see, these arguments against term limits hold important sway throughout our political history. The argument about depriving the nation of experienced leadership in a time of crisis would be particularly important to Franklin Roosevelt's challenge to the two-term tradition in 1940.

At the risk of belaboring the point, it should be noted that Hamilton's energetic executive was neither monarch nor "eunuch." This was an office that would possess substantial power while also being restrained within a system of separation of powers. This was an office that would be elected by the people, but only indirectly—presidents would be accountable to the people without being slavishly dependent on their will (or whims). Finally, with the four-year term and especially unlimited reeligibility, a president might (theoretically) serve for life; and yet Hamilton still feared that the president would be too subject to the influence of the people and especially the Congress, as "the tendency of the legislative authority [is] to absorb every other" and in "governments purely republican, this tendency is almost irresistible."[94] The constitutional executive was, through and through, a balancing act, an attempt to find a middle ground between the feckless Whig executive and the unaccountable and uncontrollable hereditary monarch.

Table 2 illustrates the theoretical variety in the revolutionary and constitutional periods. It also provides a larger theoretical framework for considering presidential tenure throughout American history. Employing the dimensions of power and democracy—power increasing as one moves vertically on the chart, democracy increasing as one moves horizontally—five models, or archetypes, of executive leadership can be classified, with emphasis on provisions for tenure. The Revolutionary-era sentiment—and that of the Anti-Federalists as well—on presidential tenure is represented in the bottom right, with the term "Whig Executives." The Whig executive was substantially restrained in powers and similarly was selected by a legislature with absolute limits on terms or at least rotation of some sort. This was considered by many to be good

TABLE 2—POWER, DEMOCRACY, AND PRESIDENTIAL TENURE: COMPETING MODELS

Absolute Monarchy Unlimited Tenure Unelected		Plebiscitary Presidency Unlimited Reeligibility Directly Elected
	Constitutional Presidency Unlimited Reeligibility Indirect Election	
Symbolic Monarchy Unlimited Tenure Unelected		Whig Executives Limited Tenure Legislative Election

Power→

Democracy→

democratic or republican practice; that is, making the executive readily accountable to the people through their representatives. Naturally, the American colonists and revolutionaries saw some connection between extensive powers and the undemocratic nature of the executive, given their experience with the English monarchy, represented in the upper-left-hand corner, termed "Absolute Monarchy." This was the eighteenth-century English monarchy with which the colonists and founders were quite familiar. In this model, the executive—the king—had extensive powers, was unelected, and had unlimited tenure.

Until the Constitutional Convention, these perspectives on leadership and, hence, presidential tenure, were the two main models in currency. And, as we saw, in the wake of revolution, the independent Americans clearly chose to reject the English model and embrace the Whig model. However, by the time of the Constitutional Convention, the choices were not so black and white. What emerged in the course of the Convention was a perspective on executive leadership that represented a balancing of power and democracy. Unlike the Whig executive, the "Constitutional Presidency" would give the executive the option to serve in the office for a considerable duration and, because of reelection, afford the possibility of extended service. In the eyes of Anti-Federalists, this would appear too close to monarchy, but when contrasted with the "Absolute Monarchy" model, we see that the constitutional model is still rather "democratic" in the sense of presidents being accountable to the people (or at least "electors") and subject to regular elections.

Represented in the upper-right-hand corner of the chart, the "Plebiscitary Presidency" was perhaps not unthinkable at the time of the founding but certainly not a fully developed idea of presidential leadership. Delegate James Wilson may have glimpsed something along these lines,[95] but, generally speaking, few Americans in 1787 would have articulated a view of executive leadership harnessed strongly and directly to public opinion. Nevertheless, by the early twentieth century, presidents such as Theodore Roosevelt and Woodrow Wilson would be articulating visions of presidential leadership that sought to couple—not balance—democracy and power. In this model, a president would be elected by the people directly and regularly (the "independence" of electors falling by the wayside early on), with continued opportunities for reelection. This model developed before the Twenty-second Amendment limited presidential terms. Not only the Anti-Federalists but even Hamilton would reject this model of leadership—Anti-Federalists because they saw a strong opposition between executive power and democracy, and Hamilton because the president would be too close to the people to protect the public interest. In the (Theodore) Rooseveltian model, the president can only protect the public interest through a close connection with the people.

Finally, in the lower-left-hand corner of the chart is "Symbolic Monarchy." It is fair to say that this was inconceivable to many at the time of the Revolution and thereafter. A monarch who was unelected and served an unlimited term but who was not powerful? This would have made little sense to the Revolutionary and founding generations of Americans. Yet this is clearly what the English have today: a formal yet symbolic monarchy where the monarch, currently the Queen of England, retains many of the trappings of the traditional (absolute) monarchy, with none of the powers, those powers being wielded solely by the British parliament and prime minister.

It is important here to more fully develop the three models that still have theoretical saliency today—the Whig, constitutional, and plebiscitary models—and, especially, to remark upon the divergent assumptions made about leadership, democracy, and their connection to executive tenure. The Whig and plebiscitary models are both generally trustful of the people, but they make different assumptions about the people's ability to ultimately restrain leadership. Whigs believe that, given the opportunity, leaders will work to abuse their power in ways that may not always be easily noticed by the people, or that leaders may so quickly consolidate their power that the people will not be in a position to stop further accretions of power and, inevitably, abuses of that power. While Whigs support the role of the people in governance, then, they are cynical about the motivations of leaders and worry about the tools available for leaders, especially executives, to mislead the people. It is from this Whig perspective that many—Jefferson key among them—opposed the lack of term limits on federal officials, especially the president, under the Constitution. Adherents of both the constitutional and plebiscitary models, however, would argue that Whigs are naïve in that they downplay the need for strong executive leadership, choosing instead to see legislatures as the engines of political systems.

The plebiscitary model is far more sanguine about the prospects for the people to control leadership and is also more trusting of leadership. Although executives may certainly err in their ways, it is not necessarily their raison d'être to quest after power and to abuse the rights of the people. In fact, in Theodore Roosevelt's "stewardship" model, presidents are there to protect and look after the people. This is, of course, why supporters of this strong model of the presidency—what is often termed the "modern presidency" among presidency scholars—do not support term limitations. In their view, it is perfectly conceivable that a president may come along who is long-serving *and* an agent of the people. In the minds of many supporters of the modern presidency, Franklin Roosevelt was precisely this sort of figure. Not only might forcing the president to step down deny the people of a faithful steward in a time of emergency, but even in ordinary times it would reduce an agent of the people to private station, thereby depriving the people of a champion of their interests.

Critics of the plebiscitary model, however, dispute the ostensible magnanimity of leaders as well as the ability of the people to distinguish between legitimate attempts to promote the public interest and cynical ploys to promote a president's interests. Additionally, critics worry that presidents, especially long-serving ones, can consume so much political oxygen that not only other leaders but the people themselves are deprived of a robust role in formulating public policy. Thus, while proponents of the plebiscitary model see democratic advancement in strong plebiscitary presidents, others see considerable jeopardy for the people's interests and democracy.[96]

The constitutional model of leadership is probably the most complex in its view of leadership and democracy. The Hamiltonian view of the presidency saw the electoral college—given that in its original conception electors would be independent agents expressing their own, not the people's, judgment—as grounding the office of the presidency in the "filtered" or mediated consent of the people. In Hamilton's rendering, firmness and power, especially executive power, might be necessary to serve the long-term interests of the public, democracy and democratic forms being not always conducive to good public policy. The four-year term—longer than any state governor's term—would further provide distance from the people while still allowing their control every four years, with no term-limit restrictions. Although not untroubled by continual reeligibility, Hamilton saw far more advantages than disadvantages. Chief among the advantages were that the people would be able to retain a president in times of crisis and that they would be able to have continuous, stable administration if they so desired. But this support of reeligibility points to one of the central ambiguities or contradictions of the Hamiltonian philosophy: although distrustful of the people as a general rule, Hamilton somehow seems to trust that the people will be able to distinguish between a virtuous leader and one who may cunningly affect the appearance of virtue while working to undermine the people's interests.[97]

Although there is ambiguity or tension in this model of the constitutional presidency, this attempt to balance democracy and executive power is really not as unique as we might think. While John Locke is predominantly viewed as a Whig theorist and promoter of legislative supremacy, he is also arguably a key intellectual forebear to the executive office created in 1787. As Harvey Mansfield has shown, "Locke established the weak, theoretical executive conformable to the antimonarchical animus of his day," but thereafter "in the *Second Treatise*, the weak theoretical executive is built up, casually as it were, to the more powerful practical and informal executive we know today."[98] Just as Locke, despite his profession of faith in legislative supremacy, saw the need, at times, for strong executive leadership—evidenced through his idea of "prerogative"[99]—so were the American framers compelled by the realities of practical governance to create an executive not entirely unlike the English king that they had so opposed only a decade earlier. Of course, this American president would be restrained not only by a set term of office and regular elections but through counterbalances in the other two institutions within the constitutional framework. But far more than the Whig model, which clearly supports a weak executive, or the plebiscitary model, which undeniably supports a powerful executive, the constitutional model seeks a balance between empowering and restraining the executive. In some ways, we might think of subsequent U.S. political history as a continual battle over striking the appropriate balance between executive authority and democratic restraint.

Indeed, notwithstanding the founders' clear provision of unlimited reeligibility, the constitutional view would be modified almost immediately by the actions of Presidents Washington and Jefferson, and these actions would be reinforced by successors Madison, Monroe, and, later, Jackson. Although Washington, as we will see in the next chapter, did not step down after two terms out of deference to the principle of "rotation," Jefferson and his successors clearly did. And with Jefferson claiming Washington as a supporter of rotation, the two-term tradition was born; even though the Constitution was not changed, the two-term limit became a "virtual postscript to the Constitution," as a number of congressmen noted in the debates over the Twenty-second Amendment in 1947.[100] This "postscript" well illustrates the ambivalence of the constitutional view regarding leadership and its relationship to democracy. The two-term tradition strongly counsels against seeking a third term—expressing skepticism of leaders' motivations and the ability of the people to restrain them through elections—while allowing the possibility for continued service in the case of necessity and emergency, thereby acknowledging the rare need for strong leadership and trusting the people to make the proper decision in these unusual circumstances.

This chapter has viewed the issue of presidential tenure from the perspective of the founding generation, examining the tenures of royal governors and then state governors after them, elaborating their main ideas on executive tenure, power, and democracy. The dominant conceptual view during this time, the Whig view, was that executive power was in conflict with democracy and therefore should be constrained. With regard to executive tenure, this meant legislative selection, short terms, and term limits or rotation. By the time of the Constitutional Convention, assumptions and conceptions of power, democracy, and tenure had changed, with Hamilton's "energetic executive" offering a compromise between power and democracy, a compromise still challenged heartily by opponents of the Constitution. The constitutional view, though, quickly came to be modified by the informal provision that we now refer to as the "two-term tradition." The next chapter will examine this tradition—its establishment and development as well as challenges to it. These challenges came not only from those, such as Theodore Roosevelt, who wished to serve more than two terms, but those who, harking back to the Whig view, insisted on a one-term presidency or at least a form of rotation in the office. As I discuss Theodore Roosevelt's challenge to the tradition in his pursuit of a third term in 1912, I will also elaborate more fully the plebiscitary model of presidential leadership.

"SOUND PRECEDENT"

The Development of the Two-term Tradition

It is fully imbedded in the minds of the people as if it were written in the Constitution that no man shall serve more than two terms.

Joseph Hawley, 1875

Despite the decision of the convention delegates in favor of unlimited reeligibility, the Whig preference for executive restraint proved resilient, and by the early nineteenth century the two-term tradition would be established. In fact, by the middle of the nineteenth century, the main political parties would be inclining toward a one-term rule for the presidency. This chapter examines the development of the two-term tradition, variations on it, and especially challenges to it. The chapter begins with a brief examination of Washington's decision not to seek reelection in 1796. Although sometimes misinterpreted as the founder of the two-term tradition, Washington refused a third term more for personal reasons than those of principle or philosophy, as scholars have shown. Jefferson, then, will receive fuller attention, as he clearly defended his decision not to seek reelection in 1808 on the grounds of political philosophy. What is more, by linking his action to that of his predecessor, Washington, Jefferson created a powerful tradition that would be followed throughout the nineteenth century and into the twentieth.

This chapter also focuses on the challenges to the tradition. One of the first challenges came not from those seeking more than two terms; rather, it came from those seeking to establish a one-term tradition. While this perspective had its origin particularly in the Whig Party in the antebellum era, the one-term idea was shared by Democrats and Republicans alike and persisted into the twentieth century. The most prominent challenges came from those presidents (and especially their supporters) who wanted to serve longer than two terms. The chapter considers in some detail the case of Ulysses S. Grant and his quests—mainly orchestrated by his friends and supporters—for a third term, first in 1876 and then more aggressively in 1880. A little-known drive for a Cleveland third term in 1896 will also be explored, as will the speculations surrounding a possible third term for Wilson in 1920 and Coolidge in 1928.

President Theodore Roosevelt's unsuccessful quest for a third term in 1912 is a key part of this story (the following two chapters address Franklin Roosevelt's successful third and fourth terms, respectively). Theodore Roosevelt's pursuit of a third term in 1912 is an intriguing case. Here was a president who refused to run for reelection in 1908 in deference to the two-term tradition; yet by 1910 it was clear to most observers that Roosevelt had changed his mind and would pursue a third term. Like Grant's supporters in 1880, Roosevelt made a famously disingenuous argument that the two-term tradition only prohibited three *consecutive* terms. Having vacated the office for a term, Roosevelt argued, he was not breaking with the tradition in seeking the office in 1912. What makes Roosevelt's case challenging is that, despite his insincerity regarding the idea of consecutive terms—he mentioned no such subtlety regarding consecutive terms in his refusal to seek reelection in 1908—his argument did tap into a long tradition in support of rotation.

What is more, Roosevelt had never actually been elected to the presidency twice, having assumed the office as vice president after President McKinley's death in September of 1901. This complicated the question of whether Roosevelt had really served two *Roosevelt* terms and thereby opened up the possibility that Roosevelt's reelection in 1912 would constitute only a second term. These factors would combine to mute the impact of the two-term tradition on the election of 1912, although the issue did influence the campaign in important respects. While few Republican primary voters objected to Roosevelt's third-term attempt—his candidacy thrived in the primary states in 1912—one key Republican, sitting President William Howard Taft, was deeply troubled by Roosevelt's violation of all things traditional, particularly the two-term tradition. And ultimately it would be Taft who would foil Roosevelt's attempt to win reelection in 1912 and thereby preserve, at least temporarily, the two-term tradition.

In the establishment of the two-term tradition and in the challenges to it, we witness the further development of the debates over executive tenure. The considerable fluidity in the debates over time—from supporters of a single term to those promoting the two-term tradition to those advocating unlimited reeligibility—suggests the ambiguous nature of executive tenure within the American political tradition. While we rightly speak of a two-term tradition governing the behavior of nineteenth- and early-twentieth-century presidents, this tradition had substantial competition, both practically and theoretically speaking. Furthermore, we see in many cases how quickly principles of executive tenure are adopted or abandoned based upon the political advantages of the situation, with individuals, parties, and even newspapers changing their minds once the reelection of a particular president comes into question. This is not to say that politics trumps principle in the debate over presidential tenure but that it must be accorded its proper place.

A "Sound Precedent Set by an Illustrious Predecessor"

Among the many precedents that Washington established as our first president, his decision to step down after two terms was respected, willingly or not, by subsequent presidents for nearly 150 years. Yet, although it is accurate to ascribe to Washington this precedent—he was the first to do it, after all—it is problematic to assume that Washington intended for subsequent presidents to follow his example. Indeed, Washington's two-term precedent took on a life of its own thanks largely to Jefferson, who somewhat disingenuously ascribed to Washington's action a theoretical foundation that Washington himself would have disavowed. In a well-known letter to the legislature of Vermont in 1807, Jefferson said: "Believing that a representative government, responsible at short periods of election, is that which produces the greatest sum of happiness to mankind, I feel it a duty to do no act which shall essentially impair that principle; and I should unwillingly be the person who, disregarding the sound precedent set by an illustrious predecessor, should furnish the first example of prolongation beyond the second term of office."[1] Jefferson, in good Whig fashion, had for much of his career publicly espoused a fear of executive authority, and he thereby supported term limits for executives (as well as legislators). In linking his decision, largely a product of his "republican" political philosophy, to Washington's, Jefferson created the impression that Washington had also stepped down for reasons of political principle.

Although the record is abundantly clear that Washington was not an advocate of term limits for the presidency, even to this day—in part for political reasons, but also because of Jefferson's successful co-optation of him to the cause—Washington is often considered to be the intellectual "founder" of the two-term tradition.[2] While Washington on a number of occasions expressed support for presidential reeligibilty—particularly in a famous 1788 letter to the Marquis de Lafayette in which he stated that he saw "no propriety in precluding ourselves from the services of any man, who on some great emergency shall be deemed universally, most capable of serving the Public"[3]—perhaps most important is his own explanation of his retirement, in his farewell address. Washington began the address by explaining his personal reluctance to hold public office and even to accept a second term: "The acceptance of, and continuance hitherto in, the office to which your suffrages have twice called me have been a uniform sacrifice of inclination to the opinion of duty and to a deference for what appeared to be your desire. I constantly hoped that it would have been much earlier in my power, consistently with motives which I was not at liberty to disregard, to return to that retirement from which I had been reluctantly drawn. The strength of my inclination to do this, previous to the last election, had even led to the preparation of an address to declare it to you; but mature reflection on the then per-plexed and critical posture of our affairs with foreign nations, and the unanimous advice of persons entitled to my confidence, impelled me to abandon the idea."[4] Although unusual by today's standards, Washington's eagerness to retire from office—and his reluctance to serve in the first place—is less important than his justification for it. He clearly explained that he was fully prepared to retire at the end of his first term but that the uncertain nature of the international world, and the advice of advi-sors, persuaded him to accept a second term, if granted. Here we can see that Washington linked the length of public service to the political or environmental context. Had the international world not been unsettled, Washington presumably would have retired after one term. It should be noted further that Washington ascribed no reason other than personal inclination for wanting only one term.

By the end of his second term, though, Washington found the politi-cal context compatible with his strong desire to retire: "I rejoice that the state of your concerns, *external as well as internal*, no longer renders the pursuit of inclination incompatible with the sentiment of duty or propriety, and am persuaded, whatever partiality may be retained for my services, that, in the present circumstances of our country, you will not disapprove my determination to retire."[5] Interestingly, Washington listed not only "external" but also "internal" concerns as factoring into his decision making. It is well known that Washington worried greatly about the rise of partisanship during the 1790s—indeed, this subject occupies a key part of the farewell address. Had partisanship or factions been at a fever pitch (had the Whiskey Rebellion occurred in early 1796) or had relations with the European powers been more precarious, we are led to believe that Washington at least would have considered serving a third term.

From Washington's own farewell address, then, we gain a rather straightforward statement of his view on presidential tenure: a president's tenure should be dependent upon the political situation and the good of the nation, not preset restrictions on service. Of course, it is common to worry about a leader sacrificing the good of his nation for his own political survival—that is one of the key arguments for term limits. But Washington showed that an equally legitimate—if rare—concern is a leader who sacrifices his nation's interests to his own inclination to shun or avoid public service or, in the case of term limits, is compelled to sacrifice the nation's interest because of a forced retirement.

This is not to say that Washington saw no danger in long presidential tenure, nor that he saw no benefit in his example of stepping down. As Bruce Peabody has pointed out, "Washington perceived the utility of stepping down from office as a means of alleviating lingering concerns about the nascent presidential office."[6] Being a member of the Constitutional Convention, Washington had heard firsthand critics' concerns that the presidency's lack of term limits would degenerate into a presidency for life or, in other words, a pseudo-monarchy. That the presidency had not turned into a monarchy—through the president's own restraint rather than through institutional restrictions—was an important lesson to teach the American people and, perhaps more importantly, America's political elite. Nevertheless, that Washington inclined toward a model of presidential restraint with regard to tenure does not mean that he supported predetermined limits on service. It would be the political context, the president himself, and ultimately the American people through their votes that would determine whether a second or third or fourth term would be necessary.

With Thomas Jefferson, however, no such subtlety of interpretation is necessary. Jefferson was long a believer in term limits or rotation for the presidency, even before he held the office. In fact, in a 1787 letter to James Madison regarding the proposed constitution, Jefferson declared that he "greatly dislike[d]" the "abandonment in every instance of the necessity of rotation in office, and most particularly in the case of the President." He continued that "[e]xperience concurs with reason in concluding that the first magistrate will always be re-elected if the constitution permits." What is more, the "power of removing him every fourth year by the vote of the people is a power which will not be exercised."[7] In another letter commenting on the new constitution, Jefferson further elaborated, "I own I should like better . . . that he should be elected for seven years, and incapable for ever after."[8] The plan that the Virginia delegation had submitted to the convention, although providing no recommendation on term length, also expressed support for ineligibility and was clearly rooted in pre-constitutional concerns with restraining executives through term limitation, in addition to preserving their independence from the legislative branch.

Jefferson, however, came to revise his view regarding a nonrenewable seven-year term. As he put it in an 1805 letter: "I have since become sensible that seven years is too long to be irremovable, and that there should be a peaceable way of withdrawing a man in midway who is doing wrong. The service for eight years, with a power to remove at the end of the first four, comes nearly to my principle as corrected by experience; and it is in adherence to that, that I determine to withdraw at the end of my second term."[9] While a cynic might see this as a crass rationalization for his own actions—that is, having sought and won reelection in 1804, despite his seeming commitment to the ineligibility of the president—we must remember that provisions for term limits in the states, including Virginia, often included the possibility of reelection to a second term but then barred the officeholder from service again entirely or until a certain passage of years or terms.[10] At any rate, once Jefferson adopted this modified view of rotation—what would become the two-term tradition—his support for his position remained steadfast until the end of his life.

But what were the reasons for Jefferson's commitment to rotation, in whatever form? It is clear from Jefferson's own words that he worried greatly about presidents serving long terms. Yet this just begs a further question: what is so problematic about long tenure in office, according to Jefferson? Jefferson seems to have had three principal justifications for limiting tenure, especially that of presidents, and these justifications are quite consistent with what we have termed the Whig perspective on executive power. First, Jefferson saw little distinction between a long-serving executive in an elective position and a hereditary monarch—the crucial similarity was the long tenure, which tended to promote arrogance and overreach on the part of the executive, not to mention facilitate the consolidation of power, all of which caused great jeopardy to the rights of the people. A president, for instance, might be tempted to secure his continuance through the suspension of the rights of the opposition. As Jefferson put it, discussing his own retirement, he "believ[ed] that a definite period of retiring from this station will tend materially to secure our elective form of government."[11]

Second, Jefferson seemed to worry quite a lot about the advancing age of a president or officeholder and how term limits would secure more competent administration. Even commenting on his own decision to step down, Jefferson declared that he was "sensible of that decline which advancing years bring on; and feeling their physical, I ought not to doubt their mental effect."[12] Indeed, from Jefferson's standpoint, a "danger is that the indulgence and attachments of the people will keep a man in the chair after he becomes a dotard."[13] Again, only term limits can assure that a president does not stay in office too long—the people, in Jefferson's view, cannot be trusted, for they "indulge" themselves and officeholders. What is more, from Jefferson's perspective, "[i]n no office can rotation be more expedient; and *none less admits the indulgence of age.*"[14] Here Jefferson makes an insightful point about the burdens of the presidency requiring a certain degree of physical and mental fitness that, in his opinion, is likely to be compromised by advanced age. Given the need to fill the office with men of preeminent reputation and character, it was reasonable for Jefferson to assume that presidents generally would be in the later stages of their public careers when elected to office, as the presidencies of Jefferson himself, Adams, and Washington attested.[15] Jefferson's point about the burdens of the presidency would only become more apposite as the power of the office and the federal government grew over time. As we will see in chapter 5, during Franklin Roosevelt's third term, the burdens of the office, age, and health wore down the president and, arguably, compromised his decision making, especially regarding the pursuit of a fourth term.

Third, and following from this second point, Jefferson believed strongly that a change of administration would often be a good thing for the American people. Jefferson is, of course, well known for his tolerance of rebellion[16] and even the excesses of revolution.[17] But on a less grand scale he also believed that a turnover of administration and particularly a changing over to younger hands would be beneficial to the political system: "It is a duty, as well as the strongest of my desires, to relinquish to younger hands the government of our bark [ship] and resign myself as I do willingly to their care."[18] Even if a president of advanced age is not a "dotard," a younger president—younger leaders in general—would inject a fresh perspective and energy into the management and governance of the nation.

It is somewhat ironic that Jefferson, who believed so strongly in republican government, was rather cynical about the abilities of the people to hold their leaders accountable through elections, leaning instead on arbitrary procedural devices to hold leaders at bay. It is important to emphasize, however, Jefferson's supreme distrust of officeholders and their ambitions. In fact, it was for this reason that Jefferson actively worked to see the two-term tradition established: "But if the principle of rotation be a sound one, as I conscientiously believe it to be with respect to this office, no pretext should ever be permitted to dispense with it, because there never will be a time when real difficulties will not exist, and furnish a plausible pretext for dispensation."[19] For Jefferson, leaders could always convince themselves that their continued service was necessary, even indispensable. Although Jefferson early on hoped that the practice of presidents retiring after two terms would "beget a disposition to establish it by an amendment of the Constitution,"[20] after Monroe's retirement in 1821, he concluded that with the "example of four Presidents voluntarily retiring at the end of their eighth year, and the progress of public opinion, . . . the principle is salutary[.] . . . [S]hould a President consent to be a candidate for a third election, I trust he would be rejected, on this demonstration of ambitious views."[21] Although FDR would, of course, be elected to third and fourth terms—rather than being rejected for his "ambitious views"—Jefferson was right to conclude that the uniform adherence to two terms by the early presidents set a powerful example that would be hard for ambitious presidents and candidates to challenge. What is more, even given FDR's third and fourth terms—and Theodore Roosevelt's dramatic, albeit unsuccessful, run for a third term in 1912—Jefferson was correct that the question of the ambitions of the president (or former president, in Theodore Roosevelt's case) would play a role in the decisions of voters, if not a decisive one.[22]

It is true that even Jefferson, at least once, wavered in his view of rotation. Not unlike Washington, he did allow for exceptional circumstance: "There is, however, but one circumstance which could engage my acquiescence in another election [a third term]; to wit, such a division about a successor, as might bring in a monarchist. But that circumstance is impossible."[23] Jefferson seemed to consider that there might be conditions that would require the continuance of leadership beyond a second or perhaps even third term. Nevertheless, his example is such an extreme one—the election of a monarchist and thereby the possible destruction of the republic—that he may be forgiven for lack of commitment to rotation in the face of a threat to the very foundations of republicanism.

A SINGLE-TERM PRESIDENCY

Although James Madison at the Constitutional Convention had been persuaded that there should be no limitation on the terms a president could serve, the examples of Washington and Jefferson would be such that neither Madison nor his Republican Party appears to have even considered whether he should serve a third term or not. Madison's biographer Ralph Ketcham, for instance, simply describes the succession of James Monroe accordingly: "Endorsing Madison's leadership, the Republican Congressional caucus nominated Monroe for the presidency."[24] President Monroe, however, strongly held to the idea of rotation, through not only his actions (stepping down after two terms[25]) but also his words. As a delegate to the Virginia ratifying convention in 1788, Monroe had opposed the Constitution and, in fact, "delivered a stirring speech in which he opposed the reeligibility of the president under the new Constitution." What is more, "[m]any of his arguments [were] those which Jefferson used" in his own opposition to reeligibility.[26] At any rate, once the "Virginia dynasty" had come to an end, the weight of tradition was undoubtedly on the side of presidents serving no more than two terms. Despite the framers' decision to allow unlimited reeligibility, opposition to long executive tenure had persisted and in fact had been incorporated, if only informally, into the American political tradition.

With John Quincy Adams being denied a second term (by the voters), it is with Andrew Jackson that we next see a president negotiate the question of presidential tenure. Jackson's vacillation or even inconsistency on the matter is particularly interesting for it illustrates a key tension within the Jeffersonian tradition and canon. As we saw, Jefferson first opposed reeligibility entirely and then later settled on a modified form of reeligibility—one reelection. Monroe similarly opposed reeligibility at the time of ratification but, once president, agreed to be reeligible, at least for one additional term. Of course, one might attribute this modification to opportunism, but one might also see it as a reflection of the tensions within Jeffersonian republicanism itself. On the one hand, Jeffersonian republicanism envisions an informed electorate that can not only hold office (if called to serve) but also hold their leaders accountable—which would seem to condone or at least tolerate reeligibility. Yet, on the other hand, Jeffersonianism embodies a suspicion of leaders and government power that raises serious questions about the abilities of the people to hold their leaders accountable in the absence of term limits of some type. Jackson in some ways perfectly embodied this tension during his presidency.

Although "Jackson did not enter the office of President with any previous commitment against indefinite executive reeligibility,"[27] once president, through his actions and words, he gave mixed signals regarding reeligibility. Of course, since Jackson did pursue and win a second term, his actions indicate that he, at a minimum, supported reeligibility to a second term. Similarly, his retirement at the end of his second term may also be taken to suggest his adherence to Jefferson's modified view, the two-term tradition. Yet in his words—in official presidential addresses, particularly his State of the Union messages—Jackson often advocated a single term for the presidency. For instance, in his first annual message to Congress, reflecting on the election of 1824—wherein Congress selected Adams instead of Jackson—Jackson suggested several reforms for insuring "that the office of Chief Magistrate may not be conferred upon any citizen but in pursuance of a fair expression of the will of the majority." He continued: "In connection with such an amendment it would seem advisable to limit the service of the Chief Magistrate to a single term of either 4 or 6 years."[28] Jackson would reiterate this suggestion for tenure reform up through his sixth annual message. Even in his fourth annual message, coming immediately after his reelection, Jackson insisted that he was "[s]till impressed with the justness of those views" he had expressed on presidential tenure and recommended yet again that Congress pass an amendment limiting presidents to one term.[29]

Jackson gave his strongest justification for ineligibility of the executive in his second annual message: "The agent most likely to contravene this design of the Constitution is the Chief Magistrate. In order, particularly, that his appointment may as far as possible be placed beyond the reach of any improper influences; in order that he may approach the solemn responsibilities of the highest office in the gift of a free people uncommitted to any other course than the strict line of constitutional duty, and that the securities for this independence may be rendered as strong as the nature of power and the weakness of its possessor will admit, I can not too earnestly invite your attention to the propriety of promoting such an amendment of the Constitution as will render him ineligible after 1 term of service."[30] The one-term presidency, coupled with direct election by the people, another of Jackson's reform suggestions, would serve to create a presidency that was not indebted to the other institutions, particularly Congress. The temptation of a president to compromise himself and, worse, the nation's interests to achieve reelection would be eliminated, and a president would be committed to the public interest. It is not exactly clear why Jackson declined to follow his own prescriptions—arguably, with his retirement after one term, he could have done much more for his single-term idea than to advocte it in his annual messages—and probing his complicated motivations would take us too far afield.[31] It is fair to say, though, that regardless of his "reasons for so doing, both his attitude and his action in regard to the President's term of office designate Jackson as one of the chief opponents of *indefinite* executive reeligibility."[32]

The Whig Party that rose up in opposition to Jackson and his policies in the mid-1830s, like the "Whigs" of the Revolutionary and constitutional periods, displayed no such ambiguity with regard to executive tenure. Composed partly of former "nationalist" Democratic-Republicans, these Whigs were typically wary of the states' rights philosophy of Jackson's Democratic Party. But they were also staunch critics of what they perceived as the monarchical tendencies of "King Andrew the First."[33] True to its tradition, then, the Whig Party embraced a strong anti-executive ethos and advocated for the elimination of the veto power—one of the key tools of the Jackson presidency—and for a single-term presidency. This philosophy was perhaps best embodied in the 1840 election, that between President Martin Van Buren—pursuing a second term—and Whig William Henry Harrison. In the course of the campaign, Harrison had noted his support for a single-term presidency,[34] but his inaugural address—(in)famous for its great length—outlined in detail the Whig view of executive reeligibility.

Harrison wasted no time in highlighting "defects of the Constitution," chief among them being "the eligibility of the same individual to a second term of the Presidency." From his perspective, reeligibility tended to "create or increase the lover of power in the bosoms" of officeholders, and "surely nothing is more likely to produce such a state of mind than the long continuance of an office of high trust." The love of power "like the love of gold . . . becomes insatiable," and thus "it is the part of wisdom for a republic to limit the service of that officer at least to whom she has intrusted the management of her foreign relations, the execution of her laws, and the command of her armies and navies to a period so short as to prevent his forgetting that he is the accountable agent, not the principal; the servant, not the master." Although "Mr. Jefferson early saw and lamented this error, and attempts have been made, hitherto without success, to apply the amendatory power of the States to its correction," Harrison pointed out that "one mode of correction is in the power of every President." Of course, he had in mind the voluntary retirement on the part of the president himself and thereby renewed his pledge "that under no circumstances will I consent to serve a second term."[35]

Harrison died a month into his term, making the question of a second term, despite his steadfast refusal to accept one, a moot point. Whigs, though, throughout the 1840s and until their demise in the 1850s, adhered generally to the one-term philosophy, it being included, for instance, in their most direct statement of party principles, the 1844 Whig Party platform. However, it was not just the Whig Party that embraced the one-term principle. Even though the Democratic Party would not go on record, through its party platform, for a one-term presidency until its fusion with the Liberal Republicans in 1872 (and after that not again until the twentieth century), its antebellum presidents after Jackson would all be one-term presidents, and only Martin Van Buren would even be nominated for a second term. To some extent this was more the product of a divided Democratic Party—coupled with unpopular Democratic presidents—than a commitment to political principle. Yet in the midst of it all there were signs that at least some Democrats were seeing the utility in the Whig one-term principle. One Democratic president who undoubtedly helped to elevate this principle to prominence was James Polk.

Polk was a dark horse compromise candidate in a crowded Democratic field in 1844. Leading up to his acceptance of the nomination, Polk received several entreaties from friends and advisors to make a one-term pledge, most of which focused on the political benefits to be derived from it. For instance, a letter to Polk in late May 1844 offered this perspective on a one-term pledge: if the other candidates for the presidency "could be assured that you would only serve *one* Presidential term, they and their friends would support you[r] nomination with infinitely warmer zeal, than if the matter was left in doubt."[36] Another advisor appealed, among other things, to the need to "put us on an equality with the Whigs on that question."[37] Democratic House member Jacob Thompson even more directly put the point in a communication to Polk a week later: "We have in our ranks four to 8 aspirants to the Presidency whose souls are bent upon the over loved object. I know nothing on your part which will have so great a tendency to cause a harmonious co-operation, with them all, as an intimation in your acceptance of the nomination that your course will be to serve but a single term. The turn of events may be such to force you to deviate from such a course, but you must remember what small considerations often influence the greatest minds."[38] But Polk did not need much persuasion on this front, as he "had long been an advocate of a one-term presidency, confident that this constituted pure Jacksonian ideology."[39] In his acceptance letter, then, he pledged to only serve one term, for "I not only impose on myself a salutary restraint, but . . . I take the most effective means in my power of enabling the Democratic party to make a free selection of a successor who may be best calculated to give effect to their will."[40] Polk, of course, could not but see the political benefits to be gained from the pledge—the unity of the party and therefore his election—but for him a one-term presidency would promote republicanism, restraining executive power as well as putting the interests of the party (and hence, the people) over the interests of individual officeholders.

But Polk did not believe that he was committing the party to the principle: "I said nothing to commit the party upon the *one-term* principle, but expressed simply my own determination."[41] And, indeed, some within Polk's circle, once he became president, suggested that he violate his own pledge. Polk recounts in his diary the pressure to run again in 1848, some advisors arguing "that it might be indispensible to renominate me as the only means of restoring harmony, and of preserving harmony in the next election, and that it might become my duty to yield."[42] Although Polk did not yield to this pressure, it does show the truly conflicted nature of the Democratic Party with regard to presidential tenure in the antebellum era. Moreover, it illustrates the common intersection of politics and principles with regard to questions of presidential tenure. While it would not become a tenet of the Democratic faith, the Democratic Party after Jackson would at least incline by practice, politics, and, sometimes, principle, toward a one-term presidency.

"It Was Not Best to Swap Horses
When Crossing Streams"

The Whig Party did not survive the 1850s, but many of its former members, including Abraham Lincoln, joined the newly formed Republican Party. And even though the Republican Party did not officially adopt the one-term principle, "within the Republican party there was considerable sentiment in favor of rotation in office."[43] As John Waugh has put it in describing Lincoln's possible reelection in 1864, "[s]econd terms were rather out of style then. . . . Running again had become the thing not to do. To run again, Lincoln would have to buck thirty years of tradition."[44] Lincoln himself, as a Whig, had earlier embraced the principle of rotation, agreeing to serve only one term when he was elected to the House of Representatives in 1846.[45] Add to this that the Confederacy had established a constitution with a single six-year presidential term and it was reasonable to conclude that Lincoln would have a difficult time securing renomination, not to mention reelection in 1864.

And Lincoln most likely would not have been renominated by the Republican Party without the significant Union victories that came in 1863 and 1864, victories that followed Lincoln's promotion of General Grant to head of the Union Army. Prior to these victories, Lincoln faced considerable criticism within his party for his supposed lack of military skill, his lukewarm commitment to the anti-slavery cause, and his unconstitutional executive actions. Grant was thought by some to be among Lincoln's strongest competitors for the nomination in 1864, but Grant made it clear that he would not be a candidate.[46] Still, there were numerous other candidates within the party—particularly Lincoln's own treasury secretary, Salmon Chase—who were actively rounding up support for the nomination. Lincoln did desire reelection—he explained that he saw a second term as confirmation by the people that he "could better finish a difficult work . . . than could any one less severely schooled to the task."[47] Thus, he and his supporters worked hard, mostly behind the scenes, to promote his renomination and reelection. They were fortunate not only because of the Union victories but also because the factions within the party opposed to Lincoln could not unify themselves behind a particular candidate. Nevertheless, the opposition to Lincoln was real. For instance, a faction of the Republican Party held an alternative convention in late May of 1864, a week prior to the regular Republican Convention, nominated former Republican presidential candidate and

Union general, John Fremont, and pledged through its platform that the "one-term policy for the Presidency adopted by the people is strengthened by the force of the existing crisis, and should be maintained by Constitutional amendment."[48] Although by September these so-called Radical Republicans did come together behind Lincoln,[49] the opposition to Lincoln's renomination within the party was substantial.

It is hard to judge, however, just what role the one-term principle played in the campaign. Although second terms were indeed "out of style," neither Lincoln nor the (regular) Republican Party had pledged to the one-term principle. And previous presidents were denied second terms more for reasons of politics than principle. Furthermore, given the "emergency" circumstances present in 1864, supporters of the one-term principle were likely not only to mute their criticisms—as two-term supporters would in 1940—but possibly even to reevaluate their position. Lincoln himself linked his reelection closely to the circumstances of the country, remarking to a party delegation that a second term reminded him of "a story of an old Dutch farmer, who remarked to a companion once that 'it was not best to swap horses when crossing streams.'"[50] In an April 1864 editorial called "The One-Term Principle," the *New York Times* had spoken out similarly (and strongly) for Lincoln's reelection: "They must be very ignorant or very wild who suppose that we can yet see the end of the great undertaking, or are in any position to judge of the skill with which it is being carried out. And to commit it to fresh hands until we judge, would be a demonstration of contempt for training and experience so marked, so full of short-sighted impatience, that there are few thinking men who witnessed it who would not doubt our capacity for self-government." The *Times* went further to draw conclusions regarding presidential tenure in general and the decision of the framers of the Constitution in particular: "it was provision for precisely such a crisis as that through which we are now passing, that the convention mainly had in view when they permitted the President to serve for more than one term."[51]

Whatever the rationale behind it, Lincoln's reelection dealt a substantial blow to the nascent "one-term tradition." But advocates of the one-term principle would not go away quietly. Although a minority voice, proponents would continue to make the case over the years, and the single-term idea would find its way into party platforms, candidate pledges, and proposals for constitutional amendment with regularity. In fact, as we will see, President Ulysses S. Grant, the first elected president after Lincoln, would face significant criticism for pursuing a second term in 1872, not to mention a third term in 1876 and 1880.

"Unwise, Unpatriotic, and Fraught with Peril"

Ulysses Grant is often remembered as a great general but almost never as a great president.[52] Although Grant was popular with the public before, during, and after his presidency, he faced substantial elite opposition during his presidency, and he has not fared well with historians over the years. Probably the most lingering criticism of Grant's administration is that it was corrupt or at least that Grant allowed his administration to be hijacked by corrupt politicians, particularly party bosses. This, of course, was an era of significant party corruption, often referred to as the Gilded Age, where partisans too rarely worried about "conflicts of interest" and where "patronage"—the doling out of public jobs to political supporters—was the *summum bonum* of party politics. It is for this reason, party corruption, among others, that Grant faced opposition within his own party when pursuing a second term. Massachusetts senator Charles Sumner, for instance, introduced a resolution in January 1872 calling for a constitutional amendment limiting presidents to one term. He justified this amendment in large part because presidents, in order to seek reelection, abuse their patronage powers.[53] Although a Republican, Sumner clearly had the Grant administration and its patronage policies in mind with this amendment. But the most important figure opposed to Grant in 1872 was the newspaperman Horace Greeley, publisher of the *New York Tribune*. Greeley, in fact, was such a strong opponent of Grant that he ended up being nominated by the Liberal Republican Party, which had split from the Republicans, and then was cross-nominated by the Democratic Party.

Like Sumner, Greeley was a critic of the Grant administration's ostensible corruption and Grant's submission to the Republican Party machinery. But there is a hint of truth—and considerable irony—to the *New York Times'* characterization of Greeley and others who were "riding the 'one-term' hobby" that they had some "personal grievance to complain of, growing out of the distribution of Government patronage."[54] Yet again we see the overlap between principle and politics at the root of debates over presidential tenure. Regardless of the mix of motivations, many of Grant's Republican critics bolted the party and formed the Liberal Republican Party, nominating Greeley—who had spoken out in the past for not just civil service reform but the "one-term principle"—and adopting a platform that spoke directly to the issue of party corruption and the tenure of the president. The plank deserves to be quoted at length:

> 5. The civil service of the government has become a mere instrument of partisan tyranny and personal ambition, and an object of selfish greed. It is a scandal and reproach upon free institutions, and breeds a demoralization dangerous to the perpetuity of republican government. We therefore regard a thorough reform of the civil service as one of the most pressing necessities of the hour; that honesty, capacity, and fidelity constitute the only valid claim to public employment; that the offices of the government cease to be a matter of arbitrary favoritism and patronage, and that public station become again a post of honor. *To this end it is imperatively required that no President shall be a candidate for re-election.*[55]

An obviously sharp indictment of the incumbent president, the platform tapped into the contemporary dismay with party corruption and also the longstanding appeal of a president who would be independent and free from partisan taint. During the Gilded Age, from the perspective of the Liberal Republicans, the only way to assure such an independent office was through the limitation on service.

Democrats would adopt an almost identical platform and would nominate Greeley as their standard bearer as well, but the fusion ticket's prospects were slim from the start. Not only was Greeley an inexperienced (some might say unqualified) candidate, but Grant was very popular with the American people and he had the party machinery behind him to cement his victory in the general election. Although the one-term principle gave Greeley little traction in the election, the beliefs of the Liberal Republicans would resonate throughout the next decade. Most importantly, their call for civil service reform, which seemed prescient after the assassination of President James Garfield in 1881 by a disgruntled office seeker, would be codified in 1883 with the Pendleton Act. What is more, Grant would be followed in the presidency by Rutherford B. Hayes, a man committed to a one-term presidency in word and deed. Nevertheless, with Grant's reelection, two consecutive elected presidents had won second terms, and the country's commitment to a "one-term principle" seemed questionable at best. And before long, the country's commitment to the two-term principle would be tested by friends and supporters of President Grant.

The *New York Times* had been skeptical of Greeley's promotion of the one-term principle. It did agree that reelecting presidents brought with it certain challenges, but it was clearly not the "'root' of all the political corruption in the land." What is more, the so-called tradition was not really such: "the custom of rejecting a President after one term has been more honored in the breach than in the observance."[56] Yet, when it came to the possibility of Grant seeking a third term in 1876, the *Times* called it "wildly ridiculous" and said that "such an innovation on established precedents would be the ruin of the man or party which attempted it."[57]

Whether wildly ridiculous or not, some of Grant's supporters started promoting a third term in the summer 1874, and in September of that year, the South Carolina Republican Nominating Convention endorsed Grant for a third term. Talk of a third term would continue throughout the year and into 1875, with Grant himself saying nothing on the subject and thereby seeming to subtly promote his own candidacy. But, as the *New York Times* pointed out, a third term for Grant was not the broad position of the party: "the *party* is innocent of any complicity in the scheme."[58] Not only was there opposition to Grant within the Republican Party, but there was a sense on the part of many Republicans that the two-term—if not one-term—tradition was to be taken seriously, especially in non-crisis times. Prominent Republican Joseph Hawley, former Civil War general and then editor of the *Hartford Courant*, characterized the situation thusly: "It is fully imbedded in the minds of the people as if it were written in the Constitution that no man shall serve more than two terms. . . . Even in the case of war, it would be better for Grant to be in the field than in the Presidency."[59]

Matters came to a head in the spring of 1875, when Republican conventions in both Pennsylvania and Ohio passed resolutions opposing Grant's renomination. This would force Grant to write a letter to the chairman of the Pennsylvania Republican Convention ostensibly denying all interest in the nomination and presumably squelching all talk of a third term.[60] The letter satisfied some, like the *Times*, which thought the letter "settled for the future all controversy and doubts about the third term."[61] However, Grant's letter was not nearly as cut-and-dried for other observers. In fact, Whitelaw Reid's *New York Tribune* "openly derided the President for not flatly declaring that he was not a candidate."[62] Given this ambiguity, the issue still would not go away until, finally, in late 1875, the House of Representatives passed the strongly worded Springer Resolution—named after Illinois Democrat William Springer—which read:

> Resolved, That in the opinion of this House the precedent estab-lished by Washington and other Presidents of the United States in retiring from the Presidential office after their second term has become by universal concurrence a part of our republican system of government, and that any departure from this time-honored custom would be unwise, unpatriotic, and fraught with peril to our free institutions.[63]

"Unwise, unpatriotic, and fraught with peril": there was nothing subtle about the Springer Resolution. But it was resoundingly supported 232-18. Despite some hope among the diehard Grant supporters, this vote ef-fectively ended any chance Grant might have for the nomination. Even more, when Republicans did make their nomination, they would not choose only a reformer—rather than a "Grant man"—but an advocate of a one-term presidency. Rutherford B. Hayes spelled out his sentiment clearly in his inaugural address: "In furtherance of the reform we seek, and in other important respects a change of great importance, I recom-mend an amendment to the Constitution prescribing a term of six years for the Presidential office and forbidding a reelection."[64] In addition to being important in "other respects," the single term for the presidency, in Hayes's view, was closely related to the issue of party corruption and civil service abuses. A president who could not seek reelection ostensibly would be free from the temptation to make questionable appointments to shore up support and thereby ensure reelection. Good to his word, Hayes would not seek to be renominated in 1880.

Notwithstanding Hayes's example of presidential restraint, the Grant forces were back in support of their man in 1880. Grant had left the United States in May of 1877 for a tour of the world and did not return until September 1879. "Though he traveled as a private citizen, the former President was at every point showered with accolade and encomium truly characteristic of a great ruler."[65] On his return, Grant toured the United States and was met with a "very enthusiastic reception in every part of the country he visited."[66] Naturally, this got both Republicans and Democrats talking about his possible nomination for president in 1880.

Much of the rest of the story follows that of 1876—Grant's supporters promoting him as he maintained silence on the matter—except with more intensity and intrigue. In 1880, Grant's name was entered into the running at the convention, and he led the field for many of the ballots; however, he never got the requisite number of delegates, and eventually, on the thirty-sixth ballot, James Garfield was nominated for president. Indeed, there was a very real chance of Grant being nominated, unlike in 1876. From our perspective, though, many of the same tensions and issues were illustrated in the battle for the nomination in 1880 as in 1876.[67] The pursuit of a third term for Grant was fueled by similar forces, namely, those party bosses close to Grant who wanted to return to power, rank-and-file Republicans who thought Grant was their best chance to hold on to the White House, and average Americans for whom Grant was a wartime hero and competent president.

An important difference, however, and one worthy of attention here, was the idea that 1880 was different because Grant was not a sitting president or incumbent as he had been in 1876. On the face of it, the argument seems somewhat disingenuous and merely the position of ambitious office seekers eager to get back into office. Theodore Roosevelt, as we will see, made a very similar argument in 1912, and there was more than a hint of insincerity to it. Yet, whatever the motivations of its advocates, the argument that 1880 was to be viewed differently than 1876 (or that 1912 was different from 1908) does have some merit, and more importantly, it taps into a longstanding perspective in American political thought.

The *New York Times*, for instance, which had strongly resisted Grant's possible reelection in 1876, made an abrupt turnaround in 1880. No doubt this was partly political—as a Republican newspaper, it wanted to see a Republican elected in 1880, and by early 1880 there did not seem to be many candidates who would be victorious besides Grant. The newspaper was not above almost completely rejecting its previous criticisms of a third term: "nobody believes in the danger of a third term," it dismissively put it. The "fact is, the people are so jealous of their sovereignty" that a president who would abuse power or "prostrate his office to serve his own ambition, would insure his defeat." Yet, its position was at least partly influenced by the notion of a third term served non-consecutively: the "imaginary peril" associated with a third term "is wanting when the proposed candidate is out of office, and has no more power or influence than legitimately belongs to his character and career."[68] One of the key criticisms of presidential reelection (whether to a third or even second term) in the 1870s had been the connection between presidential patronage and the pursuit of reelection. Presidents and their supporters would use the president's official control of jobs to assure his reelection. However, with Grant out of office in 1880, and his party supporters largely on the outs with the Hayes administration, it could be somewhat fairly said that one of the key arguments against presidential reelection—corruption through party patronage—was partially nullified.

Although the two-term tradition as conceived by Jefferson placed a prohibition on third terms in general, a plan for rotation in its purest sense (allowing presidents to serve again after vacating the office for a time) would still address the issue of the consolidation of power in the presidency. Indeed, as we saw in the last chapter, rotation was not inconsistent with the traditional Whig ideal of restraining executive power. In fact, it was Thomas Jefferson's Virginia (along with North Carolina) that recommended, upon ratification, that a procedure for rotation be applied to the presidential office. Once the president was out of office for a period of time, the question of consolidating power was irrelevant because the former president was now an "average" citizen. Not only this, but officeholders, in this case presidents, would be periodically returned to the people, as it were, to reacquaint themselves with the experiences and trials of the average person. Upon assuming office again, the public benefits ostensibly would be great: the newly elected former president would have considerable experience on which to draw but would be refreshed in terms of the people's interests, and, most importantly, he would not have compromised himself through questionable political decision making (especially patronage appointments) to secure the office.

Grant supporters undoubtedly were dissembling somewhat in making their arguments for non-consecutive terms. Whether worthwhile or not, the idea had not been in currency. The one-term principle had been, though. In fact, some Democrats argued that 1880 nominee Winfield Scott Hancock should embrace the principle in his nomination acceptance letter and make it a campaign mantra,[69] while some even alleged that Samuel Tilden—the Democratic nominee of 1876 and popular (although not electoral) vote winner in the election—was not renominated because he had actually won the presidency in 1876. In this view, the party was merely following the one-term principle in declining his renomination.[70] At any rate, there was certainly no hint in

1876 that Grant and his supporters would be back legitimately in 1880 after having dutifully waited out a term. Similarly, Theodore Roosevelt, in retiring in 1909, made no reference whatsoever to a conception of "rotation," nor did he suggest even obliquely that he would be back in contention after the passage of a term or two. Nevertheless, Grant's run in 1880 provides an interesting commentary on the concept of rotation, as does Roosevelt's 1912 bid.

Although I will go into more detail on this front in the section on Theodore Roosevelt, the experiences of 1880 and 1912 do provide some ammunition for proponents of rotation, at least in one sense. In each case, the former president was defeated by his own party rather than the American people themselves. In each case, had the party not opposed the former president, the American people would almost assuredly have reelected him. Because Grant and Roosevelt did not have access to the machinery of the party, both were unable to marshal sufficient support for their nomination bids, which even in 1912, were in the hands of party leaders and bosses.[71] This does reinforce the argument made by proponents of rotation that once a president is out of office, it is difficult to "fix" the election through the patronage or appointment process. Yet these examples also suggest a key problem associated with term limits: in both cases, the ostensible choice of the people was not renominated. The typical view of the proponent of rotation is that the president is forcing himself on the people through the powers of the office, but clearly, especially with Theodore Roosevelt in 1912, rank-and-file party voters, not to mention the American people, were inclined toward the former president—they did not need to be coerced through party patronage or corruption. I will address these tensions more fully in the concluding chapter.

"MEANING, OF COURSE, THIRD CONSECUTIVE TERM"

With Grover Cleveland's nomination in 1884, the one-term principle briefly returned to the public view. In his letter accepting the Democratic Party nomination, Cleveland publicly and strongly advocated a one-term amendment to the Constitution, linking it closely with the issues of party patronage and corruption. "When we consider the patronage of this great office," he argued, "the allurements of power, the temptation to retain public office once gained, and, more than all, the availability a party finds in an incumbent[,] . . . we recognize in the eligibility of the President for re-election, a most serious danger." This "danger" could best be remedied by an amendment to the Constitution "disqualifying the President from re-election."[72] Although Cleveland's advocacy was high-profile, there is little evidence that the issue was an important one in the campaign of 1884. Even more importantly, unlike Hayes, who backed his rhetorical support for one term with the action of refusing to run for renomination or reelection, Cleveland promptly ignored the sentiment of his 1884 letter and sought renomination and reelection in both 1888 and 1892. Additionally, there was considerable pressure on Cleveland to run again in 1896, at least from some factions of the Democratic Party.[73] Although he declined, his unpopularity within the Democratic Party at the time undoubtedly influenced his decision.

In his well-known taxonomy of presidents, Stephen Skowronek is reluctant to classify Cleveland, calling him a "hard case."[74] With regard to presidential tenure, Cleveland is similarly a bit of a hard case. Cleveland was nominated by the Democratic Party three times for the presidency, and he won the office twice, being elected in 1884 and then 1892, thereby becoming the only president to that time—and since—to hold two nonconsecutive terms. An iconoclastic president in many ways, Cleveland became the central figure in the Democratic Party, yet he was widely perceived to be independent of the party, and certainly not subservient to it. His notoriety as a reformer and his relative scrupulousness in his civil service appointments more than likely inoculated him against his own criticisms of presidential reelection, particularly in 1888, when he was an incumbent president seeking reelection.[75] And his non-consecutive terms even opened up the door for reelection—had he been popular enough within the party—in 1896, without an obvious violation of the two-term tradition (at least following the logic that the two-term tradition only prevented more than two *consecutive* terms).[76]

Although for more than a decade "Cleveland's party," the Democratic Party would abandon the incumbent president in 1896 in favor of newcomer William Jennings Bryan. Not only that, but the Democratic Party platform that year would warn, in a direct jab at Cleveland, that "no man should be eligible for a third term of the presidential office."[77] Bryan would himself be three times nominated by the Democratic Party for president (1896, 1900, and 1908), but never elected. He would come out strongly in favor of a one-term presidency in his failed bids for the office and would influence the 1912 Democratic Convention to include a plank supporting a one-term presidency, which Woodrow Wilson promptly abandoned in 1916.[78]

Bryan's case for a one-term presidency would be especially pointed in 1900, as he faced Republican incumbent William McKinley, then pursuing his second term.[79] But, as usual, the one-term principle had little effect on the race, and McKinley was reelected by a substantial majority. What is interesting, however, is that not long after McKinley's reelection, a drumbeat was sounded in favor of a third term for McKinley.[80] Unlike Grant, McKinley effectively ended all speculation when he unequivocally stated, in an official statement to the American people, that he would not accept a third term: "I not only am not and will not be a candidate for a third term, but would not accept a nomination for it if it were tendered me."[81] With McKinley's assassination in September 1901, the issue would become merely one of conjecture, but there is no reason to believe that McKinley would have changed his mind between 1901 and 1904. Doubtless ambitious politicians and McKinley supporters would have tried to persuade him to run again ("for the good of the party"), but his declaration was firm and decisive.

McKinley's successor, Theodore Roosevelt, would issue a similar declaration regarding a "third" term. Roosevelt's circumstances were somewhat complicated because while he had served almost all of McKinley's second term, one might have argued that he was completing McKinley's second term and that with his own election in 1904, his own first term began in March of 1905. Roosevelt himself, however, would have none of this ambiguity and announced, on the night of his 1904 election, that he would not seek reelection in 1908. Tying his decision strongly and clearly to the two-term tradition, he cleared up any confusion about his serving out McKinley's term: "On the 4th of March next [1905] I shall have served three and one-half years, and the three and one-half years constitute my first term. The wise custom which limits the President to two terms regards the substance and not the form, and under no circumstance will I be a candidate for or accept another nomination."[82] And yet, despite this clear statement, it would not be long before Roosevelt's name would be circulating for a third term in 1908. By late 1906, a "Roosevelt Third Term League" would be created,[83] and by early 1907 newspaper editors around the country, most of them Republican, would start beating the drum for a Roosevelt third term.[84] Several state legislatures would also start weighing in on the matter during this time.[85]

Late in 1907, the speculation surrounding a Roosevelt third term would reach a point that Roosevelt would be forced to strongly reiterate his 1904 election night pledge. Roosevelt had written a letter in November of 1907 ordering several of his cabinet members, who were promoting a Roosevelt third term publicly, to stop all activity in his behalf or be subject to penalty.[86] Even though the letter leaked to the press, the third-term talk would not subside, with Roosevelt supporters holding out hope that he was only preventing campaigning on his behalf and that he would ultimately accept renomination if he had not sought it openly. Roosevelt's opponents were especially worried, and Democrats in the House of Representatives finally smoked Roosevelt out. In December 1907, they introduced an exact copy of the Springer Resolution into the House for debate and a vote, with the intention of forcing Republicans and hopefully Roosevelt to address the issue of a third term.[87] Their move worked, as Roosevelt two days later announced again that he would not be a candidate: "I have not changed and shall not change the decision thus announced."[88] From this point forward, the Roosevelt boom largely subsided, and attention was thenceforth focused on Roosevelt's heir apparent, William Howard Taft. Still, even at the Republican Convention of 1908, the crowd would cheer for Roosevelt for "forty-six minutes and fifty-five seconds," interrupting the speech of the chairman Henry Cabot Lodge.[89] Lodge would at last put an end to the Roosevelt speculation with the announcement that Roosevelt's decision was "dictated by the loftiest motives and by a noble loyalty to American traditions, [and it] is final and irrevocable."[90]

But only two years later, Theodore Roosevelt's name would be bandied about again for a third term, this time for 1912. A critical difference this second time around, though, was that Roosevelt, being disappointed in the actions and policies of his successor, Taft, and never really losing his desire for the presidency, took no steps to quell the speculation of his return to the presidency. The election of 1912 has received extensive coverage in the scholarly literature, including Roosevelt's pursuit of a third term and particularly his bolting the Republican Party to form the "Bull Moose" Progressive Party, and we need not rehash the whole story here.[91] There are three key points that warrant emphasis, however. First is the argument made by Roosevelt and his supporters that the two-term tradition only intended to prevent three consecutive terms and that therefore Roosevelt would be not be violating the tradition in 1912 if he ran again. Second is the response of President Taft to Roosevelt's candidacy. It is not too much to say that Taft's steadfastness in opposing Roosevelt's renomination was a critical component in Roosevelt's failure to achieve a third term. Finally, it is important to note the reactions within the

Republican and Democratic parties and also within the House and Senate to Roosevelt's third-term pursuit. All three of these dimensions of the 1912 election illustrate the critical combination of politics and principle that figures so prominently in the debate over presidential tenure.

Like Grant, at the conclusion of his presidency, Roosevelt left the United States to travel the world, in this case Africa and Europe. And also similar to Grant, when Roosevelt returned to the United States, in 1910, he was received warmly, thus setting off speculation that he might be a candidate for the presidency in 1912. Quite unlike Grant, though, by August of 1910, Roosevelt was touring the West and giving political speeches for his "New Nationalism," a progressive ideology that he advocated as the solution to the problems of American society. This progressivism notably included a strong role for presidential leadership. Indeed, in the 1912 campaign, he would often advance or embody what we have referred to as the plebiscitary model of the presidency, a conception of presidential leadership that is strongly rooted in presidential appeals to public opinion.

Roosevelt surely looked like he was campaigning for office, according to the *Times*, and "forces on the public mind an inevitable comparison between himself and his successor in the Presidency. And he takes no pains to make the comparison favorable to the President."[92] Although making no definitive announcement until early 1912, from this point forward, it was obvious to many observers that Roosevelt would be a candidate for the presidency in 1912.[93] And Taft's and Roosevelt's competing views of the presidency would be an intriguing subtext during the campaign.

While Roosevelt himself may well have had genuinely mixed feelings regarding his renomination, by early 1912 he had bowed to political pressure, and it was "arranged to stage the public demand" on him to run again in 1912. This came in the form of a letter from seven governors asking Roosevelt to run again.[94] Roosevelt replied that he would indeed accept the nomination if it were tendered to him because "I have always endeavored and always shall endeavor to reduce to action . . . the genuine rule of the people." He thereby urged that the people "be given the chance, through direct primaries, to express their preferences" for the Republican nominee, a course Roosevelt knew would favor himself over Taft.[95] Roosevelt further clarified his position, somewhat infamously, a day later: "My position is perfectly simple. . . . I said that I would not accept a nomination for a third term [in 1908], under any circumstances, meaning, of course, third consecutive term."[96] The *New York Times* aptly described Roosevelt's explanation as a "pitiful sophistication." Expressing the sense of many observers, Republican and Democrat alike, it continued: "There is no room for doubt that Mr. Roosevelt meant what the country understood his words to mean, that he would never again be a candidate." Unfortunately, it would henceforth be a "disagreeable necessity . . . to withhold full faith from the public statements of an ex-President of the United States."[97]

Roosevelt and his supporters had floated publicly the idea of consecutive terms earlier in the month in an editorial in the magazine *Outlook*, for which Roosevelt wrote a column and which was thought to be a "mouthpiece" of sorts for him. The editorial previewed almost exactly Roosevelt's words: his previous pledges against a third term "referred, of course, to a consecutive third term." But the editorial also provided a memorable analogy that would be discussed and sometimes lampooned throughout the campaign: "When a man says at breakfast in the morning, 'No, thank you, I will not take any more coffee,' it does not mean that he will not take any more coffee tomorrow morning, or next week, or next month, or next year."[98]

Whatever the merits of the analogy, Theodore Roosevelt was without question now officially in the race for the Republican nomination of 1912. Before we consider the actions of President Taft to derail Roosevelt's taking a third "cup of coffee," it is instructive to note the continuing legacy of the argument for a nonconsecutive third term. Despite the obviously disingenuous explanation of Roosevelt's intentions in not seeking reelection in 1908, Roosevelt and his supporters had an opening because the nonconsecutive argument did tap into the longstanding legacy of rotation, which had merit in 1880 and still did in 1912. In fact, Roosevelt would fail to win the Republican nomination precisely because the sitting Republican president was able to control the party machinery and stack the deck in his favor at the party convention. With Roosevelt on the outside in 1912, even though a former president, his attempt to secure a third term did not raise the same questions, especially about party patronage and corruption, which his pursuit as a sitting president would have raised (much like proponents of rotation argue).

For President William Howard Taft, that Roosevelt was no longer in office was not material: Roosevelt, through his pursuit of a third term, was undoubtedly assailing the traditions of the country. Moreover,

Roosevelt's philosophy of New Nationalism—especially its conception of the office of president—represented to Taft a great danger to constitutional government. Taft thereby fought hard to rally party leaders to his side and to deny Roosevelt the Republican nomination, even if it meant that Taft would split the party and lose the fall election. As Taft told an aide, speaking of Roosevelt: "He may defeat me for reelection, and he probably will, but I think I will defeat him in the Convention."[99] Taft did defeat Roosevelt at the convention, which had the effect of further radicalizing Roosevelt and ultimately pushing him, by August 1912, into assuming the leadership of a third party, the Bull Moose Progressives. In a speech delivered on the eve of the Republican Convention, suspecting what fate awaited him there—defeat at the hands of the party machine—Roosevelt lashed out against the party leaders and issued an exceedingly hyperbolic call to his supporters to fight the injustice: "We fight in honorable fashion for the good of mankind: fearless of the future, unheeding of our individual fates, with unflinching hearts and undimmed eyes, we stand at Armageddon and we battle for the Lord."[100] Surely Taft agreed with the *Times* characterization of the speech: "for any rational man it would be one more evidence of Mr. Roosevelt's utter unfitness for the high office he is so madly seeking."[101]

Not surprisingly, Taft lashed out at Roosevelt in his nomination acceptance letter: "A faction sought to force the party to violate a valuable and time-honored National tradition by intrusting the power of the Presidency for more than two terms to one man, and that man one whose recently avowed political views would have committed the party to radical proposals involving dangerous changes in our present constitutional form of representative government and our independent judiciary."[102] Not only was Roosevelt's violation of the two-term tradition indicative of an overly ambitious individual who could not be trusted with the presidency, but coupled with his progressive New Nationalist agenda, Roosevelt's election would shake the very foundations of constitutional government, in Taft's view. Taft closed his acceptance with another strong jab at Roosevelt and his mind-set: "they [the people] have not any of them given into the hands of any *one* the mandate to speak for them as peculiarly the people's representatives."[103] Taft was not only skewering Roosevelt's argument (to some degree implicit) that only he could lead the American people to the political promised land—that he was an "indispensable" leader—but also questioning that the presidency, tied strongly to public opinion, should be the central focus of the government.

It is somewhat ironic that Taft strove to prevent the election of Roosevelt only to help insure, as a by-product, the election of Woodrow Wilson, a president who would embrace and help to further consolidate Roosevelt's plebiscitary view of the presidency. Yet, in the context of the 1912 election, Wilson and the Democratic Party were rather more moderate than Roosevelt and his Bull Moose Progressive Party. Wilson, after all, issued no messianic calls to "battle for the Lord." In fact, echoing in some ways Taft's own perspective, Wilson explained in his acceptance of the Democratic nomination, "There is no indispensable man. The Government will not collapse and go to pieces if any one of the gentlemen who are seeking to be entrusted with its guidance should be left at home."[104] And whatever Wilson would become as president, many Democrats in 1912 shared Taft's concern about long presidential tenure, going so far as to include in the Democratic platform a plank calling for "a single Presidential term." The plank "urge[d] the adoption of an amendment to the Constitution making the President of the United States ineligible to reelection, and we pledge the candidates of this Convention to this principle."[105]

The Democratic and Republican Party responses to Theodore Roosevelt's candidacy for a third term are particularly important for our purposes here, as they illustrate the critical roles that principles, personalities, and especially politics play in the debate over presidential tenure. The Democratic Party made an issue out of the third term, at least implicitly, by advocating a single term for the presidency in its platform. Undoubtedly, this was an issue that Democrats had embraced in the past and especially in their nomination of William Jennings Bryan, an advocate of a single presidential term, in three previous elections. While this would seem to be a "principled" response, it was only partially so. For instance, when the House proposed to debate an amendment to the Constitution for a single presidential term in February 1912, the proposal stalled, in part because Democrats worried about the political ramifications: they didn't want it to look as if "the Democratic Party is afraid of Roosevelt."[106]

Republicans, for their part, had a quite mixed reaction to Roosevelt's candidacy for a third term. As we have seen, Taft was strongly opposed not just to Roosevelt's policies but also his challenge to the two-term tradition. Taft in some ways perfectly demonstrates the roles of personality—it was partly the personal conflict between Taft and Roosevelt that fueled his opposition—and principle in response to the third-term issue. Taft generally set aside politics, though, in the course of his opposition. After all, if

Taft had been purely concerned with the politics of the situation, namely, his party succeeding, he would have favored Roosevelt and promoted his election in 1912. With Taft's support, there is no doubt that Roosevelt would have captured the White House in 1912. More progressive-minded Republicans, of course, welcomed Roosevelt's candidacy, hoping to ride the popularity of the former president to preeminence within the party and the country.

Perhaps the best reflection of the competing perspectives within the Republican Party came with the Senate's consideration of a six-year, single presidential term in 1912 and 1913. While the House, as we saw, balked, the Senate continued to debate the provision through the heat of the election cycle. Obviously a "direct hint to Col. Roosevelt," the proposed amendment set off much debate and "aroused deep resentment among the Roosevelt Senators."[107] Mainstream Republican senators—most of them supporters of Taft—were, of course, debating an amendment to the Constitution for a single-term presidency at the same time as they were supporting Taft for a second term. This put them in a somewhat awkward, if not hypocritical position. What is more, Roosevelt was still very popular with the public at large, and an amendment obviously directed against him had its potential pitfalls. But Republican senators surely enjoyed pushing Democrats on the issue: they had declared for a single presidential term in their platform but now saw the prospects of electing a Democratic president. Moreover, the Democratic nominee, Wilson, in his writings (he had been a college professor) "favored long tenure of the Presidential office."[108]

The Senate would eventually pass the resolution in February 1913. Yet, when it came before the House, as it had a year earlier, Democratic representatives balked. Not only was *their* president taking office in the next month, but Democrats worried that it might cause a backlash against them—Theodore Roosevelt, despite losing the election in 1912, was quite popular among the people. They also preferred to keep Roosevelt around, as "his elimination through the adoption of the constitutional amendment would be mighty bad politics."[109] What is more, it later emerged that Wilson himself had urged House Democrats to block passage of the amendment.[110] And, of course, Democrats would abandon the single-term principle in the 1916 election when incumbent Democrat Woodrow Wilson would seek and win reelection. The *New York Times* summed up the critical role of politics in its report on Senate passage of the proposed amendment: "It would be foolish to deny that the movement for the amendment is largely influenced by the ordinary motives of party politics."[111]

"I Do Not Choose to Run"

There is no evidence that Woodrow Wilson ever felt himself bound by the Democratic platform of 1912 with regard to presidential tenure. He had supported in his pre-presidential writings a strong presidency—with a long term—and had made no public declarations for the single-term principle.[112] That he urged House Democrats to block the one-term proposed constitutional amendment speaks at least as much to Wilson's maintenance of his principles as his commitment to political or party advantage. As the *Times* saw it, if Wilson did block the amendment "he deserved well of the people. . . . [T]he plank should be left where it is, moribund, and no effort should be made to revive it." The plank was really only Bryan's "pet plank" and should not be thought to bind the party or President Wilson.[113] Although this perspective obviously understates the importance of the principle for the Democratic Party, it does provide a telling perspective on Wilson's own actions. It would be his party, rather than himself, that would have to shift its position to accommodate his second-term ambitions. Naturally, the party did not have to be prodded too hard, and by early 1914, party leaders would be laying the groundwork for a second Wilson term, arguing that "there has been much misunderstanding about the 'term of the president' plank" in the 1912 platform. It was "merely an indorsement of the proposal to amend the Federal Constitution," not a party command to the president.[114] Although this sidesteps the issue that Democrats in the House—at Wilson's request, apparently—blocked the attempt to amend the Constitution, the argument was technically accurate: the plank did not say anything about a Democratic president stepping aside after one term on his own volition, that is, without an amendment barring a second term having been passed. Clearly, though, politics and party advantage played an important role in the party's position on a second Wilson term. Democrats had not held the presidency since early 1897, and Wilson was in 1914 "immensely popular."[115] The one-term principle could not stand in the way of the return of the Democrats to national prominence.[116] Even William Jennings Bryan, the main proponent of the principle within the Democratic Party, would line up behind Wilson in 1916.[117]

And after Wilson's reelection in 1916, some within the party would even start talking of a third term. By June of 1918, the chairman of the Indiana Democratic Party (and former governor), Samuel Ralston, was declaring that "the exigencies of the times [World War I] call for the renomination and election in 1920 of Woodrow Wilson."[118] Wilson would make no public statement on the matter throughout 1918, but in a meeting with party leaders in early 1919, Wilson "let the cat out of the bag" that he would not be a candidate for reelection in 1920. Although "he did not actually say he would not be a candidate," the party leaders agreed that he intended not to be a candidate.[119] Since Wilson did not actually say that he would not be a candidate, he left some possible room for interpretation, and thereby speculation would continue about his intentions for 1920. What is interesting is that this speculation regarding a third term continued even after his stroke in early October 1919.[120] And although Wilson appears to have been open toward a third term even after the stroke, for all intents and purposes the stroke ended his pursuit of a third term.[121] Surely his health would have been a concern and even a prominent issue in the 1920 election.[122] The Democrats also would have had a difficult time overcoming their longstanding commitment to limiting the term of the president. Although they modified their principles somewhat to get a second term for Wilson, their arguments for a second term were in part defended through appeal to the two-term tradition. While a second term might be squared with tradition and finessed with regard to the party's commitment to limited terms for the president, clearly a third term would expose the party to charges of hypocrisy and rank partisanship. Moreover, with the war ending in late 1918, the argument for crisis leadership would evaporate to a large extent before the election. And yet, until Wilson's death in February 1924, he would even be promoted by some Democrats to run for renomination and election in 1924.

As it worked out, the 1924 election, similar to that of 1920,[123] would be a tough one for Democrats, and they would lose big in the electoral and popular vote, Robert La Follette's Progressive Party candidacy splitting the opposition to incumbent Republican President Calvin Coolidge. But Coolidge himself would soon feel the power of this opposition as talk led to his possible pursuit of a "third" term. Before we discuss the issue of a Coolidge third term, it is important to briefly address the particularities of Coolidge's situation. Coolidge became president in August of 1923, after the death of President Warren Harding, and served out the remainder of Harding's term—which amounted to about nineteen months—before assuming his "own" term in March of 1925. Coolidge's path to the presidency was very similar, on the surface, to that of Theodore Roosevelt. Yet an important difference—a difference that would inform the fine print of the Twenty-second Amendment,[124] in fact—was that Coolidge served far less of Harding's term than Roosevelt did of McKinley's. Whereas Coolidge served a little over a year and a half as president after Harding's death, Roosevelt served three and a half years after McKinley's death. Even though, as we saw, there was controversy at the time as to whether these three and a half years should be thought of as Roosevelt's or McKinley's term, the argument was much more straightforward with regard to Coolidge's situation. By the time of the 1924 election, Coolidge had been in office for only a little over a year; it was not unreasonable for some supporters to think that only in 1925 had his presidential term begun.

And so immediately upon Coolidge's inauguration in 1925, we find politicians discussing 1928 and floating Coolidge's name as a possible candidate. Not surprisingly, it was Coolidge's "strength with the masses" that had Republicans with "no great interest in Mr. Coolidge" touting his possible renomination and reelection in 1928.[125] One suspects that with Coolidge's great popularity, it would not have mattered to Republican supporters how much of Harding's term he had served. Nevertheless, this was a powerful part of the argument: his "political associates . . . do not regard the one year and seven months he served on President Harding's term as a Presidential term." Perhaps a commentary on the ambiguity of Coolidge's situation, there was to be little organized opposition to a third term within the mass public.[126]

But, naturally, not all Republicans, especially leaders, were in favor of Coolidge's reelection in 1928, and Democrats were wary of Coolidge's power with voters. Coolidge faced an especially strong threat in his own party from western farmers, who disagreed with the administration on policy grounds.[127] What is more, Democrats and "insurgent" or progressive-minded Republicans in Congress would increasingly make noise on the question of a third term, beginning in early 1927.[128] All the while, Coolidge would issue no statement on the third-term issue nor would he take any obvious steps to promote his candidacy. But neither would he openly discourage his supporters.[129] Surely Coolidge's reticence may have been intended simply to preserve his position relative to congressional and party leaders—had he announced he would not be seeking reelection too early, he arguably would have made himself somewhat irrelevant and encouraged jockeying for position among prospective Republican candidates for 1928.[130] But it was not unreasonable to assume he was at least considering a third term.

However, the movement to nominate Coolidge would receive a great blow, from the president's own hand, with his famous statement, released to the press in early August 1927: "I do not choose to run for president in nineteen twenty-eight." Although a seemingly straightforward statement as to Coolidge's intentions,[131] many Coolidge supporters did not accept the declaration as definitive and continued to promote his candidacy.[132] Coolidge, after all, could have said, like Theodore Roosevelt, that "under no circumstances" would he accept renomination, or he might have opted for the absolutist approach of William Tecumseh Sherman when promoted for the presidency in 1884: "If nominated I will not accept; if elected I will not serve."[133] Coolidge would issue further clarifications of his position against reelection in 1927[134] and 1928,[135] but calls would persist up to the Republican Convention.[136] Yet after a strong vote against a third term—56 to 22—in the Senate in February of 1928, Coolidge's possibility for nomination and election was thereafter remote. Obviously directed at Coolidge, the resolution expressed merely the "sense of the Senate" and had no true legal effect. But the size of the vote and the numerous Republicans who voted for it suggested that "practical politicians would be staggered at the thought of flying in the face of such a record indicating so deep a popular feeling."[137]

It is difficult to say what Coolidge's true intentions were. He would later claim in his autobiography that he stepped down for principled reasons, saying that presidents "are in grave danger of becoming careless and arrogant" and that the "chances of having wise and faithful public service are increased by a change in the Presidential office after a moderate length of time."[138] Perhaps Coolidge saw how quickly other leaders were willing to jump on the bandwagon to ride him to another victory and how easily principles could be massaged or compromised when it came to keeping a president in power.[139] On the other hand, perhaps Silent Cal really did think it justified that he run for a "third" term, given the brevity of his first one, and maybe he was deliberately ambiguous so as to leave his possible renomination and reelection an open matter. There is some evidence that points in this direction, but the "bulk of the evidence seems to favor the opinion that President Coolidge's renunciation was a genuine one."[140]

Although the framers of the Constitution saw the need for reeligibility in the presidency, a tradition prohibiting third terms developed by the first decade of the ninetheenth century. And until Grant's attempts at a third term in 1876 and 1880, most nineteenth-century arguments over presidential tenure thereafter were whether a president should serve a second term let alone a third. But during the second half of the nineteenth century and for much of the early twentieth (with Presidents Grant, Cleveland, McKinley, Theodore Roosevelt, Wilson, and Coolidge), the issue of a third term returned as a key question of presidential politics. Presidents, candidates, members of Congress, and many public commentators weighed in on the desirability of presidential third terms. Despite the seemingly principled nature of many of these debates and discussions, political advantage and even caprice played a role in the outcomes as well. Indeed, it is striking how quickly partisans and presidents themselves revised their views on presidential tenure once their political benefit clashed with their principles, not just in the post–Civil War period, but even prior (for example, Jackson's embrace of a one-term rule while winning a second term). Charles W. Stein has claimed that it was "all luck and no maneuvering that . . . kept the no-third-term tradition on its feet" during this period. It was "luck in the shape of sickness, deaths, close elections, barely missed nominations, party splits, and even personal whims."[141] This characterization is at least somewhat apposite.

Yet, despite the influence of politics and chance in many of these debates, these factors explain only so much, even with regard to the post–Civil War period. Undoubtedly we have critical examples of several presidents holding to their principles in the face of their political interest, suggesting the very real power of the two-term (and even one-term) tradition. Hayes's refusal to pursue a second term, McKinley's clear declaration that he would not accept a third renomination or term, and Coolidge's steadfastness in the face of third-term demands cannot be explained merely by appeals to politics, political advantage, or whims. And in the antebellum period, the actions of Jefferson (not to mention Madison and Monroe), Jackson, and even Polk, in his adherence to the one-term tradition, point to the powerful restraint that the traditional

Whig skepticism of long presidential tenure has had on our political system. Certainly, chance and politics had something to do with no president serving a third term prior to Franklin Roosevelt, but tradition and principle were vital as well. And, as we will see in the next chapter, luck, politics, and appeal to the founders' views and principles on executive reeligibility undoubtedly all played roles in FDR's shattering of the two-term tradition.

THE TRADITION FALLS

Roosevelt's Third Term

The forces and influences which push Mr. Roosevelt toward answering affirmatively the importunings of the zealous third-term advocate are many and mighty. But there are also mighty deterrents, not the least of which is the anti-third-term tradition together with the American principle of rotation of honors and office which it seems to symbolize.

Turner Catledge, 1939

With the exception of the framers' original decision against presidential term limitations, the most significant event in the history of the presidential tenure debate is naturally the election of 1940, the first successful challenge to the two-term tradition. Not only was the tradition shattered, but the wheels were set in motion—fueled also by the successful pursuit of a fourth term in 1944—for a backlash movement that would seek to prevent future violations of the two-term tradition. This reaction would reach its fulfillment in the Twenty-second Amendment to the Constitution.

Although, as described in the previous chapter, other presidents had challenged the tradition before Franklin Roosevelt, all of them faced significant opposition within their own parties leading up to the possible third term and hence either were denied nominations that they passively (Grant) or actively (Theodore Roosevelt) sought or did not even seek renomination (Cleveland and Coolidge). Although Theodore Roosevelt ran in the general election of 1912 as a third-party candidate—prior to 1940, the most substantial threat to the tradition—the Republican Party's denial of its renomination proved critical to his failure.[1] Furthermore, Franklin Roosevelt's third-term pursuit was unique in that a looming crisis in Europe—and then all-out war—helped to fuel speculation about and support for a departure from the two-term tradition. No other previous third-term candidate had had his party's support, nor did any have the pretext of "crisis" to legitimize his pursuit. As we will see, FDR's party and supporters were clamoring for a third term quite some time before hostilities began in Europe; however, public opinion was decidedly lukewarm on a third term until the European crisis escalated. When public opinion softened in the face of the outbreak of World War II, it was then only a matter of finding out whether Roosevelt would run for and serve a third term. It is probably too much to say that "[h]ad there been no Second World War, the election of Franklin Roosevelt to a third term would have been as likely as the return of prohibition to the American scene."[2] Nevertheless, it is important not to underestimate the role of war in Roosevelt's pursuit of a third term.

Determining Roosevelt's intentions is not easy. FDR himself would contend that he did not decide to run until right before the Democratic Convention in the summer of 1940. However, others would suspect his intention to serve a third term from the very beginning of his second term. It is undeniable that Roosevelt's silence on the issue made his eventual nomination much more likely. Until FDR declared his intentions, few other Democrats would actively seek the nomination, thereby clearing the way for a "draft" at the Democratic convention. Unlike President James Polk, who declared at the outset of his term in 1845 that he would not seek a second term, it is quite possible that Roosevelt was simply preserving his political power and trying to avoid becoming a lame duck early in his second term. However, there are a number of signs that seem to suggest that lame duck concerns coexisted with Roosevelt's desire to remain in office.

Regardless of Roosevelt's intentions, the heart of this chapter is the vigorous debate over the wisdom of the third term. This was a debate naturally driven by FDR's opponents, who were scandalized that he would break the venerable two-term tradition. FDR would have very little directly to say on the tradition, but his supporters would have much to say in defense of the third term and Roosevelt's continuing leadership. Although this debate occurred over 150 years after the tenure debate at the Constitutional Convention, it is fascinating to see the similarities across the years. Supporters of the two-term tradition especially parallel those who recoiled at the absence of term limits in the Constitution. In their arguments, they embody what we have termed the Whig model of the presidency. The Roosevelt supporters in many ways reflect the thinking of the "constitutional" model and particularly Hamilton's spirited defense of continuity of administration in time of emergency. Yet the Roosevelt supporters surely do not embody Hamilton's (and other Federalists') cynical view of the public and public opinion. What is more, their conception of presidential power is considerably more robust than that conceived by even the Federalists. The arguments of the Roosevelt supporters embody both the constitutional model and what we have called the "plebiscitary" model of presidential leadership. Thus did Roosevelt supporters point not only to the crisis in Europe to justify his continuing leadership but also to his strong relationship with the American people and his role as champion of their interests against the wealthy and elite. As these debates are extensions of those of 1787–1788, so they preview as well the debates over the Twenty-second Amendment in 1947, the subject of chapter 6.

"Until or Unless the President Reveals His Intentions"

There were rumblings about a possible third term from the beginning of Roosevelt's second term. George Gallup, for instance, had polled on the question of a third term at the beginning of the second term.[3] And the *New York Times* declared in July 1937, after Governor George Earle of Pennsylvania came out for a third term, that the "issue is out for general discussion in tones above the whispers that have been heard ever since the unparalleled Roosevelt victory of last November."[4] But serious public discussion of the prospect did not really begin until later in 1938, particularly in the context of the midterm elections. For instance, the *Chicago Tribune* reported in September 1938 that "political observers in Washington" viewed Roosevelt's attempted "purge" of anti–New Deal Democrats in that year's primary elections as a clear sign of his intentions to pursue a third term.[5] A strident opponent of the president, the *Tribune* would editorialize hyperbolically at the end of 1938 that "Mr. Roosevelt wants to reign and rule. He wants to remake the political, social, and economic order of the United States. . . . Mr. Roosevelt as a third term candidate would confront the nation with dictatorship in flesh and blood, not in theory."[6] By the spring and summer of 1939, support for the third term would exhibit more and more strength among prominent Democratic leaders.

What is interesting about these early calls for a third term is how they often were only tenuously, if at all, connected to the developing European crisis. Many of the arguments for a third term in 1938 and much of 1939 were based upon the protection of New Deal economic policies.[7] One of the more significant justifications came in an article advocating a third term, published in June of 1939 by Roosevelt's secretary of the interior, Harold Ickes. Ickes had promoted a third term as early as the summer of 1938, and he continued to push the issue in late 1938 within the context of the midterm elections.[8] These earlier statements, though, were oblique compared with his outright advocacy of a third term in his June 1939 article in *Look* magazine.

The article caused a stir, as this was a member of the president's cabinet making a strong case for the president to run for a third term. Ickes, in defense of the third term, noted that "the Constitution is eloquently silent" on the matter, and he also quoted the founder of the two-term tradition, Thomas Jefferson, as saying that he (Jefferson) would have agreed to a third term, but only under one circumstance: "a successor as might bring in a monarchist." Ickes continued: "It is not too much to say . . . that if Jefferson were President today he would consent to run for a third term in order to defeat economic royalism and fascism. It is my firm conviction that, only in the continuance of triumphant liberalism in this country, can there be any real assurance of our ability to withstand fascism."[9] While Ickes linked his arguments to "fascism," then the dominant governing philosophy in Germany and Italy, his more direct concern was protecting American workers from the wealthy and big businesses; in other words, Ickes was making the preservation of the New Deal the pretext for the third term. And he was specifically worried about possible successors, either within the Democratic Party or from the Republican Party, and their propensity to be "monarchists" or "royalists."[10] Although other members of the cabinet also came out for a third term around this time—by July 1939, Attorney General Frank Murphy, Secretary of Agriculture Henry Wallace, and Secretary of Commerce Harry Hopkins, in addition to Ickes, would publicly support the third term[11]—Ickes's defense was particularly important, as he often operated as a political attack dog and even a "lightning rod" for the president on matters political.[12] Although Roosevelt refused comment on Ickes's article and advocacy of the third term,[13] it is hard to believe that he did not at least tacitly support Ickes's actions.

A long *New York Times* piece in mid-June of 1939 confirmed the centrality of preserving the New Deal to the clamor for a third term at this time. Washington was consumed by a "third-term agitation the like of which has hardly been witnessed before," and the agitation was attributed to "a campaign of zealous or interested persons to induce Franklin D. Roosevelt to stand again for election" as well as the president's own silence on the issue. The "New Dealers" did not want to give up "their tasty concoction of position, prestige, and power" and thus were "the men who were fanning the third-term agitation to a blue heat." The question, though, was whether "the American people [could] be convinced that the need for completion and perfection of the New Deal" was an "emergency" of sufficient importance to depart from the two-term tradition.[14] Notwithstanding the somewhat tendentious nature of the piece, it suggests how important preservation of the New Deal and its programs was to the pursuit of the third term, a motivation that would remain strong, even though eventually eclipsed by the crisis of World War II.

And so it continued through 1939 and 1940: more and more Democrats coming out in support of a third term while Roosevelt maintained silence on the issue.[15] What did change, however, especially in 1940, was public opinion on the issue of the third term. With the beginning of the war in Europe in September 1939, public sentiment showed a shift in favor of a third term for Roosevelt. It was not a dramatic change, but George Gallup put it this way: "although a majority of American voters are still opposed to another term for Mr. Roosevelt, the first impact of fighting abroad has apparently shortened the odds against the President if he chooses to run."[16] Showing the fluidity of opinion, however, in March 1940, a new Gallup poll would suggest, according to Gallup, that FDR "would have a hard time being elected at the present time."[17] The Nazi invasions of Holland, Belgium, and France in May of 1940, though, would again decisively shift public opinion in favor of a Roosevelt third term, with 57 percent of Americans favoring a third term compared with 47 percent in April 1940. And given that this was six weeks prior to the Democratic National Convention, the "future trend of third-term sentiment" would take on "enormous importance."[18] On the eve of the Democratic Convention, 57 percent of the public would continue to favor the third term,[19] and thus Roosevelt would be well positioned for a "draft" at the nominating convention.

What is fascinating about the increasing calls for Roosevelt's service in late 1939 and 1940 is how many still appealed to preserving the New

Deal and the Roosevelt legacy, in addition to the foreign crisis, to justify the third term. While Democratic Senator Byron (Pat) Harrison would abandon his opposition to the third term in January 1940 because of the "world crisis,"[20] and Paul McNutt—federal security administrator and Democratic presidential aspirant in 1940—would pledge his support to a Roosevelt third term due to "the threat of total war,"[21] others would persist in appealing to the preservation of the New Deal and the Roosevelt domestic legacy. Third-term supporter Sidney Hillman, vice president of the Congress of Industrial Organizations (CIO), would appeal in January 1940 to not only the world crisis, but the need to preserve the New Deal and "make sure that the progressive legislation of the last few years be continued."[22] Secretary Ickes would reassert his support of a third term in May 1940 based in part on the world crisis but also in order to prevent "counter-revolution" and the "abandonment of the New Deal."[23] As the *Chicago Tribune* observed, when Roosevelt's "place men" argued for his renomination, "[t]hey didn't say it was for war; they said it was for continuance of the New Deal revolution."[24]

Roosevelt's silence throughout the third-term buzz made it very difficult for other Democrats to declare for the presidency.[25] To come out before Roosevelt declared his own intentions would represent a show of disloyalty and would bode ill for the candidate whether Roosevelt ran in 1940 or not. If Roosevelt did run and win in 1940, the candidate would risk punishment during a Roosevelt third term. If Roosevelt ultimately chose not to run, the candidate likely would not gain Roosevelt's blessing for the nomination because of the disloyalty. Candidates, therefore, were forced to quietly campaign for the nomination, all the while pledging their support for Roosevelt. The publicity director of the Democratic National Committee, Charles Michelson, put it best when he said in June of 1939, "[t]here will be nothing doing worth while in Democratic politics until or unless the President reveals his intentions."[26]

And by early 1940, there was considerable tension within the Democratic Party over Roosevelt's silence. Arthur Krock noted breathlessly in the *Times* that the "situation is so incredible to many Democrats, so destructive to their nerves and their hopes, that the President may have taken action before this dispatch is published." Of course, the president did not take action before the story appeared, but surely Democratic leaders and especially presidential aspirants were in a fit by February 1940. At this time, only one candidate—Vice President John Garner— had actively declared that he would seek the nomination regardless of whether Roosevelt sought reelection, but others, particularly Postmaster James Farley, were left in the lurch by Roosevelt's silence.[27] By late March of 1940, Farley could wait no longer. On his account, Roosevelt had promised to state his intentions by February 1940;[28] in the face of Roosevelt's continued silence, Farley decided to throw his hat into the ring. This development apparently worried third-term advocates—Farley had considerable support within the party—but did nothing to dampen their efforts to promote Roosevelt in the drive to accumulate convention delegates, a drive that commenced in early 1940.[29] In the weeks prior to Farley's announcement, for instance, Secretary Ickes had been working overtime to assure that Roosevelt would win the convention delegation from California. Notwithstanding his denials, "Washington reports persisted that [Ickes] . . . had acted as peacemaker here [in California] with 'full authority.'"[30] Many observers pointed to Roosevelt's acquiescence in having his name entered in various primaries in early 1940 as strong evidence of his intentions to pursue a third term. In particular, "his failure to withdraw his name from the April Illinois primary was interpreted by Washington analysts to mean that this was the signal to draft him."[31]

But it is inaccurate to say that Roosevelt maintained complete silence on this issue of the third term. Rather, he told different things to different people and seemed genuinely to be confused about what he might or should do. Early in the second term, Roosevelt seemed to be cultivating his close friend Works Progress Administration (CIO) director Harry Hopkins as his successor.[32] After Hopkins's poor health eliminated him as a serious candidate, it was "generally accepted" that Secretary of State Cordell Hull was Roosevelt's personal favorite as successor, although Attorney General and ardent New Dealer Robert Jackson was believed to be a close second.[33] Moreover, in discussions with Farley and Secretary of Labor Frances Perkins, "he said not only would he refuse to be a candidate but actually he had made other plans." His agreement with *Collier's* magazine to write a column after his presidency was over lent credence to this interpretation.[34] And according to advisor Samuel Rosenman, Roosevelt during the second term seriously discussed the prospect of Rosenman "buying a piece of property near Hyde Park in order to spend some time up there and help him in writing his memoirs."[35] Surely these are signs of one at the very least ambivalent about, if not opposed to, a third term.

Still, upon learning in February 1940 that the nominating convention would be held in Chicago, Roosevelt approvingly told Ickes, "I am not overlooking the fact that [Democratic Mayor] Kelly could pack the galleries for us."[36] What is more, on a number of occasions Roosevelt discussed the possibility of successors and what type of candidate he would support. More than one keen observer noted that Roosevelt seemed to be painting a "self-portrait."[37] FDR also seemed to find fault, especially in discussions with his political advisors, with most of the existing candidates, fueling his supporters' belief that he was the best (or only) alternative in 1940.[38] A particularly nasty public commentary came regarding Farley's candidacy. Roosevelt ostensibly relayed through a member of Congress—who then relayed the sentiment to the press—that he doubted Farley as a strong candidate given his Catholic faith and worries about his allegiance to the pope.[39] At the very least, it was widely acknowledged that Roosevelt was not going too far out of his way to aid other candidates for the nomination of 1940.

Roosevelt biographer James MacGregor Burns probably came closest to the truth when he said of Roosevelt's intentions that "the President was genuinely unsure of his own desires." Not only did Roosevelt want to keep his options open, as was his method of leadership, but he also apparently believed that his silence would aid him in his dealings with Congress in the final two years of his second term.[40] According to Farley, Roosevelt defended his silence until the Democratic Convention thusly: "It would have destroyed my effectiveness as the leader of the nation."[41] Even the sometimes critical *New York Times* would see the wisdom of this position. As early as 1937, for instance, the *Times* recognized that previous "presidents who have 'called their shots' too far in advance . . . have almost invariably run into serious difficulties."[42] The *Times* would continue to hold this position in June of 1939, saying that Roosevelt's "influence on Congress, none too constant during the last two years, might be materially weakened" were he to announce his retirement prematurely.[43] A month later, the *Times* further elaborated that if "he disclosed and made irrevocable any design he might have to leave office in January 1941, he would lose his grip on Congress and become immediately a 'lame duck' President, and thereby surrender his program to the prey of shifting opposition blocs." Despite the advisability of the strategy, "the time has come, in view of some of his most ardent well-wishers, to change [it]."[44]

But with the commencement of war in Europe, Roosevelt's decision to keep quiet about his intentions became even more defensible. Given Roosevelt's strong stance with the "democracies" of Europe, his announcement of retirement might give encouragement to the German and Italian governments. While some Roosevelt supporters would go too far and suggest collusion (or at least sympathy) between the Republican Party and the Nazis and fascists of Europe, a weakened Democratic Party (or at least one with a leadership vacuum) might very well usher in a Republican president committed to the principles of "isolationism." Although Wendell Willkie, the eventual nominee, would not be an isolationist, the prospect of an isolationist receiving the nomination and winning the general election was certainly feasible throughout 1939 and 1940. Roosevelt's reticence on the issue of the third term could easily, then, be justified in terms of buoying the spirits of the English and European democracies as well as keeping Roosevelt's political position strong.

"AN INVITATION TO A DRAFT"

Whether Roosevelt was already leaning toward a third term or not, Willkie's nomination evidently convinced Roosevelt's supporters, and then Roosevelt himself, that only he could win the upcoming election. The *Times* relayed that, according to administration officials, "if there had been doubts in his mind of his intentions they had been dispelled by the nomination of Mr. Willkie."[45] Willkie presented a unique challenge to the Democrats and to Roosevelt. He had not been a front-runner like New York Governor Thomas Dewey (who would be the nominee in 1944) or Ohio Senator Robert Taft. In fact, he had been a dark horse candidate, a former Democrat and businessman with little experience in politics. Despite his "amateur" status, Willkie was "an attractive antagonist. Glamour had, in the past, been a Roosevelt prerogative." Willkie was also a committed internationalist—not an isolationist like others in his party—and therefore the campaign would likely center on domestic politics and the New Deal. Roosevelt, like his advisors, concluded that while "a Dewey, Taft or [Michigan Senator Arthur] Vandenberg might have been stopped by Cordell Hull or someone else, Willkie presented a mandate for four more Roosevelt years."[46]

That Willkie's nomination forced the hand of Roosevelt says something about the calculations that went into the third term. Undoubtedly, preventing a political neophyte like Willkie from winning the office at a time of foreign crisis—even though he was not an isolationist—would be part of the rationale for pursuing a third term. But the political jeopardy into which the New Deal and the Democratic Party were thrown with the nomination of this attractive—and seemingly electable—candidate was also in the minds of Roosevelt and his supporters as the bid for a third term became a reality.

Not long after the nomination of Willkie, Roosevelt would hold a meeting with Secretary of State Cordell Hull. As Burns tells it: "The secretary of state immediately noticed a whole change of manner. To be sure, Roosevelt still deprecated the idea of running for a third term. But he talked in a 'sort of impatient, incredulous tone' of the pressure on him not to let the party down. He explored Hull's weak points as a candidate. His guarded tone convinced the old Tennessean that the President would run again."[47] At this point, only a few weeks prior to the Democratic nominating convention, there was little that Hull could do. His only chance at the nomination at this late date had been an endorsement from Roosevelt. The only remaining obstacle to Roosevelt's renomination was James Farley, as Vice President Garner had done quite poorly in the primaries and thus was largely out of the race. When Roosevelt met Farley in early July, it was obvious to Farley that the president had decided to run again. Farley implored the president to make clear to the convention that he was not a candidate and would not accept the nomination. Roosevelt said that he could not decline the nomination even though "I don't want to run and I'm going to tell the convention so."[48]

Farley himself was quite opposed to a third term, worrying especially, according to his close friend and newspaper reporter Walter Trohan, that "taking a third term would stop younger men from coming up in the party and wreck the whole structure."[49] Therefore, he would not pull out of the running, despite no chance of beating Roosevelt. The question, rather, was how many votes he would take away from Roosevelt, for despite Roosevelt's broad popularity within the party, there was a sizeable minority in the party that was anti–New Deal or anti-Roosevelt—or both. There were also some who, despite their warm feelings for Roosevelt, did not want to see the two-term tradition broken.

Roosevelt was overwhelmingly renominated, but it was not in the fashion that he had hoped. As Roosevelt had authorized, convention chairman Senator Alben Barkley "informed the delegates that he [Roosevelt] had no wish to run again, and released all delegates pledged to or instructed for him to vote for any candidate they might be pleased to support."[50] But this move itself was interpreted by many, in the words of a *New York Times* editorial, as an "invitation to a draft." "He could have said, not merely that he had 'no desire or purpose' to be a candidate, but—simply and flatly—that he would not accept a renomination if it were offered to him."[51] What is more, Roosevelt political operatives like Ickes and Hopkins were closely monitoring activities at the convention, which further gave the lie to Roosevelt not seeking—at least in a limited sense—the nomination. And in the end, Farley (and Garner) would deprive Roosevelt of the unanimous support of the convention.[52]

Nevertheless, Roosevelt would be renominated resoundingly if not unanimously, and then he would move on to control the vice presidential nomination. Garner, having openly opposed his boss, now had no chance of being renominated, but there were many others who were trying to secure the second spot. Yet Roosevelt, to the shock and dismay of his advisors, was adamant: the vice presidential candidate was to be Secretary of Agriculture Henry Wallace. Wallace was a notable liberal within the party, and one who, according to Roosevelt, "would appeal to the farm states, where isolationist feeling was strong."[53] But national tickets generally are characterized by balance. That is, with the New Dealers winning the presidential nomination through Roosevelt, many at the convention expected a more conservative figure within the party to be nominated as vice president. But Roosevelt was steadfast, even going so far as to draft a statement to the convention "refusing the nomination . . . if Wallace was not chosen."[54] Roosevelt won the fight, but in the process he alienated many within the party, regular delegates as well as leaders such as Farley, Garner, and the vice presidential hopefuls.[55] As Burns has put it, the "show in Chicago had not quite come off: he had won his draft in such a way as to intensify popular suspicion of his deviousness. It was not surprising that polls showed a Republican resurgence."[56]

Predictably, Roosevelt would face opposition from anti–New Dealers such as Democratic Senator Edward Burke of Nebraska. Not only had Burke been consistently opposed to New Deal legislation, he had failed to win renomination in his party's 1940 primary. He spearheaded plans for a "nation-wide organization of Democrats, Republicans and independents to fight the third-term candidacy of President Roosevelt."[57] Also among the Democratic opponents of the third term was former New York Governor Al Smith, a conservative who became estranged from Roosevelt and who had supported Republican Alf Landon in 1936.[58]

But it would be a mistake to see the opposition to Roosevelt's third term as merely a collection of those already unfavorable to Roosevelt's candidacy. In fact, the *New York Times*, which had supported Roosevelt in both 1932 and 1936, came out in opposition to his candidacy of 1940, mainly because of the third-term issue. The editors were skeptical of the "draft" of Roosevelt: "he has not accepted the nomination because he really believes he has been 'drafted,' [since] he has seemed so carefully to plan this 'draft,' and could so easily have resisted it."[59] Indeed, in a news item of the same day, *Times* correspondent Krock characterized the ultimate "draft" at the Democratic Convention as one that was "never able to shake off the quotation marks." Instead, the renomination could be traced to the "inner circle of the New Deal" and was "[a]ided from the beginning by the passive acquiescence of the President—expressed by silence."[60] Furthermore, noting that "the position of the two parties is now practically identical" with regard to "issues of war," *Times* editors perceptively saw the key role of protecting the New Deal in Roosevelt's pursuit of a third term. They concluded that Roosevelt and his party "must now recognize that there are large numbers of independent voters to whom the doctrine of any man's indispensability is distasteful, and for whom the third-term issue will be important and decisive."[61]

And while the anti-Roosevelt and anti–New Deal opposition may have seized upon the third-term issue as a reason to oppose Roosevelt, Roosevelt supporters were not immune to skepticism regarding their motives. The most obvious charge of inconsistency could be leveled at Democratic senators. Indeed, Senator Burke challenged his fellow Democrats "to explain why they were supporting President Roosevelt for re-election after voting for a 1928 resolution opposing a 'third term for any President.'"[62] Only four Democrats had voted against the resolution in 1928, which was aimed at Republican President Calvin Coolidge, while thirty seven had voted for it.[63] And of those thirty seven, fourteen were still serving in 1940. Not one of these fourteen actively opposed Roosevelt, not even Maryland senator Millard Tydings, who had been targeted unsuccessfully in the failed "purge campaign" of 1938.[64] Despite strong arguments in favor of a third term, such as experienced leadership in a time of crisis—the most common mantra of the campaign—surely that Roosevelt was a Democrat and not a Republican had helped them change their minds on the issue.

What is more, as we will see, competing with this appeal to experienced leadership were not-so-subtle arguments in favor of simply preserving the New Deal, suggesting the strong political nature of the support of the third term. Indeed, Senator Kenneth McKellar, one of the Democratic senators who had opposed a third term in the 1928 resolution, justified his support for Roosevelt's third term because "our people have no intention of turning our government over to the same old interests that ran it prior to the Roosevelt era."[65] Roosevelt and his administration usually would be more careful in linking the New Deal—and its advancement of democracy—to the conflict in Europe, but even they would sometimes lean so heavily on class-based appeals and the language of social progressivism that the war in Europe would seem secondary to preserving the New Deal in Roosevelt's quest for a third term.

"IF THIS PRINCIPLE DIES, IT WILL BE DEAD FOREVER"

Although the election of 1940 would prominently feature debates over the course of American foreign policy and the continuing efficacy of the New Deal, the question of the third term would also play an important role. An examination of the major campaign speeches reveals the general contours of this debate over the third term, the most significant public debate over presidential tenure in America since the constitutional period of 1787–1788. The debates of 1940 track well those of 1787–1788, with Roosevelt's supporters finding solace in Hamilton's arguments, and with Willkie and Republicans inclining toward the Anti-Federalist (or Whig) view.[66] Yet there are also important variations that relate to changing conceptions of government and especially presidential leadership.

At no time after his renomination did Roosevelt address the so-called two-term tradition or the question of term limits in anything but implicit or elliptical terms; in fact, the record does not indicate FDR discussing in a meaningful way, even with his advisors, the theoretical or philosophical issues associated with a third term.[67] Indeed, late in the campaign, Willkie was still clamoring for a defense of the third term: "Mr. Third Term Candidate, will you not please before you conclude your campaign speeches tell the American people as to why you believe you should be permitted to violate this sacred principle of free government?"[68] Willkie, however, made the third term the centerpiece of several of his campaign speeches and, throughout many of his speeches, did not refer to Roosevelt by name but rather as the "third term candidate" or some such variation. Thus Willkie will get more attention in what follows, while we will have to lean somewhat on FDR's supporters to flesh out the arguments in favor of the third term. As Willkie was nominated before Roosevelt and initiated much of the criticism of the third term, the speeches of Willkie will be addressed first.

Nominated in July 1940, Wendell Willkie would not deliver his official acceptance until the middle of August. Interestingly, the speech would spend very little time discussing Roosevelt's pursuit of a third term. Rather, Willkie would focus on points of difference in the policies of himself and FDR, setting the tenor of the coming campaign. However, anticipating themes to come, Willkie would question the president's decision—announced in his address to the Democratic Convention—to avoid "purely political debate" and make an offer to engage in face-to-face debates in the coming months: "I do not think that the issues at stake are 'purely political.' In my opinion they concern the life and death of democracy." What is more, in these debates, Willkie wished to inquire why Roosevelt thought he, in his pursuit of a third term, was entitled to "a greater public confidence than was accorded to our Presidential giants, Washington, Jefferson, Jackson, Lincoln, Cleveland, Theodore Roosevelt, and Woodrow Wilson."[69] But beyond these quick remarks, little would be said substantively on the issue of the third term.

Surprisingly few of the many speeches Willkie gave during the campaign would be devoted primarily to the issue of the third term, despite many references to Roosevelt as the "candidate for the third term" or "Mr. Third-Term Candidate."[70] Willkie would also occasionally lambaste Roosevelt for his pretense to "indispensability" amidst discussions of domestic and foreign policies. But many of Willkie's speeches make little or no reference to the third-term issue—one might guess that Roosevelt was merely running for reelection to a second term. The speeches that do make the third term their centerpiece are instructive, though.

It should be noted at the outset that Willkie occasionally engaged in rather hyperbolic warnings about the results of a Roosevelt third term. At times he characterized the decision of 1940 as one between democracy and dictatorship, with Roosevelt's election bringing the latter. Indeed, in his first major speech of the campaign, Willkie admonished that if Roosevelt were to be elected, "you will be serving under an American totalitarian government before the long third term is finished."[71] And later in the campaign, Willkie would see in the election of Roosevelt the coming of not just dictatorship but "state socialism."[72] Although these exaggerated characterizations are unfortunate—and tend to detract from the overall persuasiveness of Willkie's criticisms—they were not merely the domain of the Republicans. Not only his supporters but Roosevelt himself would characterize the election of Willkie as perilously close to a victory for Hitler and Nazism. Looking past these overheated polemical statements, Willkie made several incisive criticisms of Roosevelt's third-term pursuit.

First, Willkie made the typical conservative argument that Roosevelt was not respectful of the traditions of U.S. government, in particular the storied tradition, that began with Washington, of stepping down after two terms. Not only was this a long tradition among American presidents, but it had been "among the deepest traditions of the Democratic party."[73] And once broken, the "decision on that point will be irrevocable. . . . If this principle dies, it will be dead forever. . . . Once we have broken down the third-term tradition what is to prevent a fourth and a fifth term?"[74] Of course, little about Roosevelt's first and second terms was traditional, so this criticism was somewhat limited in shock value. Nevertheless, in Willkie's estimation, a person who would be willing to break a tradition 150 years in the making was someone who could not be trusted to wield responsibly the substantial powers of the American presidency. Willkie enlisted the support of Thomas Jefferson on this front: if a president, Jefferson said, should "be a candidate for a third election, I trust he would be rejected on this demonstration of ambitious views."[75]

This leads to a second major concern of Willkie's. Not only had Roosevelt demonstrated a dangerous ambition, an excessive immodesty, in his willingness to reject a time-honored tradition, but the powers of the presidency—already vastly expanded in Roosevelt's two terms— would grow even more in a third term and further upset the delicate constitutional balance of the American system. This line of argument could occasionally send Willkie veering off into paranoid accusations of the coming of dictatorship and even the suspension of elections, but his underlying point had considerable merit. The powers of the presidency had indeed grown in Roosevelt's two terms in office, and in his second term he had even attempted to "pack" the Supreme Court and "purge" congressional Democrats who did not agree with him from the party. One did not have to be a Roosevelt-hater to be concerned about these actions and to worry about the balance of powers in American government, especially if one were a member of Congress or the federal courts. Willkie rarely questioned Roosevelt's motives outright—he even allowed that they were "pure"—for one acting from good motives would be just as dangerous, if not more so, as one acting from bad motives: "he will more easily convince himself that further increase of power and greater release from constitutional limitations are required."[76]

But Willkie did not hesitate to critique the motives of Roosevelt's supporters, especially the "New Dealers" and also the big city political bosses that were essential to Roosevelt's and the Democratic Party's successes. This line of argument constitutes a third main critique of the third-term pursuit: long tenure in office tended toward corruption in administration and insulation from the people's interests. Although Willkie rarely did more than insinuate that Roosevelt himself was insulated or corrupted, Roosevelt's supporters had used the Democratic Party's hold on the presidency and its considerable powers to sustain their own ends, as against the public good. Of course, the political machines were an easy target, but even the New Dealers around Roosevelt had become removed and distant from the people's interests. What had started as a relatively noble-minded group had become a "petty little group"—which was "largely unknown to our people."[77] These New Dealers, according to Willkie, "do not trust us," the American people, and thus "have constantly sought more power for themselves and for the Chief Executive." The administration in general had "lost faith in the people" and had become dependent on "the corrupt political machines of Boss Kelly, Hague, Pendergast, and Flynn."[78] And the not-so-subtle implication was that these groups operated with the tacit support of Roosevelt, further suggesting his unfitness for extended service.

Finally, Willkie worried that the third term represented a lack of faith in democracy. While supporters of the third term would cite the rights of the people and democratic principles to justify it, Willkie and Republicans would see an abandonment of democracy in the third-term pursuit. For one thing, since Willkie questioned whether Roosevelt's renomination was truly a "draft," it was not clear in his mind that the Democratic Party's rank and file had exercised their own choice in renominating Roosevelt. Rather, "those self-styled noble liberals Harry Hopkins and Harold Ickes, conferred with Bosses Kelly, Hague and Flynn behind . . . bulletproof windows. That is the way the third term candidate was nominated."[79] More substantively, Willkie critiqued the assumptions of the so-called "indispensable man" theory that, he argued, anchored the Roosevelt campaign. "Just think, here is a candidate that assumes that out of 131,000,000 people he is the sole and only indispensable man."[80] However, "[t]here are literally many thousands who would make effective managers of the great business of government."[81]

It should be obvious that Willkie's arguments track well with the Whig model of executive power, especially as expressed by the Anti-Federalists in 1787–1788. Just as the Anti-Federalists worried about presidents being beholden to, in our modern parlance, special interests, so was Willkie concerned about the groups and interests promoting Roosevelt. As the Anti-Federalists saw long-serving officials naturally becoming removed from the people and susceptible to the temptations of power, so did Willkie worry about Roosevelt's distance from the public interest and his accretions of further power in the executive office. Finally, as the Anti-Federalists worried about the "anti-democratic" qualities of a long-serving president, so did Willkie question that only Roosevelt could possibly lead our vast country through the European crisis. In short, then, Willkie's criticisms were strongly rooted in a longstanding American philosophical tradition that supported term limitations on government officials, particularly presidents. The arguments in favor of Roosevelt's third term, while following Hamilton's to some degree, do vary in important particulars that call attention to key twentieth-century changes in our understanding of presidential power.

"Untried Hands, Inexperienced Hands"

In his speech at the Democratic Convention, Roosevelt explained his decision making.[82] In characterizing his acceptance of the nomination Roosevelt was at pains to describe his action as one of strong reluctance, and said that "no call of party alone would prevail upon me to accept re-election to the Presidency." Indeed, he had planned to "announce clearly and simply at an early date that under no conditions would I accept re-election. This fact was well known to my friends." However, once the events in Europe developed, an announcement of retirement would have been "unwise from the point of view of sheer public duty." Roosevelt then elaborated that his announcement of retirement would have reduced his influence in the Congress and with regard to other foreign nations: "Swiftly moving foreign events made necessary swift action at home and beyond the seas." Given the inevitable partisan bickering and jockeying that would have followed his announcement of retirement, achieving unified and quick action—especially through Congress—would have been difficult if not impossible. Thus did Roosevelt plan, until only recently we were led to believe, to merely delay his announcement of retirement.

Roosevelt continued, however, employing a somewhat dicey political metaphor: "[Lying] awake as I have on many nights, I have asked myself whether I have the right as Commander in Chief . . . to call on men and women to serve their country . . . and at the same time decline to serve my country in my personal capacity if I am called upon to do so by the people of my country." It is important to remark how heavily invested Roosevelt was—in this passage and throughout the acceptance—in the idea that he was truly drafted by the convention and that he was merely responding to the will of the people. If it were to appear that Roosevelt actively sought renomination, it would of course fuel his critics' speculations that excessive ambition was at the root of the third-term pursuit and would thus reaffirm the two-term tradition. What is more, to analogize his own service to that of American troops—who were truly called to their service—would be quite crass and political had he not been actually drafted.[83] So, while the European crisis delayed his announcement, it also finally tipped the balance and forced his acquiescence in the face of the convention's draft. As Roosevelt put it toward the end of the speech, "If our government should pass to other hands next January, untried hands, inexperienced hands, we can merely hope and pray that they will not substitute appeasement and compromise with those who seek to destroy all democracies everywhere, including here."

Undoubtedly, Roosevelt's use of the war in Europe and his status as commander in chief to justify his renomination gave his political opponents fits.[84] But even more, Roosevelt would also lay the groundwork in the speech for minimal campaigning on his part. As he put it, the campaign will be "different from the usual national campaigns of recent years. . . . [T]he President of the United States in these days [must] remain close to the seat of government." Roosevelt did plan to "make his usual periodic reports to the country through the medium of press conferences and radio talks" but "shall not have the time or the inclination to engage in purely political debate." FDR did hold out the possibilities for campaign speeches "to call the attention of the nation to deliberate or unwitting falsifications of fact" on the part of his political opponents.

Although Roosevelt did not directly discuss the two-term tradition or the reasons for his breaking it, it is obvious from the acceptance speech that his justification of the third term was primarily twofold, with both justifications linked to the European crisis: the need for emergency leadership and for stability of administration, two of the main points Hamilton offered in his criticism of term limits. Roosevelt, after all, had the "experienced hands" to deal with the European crisis, and at any rate it would be disruptive to replace the administration that was currently addressing the situation (successfully, of course, in Roosevelt's opinion). Reflecting the more democratic sentiments of the twentieth century, though, Roosevelt would fully ground his decision making in the acclamation of the people: the "right to make that call [to draft the president] rests with the people through the American method of a free election."

Preserving his image as "above politics," Roosevelt commenced the campaign by commissioning his "warrior" Ickes to reply to Willkie's acceptance speech.[85] As Ickes put it, the "[p]resident cannot adjourn the Battle of Britain in order to ride circuit with Mr. Willkie." Although it was not Roosevelt speaking, Ickes's response was delivered with the blessing of the White House.[86] As Willkie had said little directly on the third term in his acceptance, Ickes's response did not contain an overt defense of the third term. Nevertheless, Ickes made a defense of the Roosevelt administration and the New Deal that was clearly grounded in the needs for emergency leadership and continuity and stability in administration. Coming close to calling his Republican opponents Nazi sympathizers, Ickes claimed that "President Roosevelt and his New Deal administration have given America seven and a half dynamic years of defense of democracy. President Roosevelt has made America the symbol of light in a darkening world."[87] More so than Roosevelt had in his acceptance speech, Ickes drew a strong parallel between the crisis in Europe and the New Deal policies of the Roosevelt administration. Ickes painted with a much broader brush and saw the New Deal domestic policies—in their promotion of democracy and social progress—as much as Roosevelt's foreign policies as crucial in the battle against fascism and dictatorship in Europe.

Roosevelt himself would not give any campaign speeches until late October, but the Democratic Party would line up numerous speakers to make the case for the third term, including Secretary of State Cordell Hull, Harold Ickes, and even the Republican mayor of New York, Fiorello La Guardia.[88] Vice presidential nominee Henry Wallace would also lend his voice to the litany of speakers. La Guardia, in some ways a Republican in name only, was a strong supporter of Roosevelt and the New Deal. And while he continued to support New Deal policies, his decision to support the third term was not merely political. In his eyes, "government administration is a science: it cannot be learned over night. In these perilous times, there can be no time lost in getting 'the feel of things' by a new Administration."[89] This mantra about crisis leadership in a time of emergency would be picked up by Wallace and in fact would be something of the "official" defense of the third term. Wallace would make an even more subtle argument, though, that would focus on the interregnum period should Willkie win the coming election: "it would be a dangerous matter to have a period of eleven weeks between the election and the inauguration of a new President, while the European war hangs in the balance."[90] Cordell Hull's defense of the third term would follow the same parameters: "This is no time for the country to be making a change from experience to inexperience—a change which, furthermore, would immediately involve two and one-half months of confusion and uncertainty."[91]

In his own speeches, Roosevelt would boldly defend his administration and criticize Willkie and Republicans—in some cases ham-handedly linking them to Nazis and enemies of the United States—but only in his last major campaign address would he come anywhere close to addressing his unprecedented decision to seek a third term as a major party nominee.[92] Sounding the typical mantra, Roosevelt said that "[t]here is a great storm raging now, a storm that makes things harder for the world . . . And that . . . is the true reason that I would like to . . . stick by these people of ours until we reach the clear, sure footing ahead." And in a line that would come back to haunt him somewhat, Roosevelt continued, "[t]hen, when that [the third] term is over there will be another President, and many more Presidents . . . in the years to come." Clearly Roosevelt was appealing to the needs for emergency leadership and continuity in administration here, the twin pillars of the "official" justification for the third term.

But Roosevelt implicitly went further in certain respects, providing a justification of the third term whether or not there was a crisis in Europe. For example, Roosevelt characterized his time in office as "our democracy mov[ing] forward." He did allow that "[y]our government has at times been checked," which may have been a self-effacing reference to his overreaching in the second term.[93] "But always, with the aid and the counsel of all of the people, we have resumed our march. And now—we are asked to stop in our tracks. We're asked to turn about, to march back into the wilderness from which we came." This is a defense of the third term that sounds quite a lot like that of Ickes and the early supporters of a third term, namely, protecting the legacy of the New Deal. While Roosevelt and others would often make a link between the security of democracy in the world at large (where it was endangered) and the security of New Deal reforms at home, one can be forgiven for suspecting that Roosevelt would have been seriously tempted to run for a third term to protect the New Deal legacy, with or without a "great storm raging" in Europe.

The arguments in favor of Roosevelt's third term clearly were indebted to Hamilton; indeed, Hamilton was even on occasion quoted in campaign speeches.[94] Roosevelt and his supporters appealed especially to Hamilton's arguments in favor of experience, crisis leadership, and stability of administration.[95] In many ways these three points were strongly intertwined in the case of Roosevelt. FDR surely did have experience in the office of presidency, and at a time when the job had changed and become more sophisticated. And few could deny, what with a world war fully under way at the time of the Democratic Convention in 1940, that the United States was facing a crisis. Who better than Roosevelt to preserve stability and continuity of administration throughout this period? In this sense, then, the defense of Roosevelt's third term is fully in line with the Hamiltonian perspective against term limits.

Yet the arguments for a third term did not stop there. In fact, in an important sense the defenders went beyond this Hamiltonian or "constitutional" view and embraced a more modern or "plebiscitary" conception of presidential leadership to further justify the third term. It is well known that Hamilton had limited faith in the average people—he believed that they would have a role in governance, but he wanted to constrain and properly direct that role. And for Hamilton, the presidency was an important office for checking or restraining the people. Furthermore, although Hamilton described it as "energetic" in *Federalist* #70, the office of the presidency fulfilled its role to a significant degree by halting or thwarting action, especially that of the legislature, the latter often too beholden to the people.[96] But Roosevelt and his supporters defended the third term in part because they believed that there should be no restraint on the people and what they want. If the people wanted Roosevelt for a third term, they should be trusted to make that decision. Although this argument is not inconsistent with Hamilton's other arguments against term limits, it is certainly not one on which Hamilton placed emphasis, given his decided wariness of the people—there were plenty of other, more important, reasons for unlimited reeligibility. However, with the rise of the modern presidency in the early twentieth century, and the concomitant strong ties between the presidency and the American people that it wrought, it is not surprising that Roosevelt and his supporters would appeal to the "democracy" of unlimited terms and the president as an agent of the people.

This is not the only difference from Hamilton's perspective. Also in keeping with a modern conception of the presidency, Roosevelt defended his silence until the last moment for reasons of preserving presidential power, especially vis-à-vis Congress and foreign nations. Although this is not necessarily an argument for a third term—Roosevelt may have chosen not to run again and still reaped benefits from this silence—it is an argument against set term limits, which, as we characterize them today, make a president or any other official immediately a lame duck upon election to the last eligible term. There is really no direct counterpart in Hamilton's writing to this lame duck argument. Again, it is not fully inconsistent with Hamilton's arguments—it has some relationship to his preference for stability in administration and his worries about term limits discouraging good behavior—but it is also anchored by a conception of presidential leadership that was not widely supported at the time of founding, either by supporters or opponents of the Constitution. Opponents of the Constitution worried greatly about a pseudo-monarchical presidency, but even the Federalists were careful to emphasize the key role of "balance" in the constitutional setup, and few of them envisioned a political system with the president as the prime mover of both domestic and foreign policy. Rather, this lame duck argument against term limits is an almost exclusively modern one, one that is informed by the changing role of the presidency in the American political system.[97]

While Roosevelt and his supporters would win the day in 1940—and again in 1944, as we shall see in the next chapter—these arguments over presidential term limits would return in sharp relief in 1947 with the debate and passage of the Twenty-second Amendment to the Constitution. The House and Senate arguments would further extend and refine those of 1940 (and also 1944), pitting especially the modern, plebiscitary presidency of the mid-twentieth century, with its extensive influence and power, against traditional and ingrained American suspicions of executive dominance and overreach. Before we move on to that discussion, however, the next chapter will address a grossly overlooked dimension of the debate over term limits. While it gets little attention in the scholarly literature, FDR's decision to pursue a fourth term adds considerable texture to debates over presidential tenure.

THE TROUBLING CASE OF

FDR'S FOURTH TERM

*It is difficult for men in high office to avoid the malady
of self-delusion. They are always surrounded by worship-
pers. They are constantly, and for the most part sincerely,
assured of their greatness. They live in an artificial
atmosphere of adulation and exaltation which sooner or
later impairs their judgment. They are in grave danger of
becoming careless and arrogant. The chances of having
wise and faithful public service are increased by a change
in the Presidential office after a moderate length of time.*

Calvin Coolidge, 1929

FDR's successful reelection of 1944 is often treated almost as an afterthought, unworthy of serious scholarly or critical scrutiny. Indeed, on the surface it is simply an extension of the election of 1940: the country needed Roosevelt in 1940 with war in Europe on the horizon and needed him perhaps even more with the war still on in 1944. The justification in both elections for breaking with tradition is the same; it is the emergency situation that necessitated Roosevelt's unconventional actions. And even though a fourth term was as unprecedented as a third term, it was *two* terms that had attained the status of tradition; once a third term was secured, the fourth term seemed almost a natural step—and now there was precedent.

But this is unfortunate, for the election of 1944 raises critical questions about presidential tenure, and long tenure in general, that are not raised, at least to the same extent, by the 1940 election. The above quote comes from Calvin Coolidge's autobiography and at least partly describes the decision making of Franklin Roosevelt and his closest advisors in the lead up to his pursuit of a fourth term in 1944, which at times seems shockingly careless. This judgment is informed by recently unearthed primary documents as well as secondary analyses of President Roosevelt's health in the last year of his life. It is today beyond dispute that FDR had alarmingly high blood pressure through much of his third term and that he also experienced, beginning at least in early 1944, congestive heart failure. What is more, his doctors knew about this condition, and he did as well, although it is unclear whether he knew the full extent of his condition.

Despite cardiologist Howard Bruenn's examination of FDR in March of 1944 that revealed serious heart problems—Bruenn would thereafter attend to FDR on a daily basis—FDR and his advisors would push on for a fourth term, seemingly oblivious to his grave health concerns. This would be especially evident in the nonchalant manner in which FDR seemed to approach the vice presidential nomination in 1944. Given Harry Truman's highly regarded presidential leadership after succeeding FDR, his choice as vice president might be seen to reflect wise decision making with an eye toward the possible death of the president. However, this is revisionist, wishful thinking. At the time of his nomination, Truman was in many quarters considered a product of the party boss system and at any rate not someone of exceptional leadership skills. Additionally, Roosevelt and his advisors seemed to be almost completely preoccupied with the politics of the vice presidential nomination—that is, who would bring the most votes in the election—rather than the leadership qualities of a potential president. This is further confirmed by Truman's lack of communication with Roosevelt and his advisors during the several months of his vice presidency. At the time of his notification of FDR's death, Truman knew next to nothing about the critical issues domestic and foreign that he would be forced to face directly now that he was president.

But the actions of Roosevelt and his advisors with regard to his health and his continuing service as president are puzzling. They by no means seem conspiratorial. If FDR and his advisors truly knew that he was seriously ill, it seems odd to say the least that they didn't place more emphasis on selecting a vice presidential nominee who would be fully committed to FDR's vision and policies. They could have stacked the deck in favor of a New Dealer or a close supporter of the president, but they did not. At the very least, FDR knew that he had heart problems. Yet Roosevelt himself seemed especially uninterested in and disengaged from the vice presidential nomination; it was a chore to complete rather than a momentous decision carrying great weight for the future of the country.

The impression one is left with is that FDR and his advisors engaged in self-delusion on a rather large scale: the president and many around him continued to believe that he would "bounce back," despite the persistence of illness, the haggard look of the president, and his frequent need for rest and vacation, not to mention Bruenn's diagnosis. Coolidge's characterization of the White House as an "artificial atmosphere" is an apposite one, even if one does not ascribe sinister motivations to the participants. This artificial atmosphere, over time, promotes arrogance and even self-deception, as if the normal rules—in this case, the simple laws of physiology—are not applicable to the president. This seems to accurately describe the perspective of FDR and his advisors on his fourth term and to partly explain their negligence in how they dealt with not only the vice presidential nomination but also their communications with Harry Truman during the first several months of the fourth term.

BEEN THERE, DONE THAT

Like FDR's reelection bid in 1940, the 1944 pursuit was shaped by World War II. Voters considered the acceptability of FDR's fourth-term bid yet again within the context of the war, but this time the key issue was not whether war was coming but whether it would be over before the election. According to a Gallup poll released in June of 1943, if the war were to be over before the election, 69 percent would be against Roosevelt's reelection, whereas if it were still ongoing, only 44 percent would vote against his reelection.[1] Despite Roosevelt's declaration in November 1940 that when the third term was over, "there will be another President,"[2] as the 1944 election approached, Roosevelt took no steps to scotch talk about his pursuit of a fourth term. It is likely that had the war ended in late 1943 or early 1944, Roosevelt would not have pursued a fourth term. The Gallup poll suggests that it would have been an uphill battle at any rate, and clearly Roosevelt's pursuit of a fourth term was motivated in part by a sincere belief in doing his duty during this time of war. Nevertheless, it did not appear that the war would be over any time soon in 1943 and early 1944, and thus the talk of a fourth term began in earnest.

In early March 1943, the "draft Roosevelt" movement commenced—not discouraged but also not orchestrated by the White House. At the completion of Roosevelt's ten years in the office, on March 3, 1943, several top Democratic Party leaders met with Roosevelt to persuade him to run for a fourth term "if the war is still on." Although Roosevelt did not respond publicly to the request, "[p]olitical leaders of both major parties proceeded on the assumption . . . that he would be a candidate. They considered the technique of a draft as merely a detail of strategy."[3] Of course, Republicans did not take long to respond to the "draft," with the chairman of the Republican National Committee, Harrison Spangler, a month later calling quixotically on FDR and Democrats to promise that FDR would not be nominated for a fourth term in 1944.[4]

By July 1943, a full year before the Democratic Party nominating convention, the *New York Times* would report that despite intra-party squabbling, "the nomination of Franklin D. Roosevelt for a fourth term as President is still taken for granted here." In a hint of the future, the same article would report that the renomination of Henry Wallace was definitely not being taken for granted.[5] While there would be no word on the renomination from the White House, numerous others would offer their opinions in the summer and fall of 1943, some arguing that Roosevelt would not run and others that he would.[6] And back and forth it would go, with columnist William Allen White speculating in October 1943 that Roosevelt would not run, although he did qualify this, saying that he was one of those "rare birds who believed that Roosevelt may not run for a fourth term." White also raised the specter of health problems requiring Roosevelt to refuse a fourth-term bid but did not make it central to his guesswork.[7] The year 1943 would end with more fourth-term speculation prompted by Roosevelt's well-known allegorical speech about Dr. New Deal and Dr. Win the War,[8] which some thought "comprised a fourth-term declaration."[9]

January 1944 would witness "Democratic National Committeemen from twelve Middle Western States" convening in Washington for a meeting, calling for a fourth term for President Roosevelt. This was considered the "first group action in that regard."[10] Several days later a meeting of the Congress of Industrial Organizations (CIO) in New York City would pass a resolution urging the renomination and election of President Roosevelt. But in early February, Roosevelt was still resisting talk about a fourth term, saying that "there's no news on that."[11] Interestingly, Senator Harry Truman would in February and March 1944 make two relatively high-profile speeches supporting a fourth term for Roosevelt.[12] "The draft-Roosevelt movement took on new impetus and greater authority [in early April] as Senator Robert F. Wagner, leading proponent of the New Deal in Congress and close personal friend of President Roosevelt" came out strongly for a fourth term.[13] But in late April, Senator Burton K. Wheeler, Democrat from Montana, would predict that "Roosevelt's health" would prevent him from running for a fourth term. Although a Democrat, Wheeler was opposed to a fourth term, saying, "I wouldn't vote for my own brother for a fourth term for President."[14] Wheeler was, however, accurately reflecting some of the concerns about Roosevelt's health that were current and that were remarkable enough to draw a spirited response from Democratic National Chairman Robert Hannegan.

At the annual Jefferson Day dinner in early May 1944, Hannegan officially kicked off Roosevelt's bid and pronounced him "'fit and ready for the fight,' despite 'malicious rumors to the contrary' and [further] declared that 'the people of the United States are determined that Franklin D. Roosevelt shall complete the assignment which destiny has given him.'"[15] (The "malicious rumors" about Roosevelt's health will be treated more fully later.) But even in May 1944 the most definitive thing that Roosevelt uttered on this front was "that he hoped to see the [British] Prime Minister [Churchill] at some time in the future, either this summer, this fall or late spring." Naturally this set reporters off to question the fourth term, as next "spring" would come only in a fourth term. And yet Roosevelt would neither confirm nor deny that he aimed to pursue a fourth term.[16]

Finally, on the eve of the Democratic National Convention, Roosevelt would break his silence. Employing a tactic quite similar to that in 1940, Roosevelt would indicate his willingness to serve again through the use of a crafty, if cloying, metaphor. Writing to Hannegan, FDR said that he was reluctant to run but that he had "as little right to withdraw as the solider has to leave his post in the line." He concluded that as a "good soldier" deferring to "the Commander in Chief of us all—the sovereign people of the United States," he would accept renomination and run for a fourth term.[17] Significantly, Roosevelt said nothing about Wallace's possible renomination, thereby preparing the way for the real battle of the convention: the vice presidential nomination.

The debate over a fourth term, before and after FDR declared his intention to run again, was muted compared with that in 1940. However, there were substantial criticisms and defenses made of the possible fourth term. For instance, in February 1943, World War I hero Captain Edward V. Rickenbacker came out against a fourth term in a speech to the New York State Assembly, warning of an "inner clique of bureaucracy" that stood to benefit from the fourth term.[18] Harrison Spangler saw the fourth term as Roosevelt continuing himself in office indefinitely, saying that George Washington and Thomas Jefferson "knew that if a President had been in office for a long time he might perpetuate himself."[19] But since their time, presidents had gained even more powers to be used to retain the office, according to Spangler: "the New Deal with millions of public money has assembled a vast and far-reaching propaganda machine which conceals and distorts, glorifies its creators and dulls and beclouds the free thinking of men and women."[20]

This talk would again pick up in the lead-up to the Democratic Convention. For instance, Republican Senator Robert Taft in March 1944 "charged that a fourth term would cause a steady enlargement of the Executive power."[21] But it would be Thomas Dewey, the Republican nominee for president, who would make some of the sharpest attacks. In his speech accepting the Republican nomination, Dewey would develop a theme he would pursue throughout the campaign: the Roosevelt administration had "become tired and quarrelsome" in office and "three terms were too many."[22] In two September campaign speeches, Dewey would bring the fourth-term question most fully into focus, with "indispensability" a key theme of both addresses:

> Let us have no more of this pretense about indispensable men. There are no indispensable men. If our republic after 150 years of self-government is dependent upon the endless continuance of one man in office, then the hopes which animated the men who fought for the Declaration of Independence and the Constitution have come to nothing.[23]
>
> The man who wants to be President for sixteen years is, indeed, indispensable. He is indispensable to Harry Hopkins, to Mme Perkins, to Harold Ickes, he's indispensable to a host of other political job holders. . . . He's indispensable to those infamous machines, in Chicago—in the Bronx—and all the others.[24]

Roosevelt himself (in accepting the Democratic nomination) responded directly to the idea that his administration was "tired" or "quarrelsome," with his assertion that his administration represented "experience" while that of his opponents would represent "immaturity." Others at the Democratic Convention would also make the same contrast between "age and experience" and "youth and inexperience."[25] Indeed, the experience of Roosevelt would be a major defense of the fourth term from the start. In Truman's call for a fourth term, in February 1944, he had argued that "[t]o entrust the winning of the war and the framing of the peace into the hands of any man with a limited outlook and without the experience needed for such a job would be the sheerest folly."[26] Similarly, Wagner's call for a fourth term was because, he said, "I do not believe that the American people will want to take the chance of turning over the Presidency to some untried novice."[27] Senator Samuel Jackson probably put this perspective in its starkest formulation at the Democratic National Convention: "A change in national administration in time of war, even when surrounded by promising circumstances, is frightening to contemplate. . . . It is dangerous."[28]

Nevertheless, even Roosevelt's defenders and advisors worried somewhat about the delicacy of the fourth-term bid. They recognized that the fourth term in and of itself was controversial: it would indeed "further entrench the Federal executive group and make the Federal judiciary almost entirely Roosevelt-appointed." And the "health issue" was also threatening to erupt into a major issue in the campaign and call into question the viability of the fourth term. Described as a "subsurface" worry, Roosevelt's "ability to carry for four more years burdens which, by common consent, will be even heavier than before" was a matter of concern to his advisors. And "Mr. Roosevelt's news pictures disturb[ed] his campaign publicity department."[29] It would only be later—and especially in recent years—that we would find out what a significant issue Roosevelt's health would be in the last year of his life.

Overall, though, in comparison with 1940 there was far less discussion of "breaking with tradition" in pursuing a fourth term. The war was foremost in campaign rhetoric and debates, with the New Deal, domestic affairs, and the fourth term especially being downplayed.[30] Dewey even remarked after the election that "the state of the war had been the one factor that made his election impossible—an analysis of his defeat with which his campaign managers and many outside observers would agree."[31] And the public, as we saw with the Gallup poll, was willing to put aside its concerns about long service of the executive because the war constituted an emergency, for which FDR's leadership was needed.

But the fourth-term issue should have absorbed more attention, especially as it related to the health problems of Roosevelt. Only under the surface, or in veiled terms, were concerns about a fourth term linked to questions about Roosevelt's health, in Dewey's remarks about "age" and the "malicious rumors" about which Hannegan complained. But, as we will see in the following section, FDR was gravely ill in the last year of his life. Although his health was mentioned here and there throughout the campaign season—more by the opposition party than the mainstream media outlets—the extent of his illness was not widely known, and much of the speculation about his health was just that, speculation based upon his physical appearance. However, much of this speculation turned out to be largely correct: the president was seriously ill. And FDR and his advisors erred greatly in not facing the very real consequences of presidential mortality, especially as far as presidential succession was concerned. To reprise Coolidge's line, the "artificial atmosphere" of the White House doubtless allowed FDR and his advisors to delude themselves that he would not be subject to the same rules as the average man: FDR was treated like some sort of superhero in the White House, someone with Herculean strength and durability.

"THE OLD 'TICKER' TROUBLE"

For much of Roosevelt's third term and brief fourth term, there were whispers and rumors about his health. Upon his death in April 1945, a debate would begin: how much did Roosevelt and his advisors know about his health, especially going into the 1944 election? Roosevelt's personal physician, Admiral Ross McIntire, would make an attempt to shape the debate almost immediately with the publication of his *White House Physician* in 1946. Consistent with his repeated declarations of FDR's good health during his presidency, McIntire would assert in his book that Roosevelt was in sound health and that his death could in no way have been predicted. However, in 1948, Roosevelt critic John T. Flynn would publish *The Roosevelt Myth*, wherein he would argue that Roosevelt's advisors clearly deceived the country in 1944, for they knew full well his serious medical condition.[32] And in 1956, scholar Herman Bateman would assess the state of the debate, concluding that the "published evidence to date shows only partial signs or traces of a deteriorated physical condition at the most critical time, the election of 1944."[33]

In the last forty years, however, important primary sources and secondary analyses have emerged that call into serious question Bateman's conclusion. Critical here is Howard Bruenn's publication, in 1970, of his clinical notes during his time as Roosevelt's cardiologist (March 1944 until FDR's death) as well as the recent release of his diary.[34] Also of key importance is the recent publication of the diary of Margaret (Daisy) Suckley, a cousin of Roosevelt's and also a close friend, who discussed, among other things, Roosevelt's illnesses with him during the last years of his life.[35] Furthermore, oral histories in the Truman Library—interviews with White House and party officials and reporters who worked for or covered Roosevelt or Truman or both—provide additional texture and support.[36] Finally, several important secondary sources have emerged recently that not only utilize newer primary sources, such as Bruenn's and Suckley's diaries, but incline less toward nostalgia when examining FDR's presidency and are less likely to airbrush the decision making of 1944.[37]

Although Roosevelt was in reasonably good health for his first two terms, during his second term, the press began to raise more questions about his health—sparked presumably by his physical appearance—and by early in the third term, the president's physical health was clearly in decline.[38] In his second term, his physicians noticed his elevated blood pressure, but it would be in the third term that Roosevelt's blood pressure would become a cause for concern if not alarm.[39] By 1944, there were serious concerns about Roosevelt's health, reflected by thirty-six articles on his health in the *New York Times* by June of that year.[40] Despite reporters raising questions about the president's health, there was generally a disconnect between what the press was reporting about FDR's health—the details of which were supplied almost exclusively by his physician, McIntire—and what we now know was happening at the time, especially in late 1943 and early 1944.

"After his return from the Teheran Conference in December 1943, the President's decline accelerated. . . . Roosevelt went to Hyde Park to recuperate and to celebrate the Christmas holidays with his family. Instead, he came down with a severe case of influenza which proved particularly resistant to treatment."[41] Because Roosevelt's condition did not significantly improve, Bruenn was called in to examine him in March of 1944. Dr. McIntire was an ear, nose, and throat specialist chosen as Roosevelt's personal physician because of Roosevelt's chronic sinus problems. Bruenn's examination at the Bethesda Naval Hospital revealed that Roosevelt suffered from "hypertension, hypertensive heart disease, cardiac failure (left ventricular), and acute bronchitis." Bruenn later claimed that this diagnosis "had been completely unsuspected up to this time."[42] Bruenn briefed McIntire on the examination, saying, according to James Bishop, that Roosevelt "could expire at any time. And yet, with proper care—and granting that Mr. Roosevelt's mental functions were not badly impaired—he might live on for months, maybe a year or two."[43] Bruenn accordingly recommended, among other things, extensive bed rest with nursing care, which was rejected "because of the exigencies and demands on the President." Ultimately, FDR's schedule would be lightened significantly, he would be placed on a diet, and digitalis treatment, for his heart condition, would be administered.[44]

Although Bruenn would continue to see to the president several times per week until his death, he was still not the president's primary physician; that role was filled by McIntire. What is more, although Bruenn, McIntire, and several other doctors—who had been called in after the Bruenn visit in March 1944 to discuss recommendations for Roosevelt's treatment—knew about Roosevelt's heart condition and high blood pressure, there is no indication that they directly confronted Roosevelt with the seriousness of his condition. As Bruenn recounted, "[at] no time did the President ever comment on the frequency of [my] visits or question the reason for the electro-cardiograms and the other laboratory tests that were performed from time to time; nor did he ever have any questions as to the type and variety of medications that were used."[45] Eminent FDR biographer James MacGregor Burns speculates that the doctors "evidently assumed that McIntire had the responsibility [to inform the president] and would exercise it, but there is no indication that he did."[46] However, it is naïve to believe that Roosevelt's lack of questions about his condition—or lack of communication with McIntire—meant that he did not know something about his condition. Indeed, we know from the recently published Suckley diary that by May 5, 1944, Roosevelt knew he had problems with his heart and blood pressure. As Daisy Suckley put it: "He said he discovered that the doctors had not agreed altogether about what to tell him, so that he found out that they were not telling *him* the *whole* truth & that he was evidently more sick than they said!" She continued tellingly, "It is foolish for them to attempt to put anything over on *him*!" Roosevelt confided, according to Suckley, that "the trouble is evidently with the heart—the diastole and systole are not working properly in unison," but he encouraged her that "there is definite improvement." And a day earlier, Roosevelt had relayed to Suckley that Bruenn was "one of the best heart men," giving the lie to some biographers' claims that Roosevelt did not know Bruenn was a cardiologist.[47] By December 1944 (at the latest) Roosevelt also began directing his physical therapist, George Fox, to take daily blood pressure readings, in all likelihood without the knowledge of Bruenn.[48] But Roosevelt's heart problems were generally a well-guarded secret, as Roosevelt's daughter, Anna, confided to her husband in February 1945: "Ross [McIntire] and Bruenn are both worried because of the old 'ticker' trouble—which, of course, no one knows about but those two and me."[49]

Numerous writers have probed McIntire's role in covering up the president's health issues during FDR's last year. Evans evaluates McIntire in the following manner: "It is difficult to sort out the optimism of a patriot, the lack of a candor of a political operative, and the professional limitations of a physician who was an ear, nose, and throat specialist, not an internist or cardiologist."[50] However we want to judge McIntire's motivations with regard to his dealings with FDR, his reports to the press on FDR's condition after the Bruenn evaluation were disingenuous at best. The press was not informed, of course, that FDR was examined by a cardiologist. Rather, the visit was simply labeled a checkup. The *Chicago Tribune*, a paper vehemently opposed to Roosevelt and a keen observer of his declining health, ultimately broke the story, in August 1944, that Roosevelt was being attended by "Howard Gerald Bruenn, a New York City heart specialist."[51] This fact was not acknowledged by the White House, and the story does not appear to have been widely reported. In response to press corps questions about Roosevelt's checkup, McIntire not only informed the press in early April 1944 that FDR's health was "satisfactory" but chalked up Roosevelt's recent illness to "influenza or a 'respiratory infection' and a sinus disturbance. . . . When we got through [with the checkup], we decided that for a man of 62-plus we had very little to argue about, with the exception that we have had to combat the influenza plus the respiratory complications that came along after."[52] Now surely Roosevelt had had bronchitis and sinus problems, but to say that they had "little to argue about" *after* Bruenn had given his heart and blood pressure diagnoses is without question a breach of the public trust. But it is hard to place the blame fully on McIntire. As Daisy Suckley said, it was "foolish" for anyone to try to "put anything over" on Roosevelt. Roosevelt must bear some of the responsibility for these misleading statements to the press.

The rosy assessments of FDR's health by McIntire would persist through 1944 and even up until Roosevelt's death. A month before the 1944 Democratic National Convention, McIntire informed the press that Roosevelt's health was "excellent in all respects." Roosevelt had recently vacationed in South Carolina, and the rest and relaxation had done him good, according to McIntire: "It was a very excellent rest period in which the President followed a very good routine." He continued that Roosevelt was administered a number of "physical checks" and that all were "well within normal limits."[53] In late September, McIntire listed Roosevelt's health as "good, very good."[54] In mid-October, "in view of rumors in political circles and elsewhere," McIntire declared that the "President's health is perfectly O.K. There are absolutely no organic difficulties at all. He is eight or nine pounds under his best weight."[55]

It is interesting to note here that McIntire was yet again prompted to make a statement on Roosevelt's health because of "rumors."[56] His comment about Roosevelt's weight was clever, suggesting that Roosevelt's weight loss was the cause of his ill health rather than a symptom. The rumors and whispers about Roosevelt's health were, of course, made by Republicans and opponents of the administration. At any rate, these criticisms would force Roosevelt into a tour of several big cities to demonstrate his good health, including a rain-drenched trip through New York that reaffirmed to many Roosevelt's vigor. Democratic National Chairman Hannegan would thereby describe Roosevelt as "very vigorous, the picture of health."[57] International News Service reporter Robert Nixon, referring specifically to the New York trip, reflected that "there were these terrific contrasts. You thought at times that the man *was* failing, but then he would spring back just like a grasshopper."[58] *Washington Star* reporter Joseph Fox voiced a similar perspective: "Roosevelt would fool you. He could bounce back. He could be in pretty bad shape and then he could bounce back."[59]

At the time of Roosevelt's fourth inauguration—a rather scaled-back affair at the White House, not the Capitol—questions of Roosevelt's health would again surface. The *Chicago Tribune* noted that "[i]n official circles . . . the switch [to the White House] was accepted as another move to safeguard the chief executive's health."[60] Harry Truman's close friend Harry Easley, who accompanied Truman to a post-inauguration party, saw Roosevelt and recalled, "by God the President had the pallor of death on his face right then."[61] But this sentiment was by no means universal. For instance, the *Louisville Courier-Journal*'s Washington, D.C., bureau chief, Robert Riggs, thought nothing of Roosevelt's appearance at the inaugural: "I was the last man to think he was dying."[62] McIntire pronounced Roosevelt in "fine shape" and said that "Mr. Roosevelt's health compared favorably with that of most men of 63." Nonetheless, even McIntire mentioned the persistence of rumors about FDR's health, saying, "he had a list of eleven different things wrong with the President— on the basis of rumor."[63]

Days after the inauguration, Roosevelt would leave for the Yalta Conference with Stalin and Churchill to determine the fate of Europe after the cessation of World War II. There has been speculation on Roosevelt's health and its role in the Yalta Conference, some concluding that Roosevelt was outmatched by Churchill and especially Stalin, and that his sickness was to blame for the supposedly poor outcome of the conference (from the U.S. perspective). The most vituperative of these critiques came early on, in 1948, in Flynn's *The Roosevelt Myth*: "A president, too ill to do more than a few hours work a day, whose hands trembled, whose energies were feeble, whose mind was weary and who, at times, was only partially conscious of his surroundings, was not the kind of representative America needed to confront the far more experienced and subtle Churchill and Stalin in the disposition of the affairs of the world."[64] Most scholars, however, have since agreed that Roosevelt's judgment was sound and that his negotiations and decisions were the result of the comparative positions of the nations involved rather than any physical deterioration on his part.[65] What is important for our current purpose is McIntire's characterization of FDR's health after the Yalta Conference. During the conference, many observers, especially the foreign ones, noted the poor physical appearance of President Roosevelt. For instance, "Churchill's physician told associates that the President had 'all the symptoms of hardening of the arteries of the brain in an advanced stage. So I give him only a few months to live.'"[66] Additionally, the White House aggressively screened photographs of Roosevelt and released only those that depicted the president in a favorable light physically.[67] And still, upon return from the conference, McIntire and others reported to the press that the president was in "great" and "excellent" health. In response to "reports from Europe that the President had been ill," presidential assistant Jonathan Daniels said that "I have never seen him looking so well." [68]

Roosevelt's March 1 address to Congress upon his return from Yalta caused alarm among observers. Not only did Roosevelt for the first time in public remain seated in his wheelchair to deliver his speech—telling the assembled that he was weary from his journey—but the speech in general was poorly delivered, and he looked quite ill. *Providence Journal* reporter Robert Walsh, who covered the speech, recalled that "his [Roosevelt's] hands were shaking and he had that sort of a gaunt look about him. . . .

On the way out, of course, we could see him going out, wheeled out. As at the inauguration, I thought, 'He will never last four years.'"[69] *Chicago Times* correspondent Carleton Kent viewed matters similarly: "I recall how wretchedly ill he looked, drawn, and pale. I had seen him a number of times as he went across the country after his first election in 1932, and I was prepared for a pretty robust looking man. And he looked drawn and distinctly ill, I thought."[70] Reporter Robert Riggs would recall, however, that "he sounded all right then and he got by with it all right."[71] And while Samuel Rosenman, close advisor to President Roosevelt, recalled that Roosevelt's health after the return from Yalta "frightened me," nonetheless "it never occurred to me that he would not be able to finish the fourth term and then go back to Hyde Park."[72]

After Roosevelt's death only a little over a month later, McIntire would still contend that there were really no signs and that it was totally unexpected. Commenting on FDR's death in an article in the *New York Times* the day after FDR's death, McIntire said that "this came out of a clear sky." "His optimistic reports of the late President's health, he declared, had been completely justified by the known tests." Indeed, Roosevelt's death was so unexpected, reported the *Times*, "that no member of his family was with him at Warm Springs, no high-ranking associate or long-time intimate." While there may have been no need for a "death watch" in April 1945, Roosevelt and his advisors undoubtedly ignored cues that many outside observers—when they had an opportunity to actually see Roosevelt—did not miss. The same article reported that "a marked change in Roosevelt's appearance and manner had brought anxiety to many regarding his health" in recent months.[73] And another *New York Times* article on the same day, titled "Roosevelt Health Long under Doubt," reported that "those in the capital who have had regular contacts with him over the last two years" saw a variance in their firsthand observations of his physical condition and the official pronouncements of the White House.[74] The *Chicago Tribune* painted a more cynical picture, not of incompetent White House physicians who did not understand what was happening but of a secretive group who, for whatever reasons, failed to take the necessary steps, given the evidence of a dying chief executive. The *Tribune* reported the day following Roosevelt's death that it was "known thruout [sic] official circles that there was a veritable parade of doctors in attendance on the chief executive" in Roosevelt's last few months. Even more, these physicians "who examined the chief executive or cardiograms, reported he could not live six months."[75]

While there has been debate over whether FDR's ill health compromised U.S. interests at the Yalta Conference, few scholars have scrutinized the nonchalant and disinterested manner with which Roosevelt approached the vice presidential nomination in the summer of 1944 and the manner by which he and his staff kept his new vice president informed (or uninformed, as it were) before his death. Given his ill health, FDR nevertheless seemed apathetic about the vice presidential nomination. In fact, of his eventual vice presidential nominee and successor, Roosevelt said right before the convention in July 1944, "I hardly know Truman."[76] While this comment surely says something about the status of the vice presidency at the time, it also reveals something of the nature of the relationship between Roosevelt and his soon-to-be vice president, as we will see.

The planning for the vice presidential nomination began as early as 1943, as Democratic Party leaders considered the possibility of a fourth term for FDR. The liberal Democrat Henry Wallace had been placed on the ticket in 1940 at the insistence of FDR. Because many leaders and insiders knew that Roosevelt's health was at least questionable—even if they discussed it only among themselves and not with him—the prospect that the vice president would succeed Roosevelt in a fourth term was a real possibility.[77] Edwin Pauley, treasurer for the Democratic National Committee and an opponent of Vice President Wallace, put it bluntly: "It was about a year before the convention that I proceeded to prevent his becoming the President. I say 'the President,' because, in my opinion, it was becoming obvious that the Vice President would become the President because of Roosevelt's health."[78] Given Wallace's liberal record—and the controversy within the party during his tenure as vice president—he would have to be replaced with a more moderate figure in the party, in the view of the party leaders. The movement to drop Wallace from the ticket would operate stealthily, at least until Roosevelt declared his intention to run for a fourth term. Robert H. Ferrell describes the maneuvering as "a virtual conspiracy to get [Wallace] out of the running."[79]

A strategy of discouraging Wallace from seeking renomination as vice president did not work, given FDR's reluctance to tell Wallace straightforwardly that he wished for him to step aside, as the party leaders hoped he would do.[80] In classic Roosevelt fashion, FDR told Wallace he would vote for him if he were a delegate to the convention; told his assistant, former Supreme Court judge Jimmy Byrnes, that he supported him for the nomination; and also agreed, at a secret meeting, to pledge support to Truman.[81] What is more, a letter he wrote in support of Truman said that he supported either Truman *or* William O. Douglas, by then a justice of the Supreme Court.[82] Nonetheless, after much politicking, the outcome was as the party leaders had hoped: Truman became the vice presidential nominee.

What is troubling about the nomination, though, is that Roosevelt himself seemed to have very little interest in this momentous decision. FDR seemed "curiously disengaged concerning the vice-presidential canvassing at the White House. At San Diego he told Jimmy [Roosevelt, his son] that he didn't give a damn whether the convention chose Douglas or Byrnes or Truman; the important thing was to get on with the war."[83] Daisy Suckley relayed prior to the convention how "harassing & wearing" the vice presidential nomination had been and how FDR was "trying to get it *out of* his hands."[84] Robert Nixon perceptively described the nomination this way: "The choice was entirely political on the basis of here is a person with no strikes on his record, who comes from the Middlewest [*sic*] where we need representation. It was just that simple, I don't think that it ever crossed Roosevelt's mind that he might be succeeded by a Vice-President."[85] And even the party leaders who orchestrated the "anti-Wallace" campaign seemed less concerned about the fate of the nation than they did about power within the party shifting to the left wing and Wallace supporters. As Truman biographer Alonzo Hamby has put it regarding the vice presidential nomination, the party leaders primarily wanted a "winning ticket; given Roosevelt's questionable health, their secondary goal was a potential successor with whom they could work."[86]

Although Truman has in the years since his presidency come to be seen as a strong, independent leader, this was not the general perception in 1944. As Donald Young put it in his analysis of vice presidents, Truman's "strongest recommendation (laughable in view of his subsequent career) was that he had offended almost nobody."[87] Reactions to his nomination betrayed the main purpose behind his selection. Although his nomination was generally received favorably, probably most accurate were these two characterizations of his selection: Truman was referred to as "the Missouri Compromise" and the "Common Denominator," surely not seizing upon his inherent fitness for the office but testifying to the mixture of qualities that made him most desirable to the various factions and leaders within the party. And many commentators were less than generous, seeing Truman as among the worst candidates ever chosen, a party hack, and a "mousy little man from Missouri." Despite the patently political character of the process, Truman biographer David McCollough concluded, "[as] time would tell, everything considered, the system, the bosses and all, had produced an excellent choice."[88] But "the system" was engaged more in producing a nominee who would bring the party votes, appease the party leaders, and be susceptible to management, than it was in producing a nominee who would easily segue into the presidential office, if necessary. It may be more adventitious than not that Truman excelled as he did at president.

For all of the speculation about party leaders and insiders knowing that they were selecting a president, not just a vice president, Roosevelt and his advisors did very little between the nomination and the president's death to bring Truman into the policy loop and explain to him the important matters that the White House was considering in terms of domestic and especially foreign policy. Roosevelt finally met with his vice presidential running mate on August 18, 1944, in a public meeting intended to show "solidarity on the ticket." He had not previously met with Truman since March of that year.[89] During the campaign, Truman would also see very little of FDR. Even more striking is that once Truman became vice president—first in line for the presidency—Roosevelt and his advisors did almost nothing to apprise him of the key matters of government.[90] *Washington Star* reporter Gould Lincoln put it bluntly: "Mr. Roosevelt had done less for him than anybody in the world."[91] Truman himself would later relate that FDR "never did talk to me confidentially about the war, or about foreign affairs or what he had in mind for peace after the war."[92] While it is true that Roosevelt was occupied with preparation for Yalta and then the conference itself for much of January and February 1945, there is no indication that Roosevelt directed any of his advisors—cabinet or otherwise—to apprise Truman of the many critical war policies of the administration.[93] Suffice it to say that when Truman assumed office, he had much to learn.

Because Truman acquitted himself so admirably in his early weeks and months as president, it has been easy to brush aside the questionable actions of the Roosevelt administration with regard to presidential succession. However, this neglect has been unfortunate, for Roosevelt's actions point us to the limitations and drawbacks inherent in long presidential and executive tenure in general. As the next section demonstrates, one does not have to be a Roosevelt skeptic or critic to be shocked at the negligence of his administration with regard to the pursuit of a fourth term and particularly the failure to prepare adequately for the possible succession of the vice president to the office of president.

"They Live in an Artificial Atmosphere"

Why have few observers over the years probed this unsettling aspect of the Roosevelt administration? Roosevelt biographers tend to minimize if not ignore the negative implications of his illness and especially the secrecy with which the White House managed his declining health. For instance, Doris Kearns Goodwin perpetuates the almost certainly false notion that FDR might not have known he had heart problems, putting blame fully on McIntire: "It was an extraordinary act of presumption on McIntire's part, depriving Roosevelt of the right to know what was happening to his life."[94] Conrad Black curiously suggests that McIntire and Bruenn had told Roosevelt that he could survive his fourth term if he cut back on his workload.[95] Surely McIntire may have told this to FDR—he persisted in claiming that the president's health was "excellent" after all—but Bruenn himself said that he did not communicate with FDR about his condition and declared also that no one asked him about the fourth term. Had they asked, though, he would have been compelled to say that it would have been impossible medically speaking.[96]

Roosevelt biographers do not completely neglect the negative but certainly do not explore the ramifications. Goodwin notes that McIntire and FDR misled the newspapers and the people but fails to go much beyond simply stating that this was so.[97] Similarly, Ted Morgan allows that a "crucial factor was kept from the voters [in 1944]—the true state of the president's health."[98] But, again, he does little with this revelation. Indeed, many of the prominent FDR biographies fail to draw the critical conclusions that are warranted by FDR's actions in the last year of his life, especially against the backdrop of the 1944 election. Most particularly, there is almost no mention—let alone critique—of Roosevelt's failure to keep his vice president up to speed on matters foreign and domestic. One can clearly disagree about whom to blame—McIntire, FDR, his close advisors, even Bruenn—but surely there were legitimate concerns about transition that FDR, among others, should have considered. Black notes about FDR's death that "for one who had cheerfully borne so much pain for so long, at the end he suffered little conscious discomfort and no fear or unnerving mortal premonitions. . . . He would not suffer the indignity of Woodrow Wilson, neither the bitterness of an ultimate defeat nor a prolonged terminal illness." Yet, Hugh Evans, a medical doctor who has studied FDR's health extensively, has suggested that it was more fortuitous than not that Roosevelt did not experience a disabling but nonfatal attack like Wilson's 1919 stroke. The possibilities of a power struggle within the White House and between FDR's advisors and Truman, in the event of a disabling medical condition for FDR, could have had grave implications for the country's stewardship and success.[99] While the Twenty-fifth Amendment subsequently addressed questions of presidential disability, the question here is not so much disability—which could befall even the healthiest of presidents—or even presidential health in general, but the misguided decision making that surrounded the pursuit of the fourth term, given President Roosevelt's health.

Doubtless the vice presidency had historically been a position of weakness, a place to relegate presidential rivals. And even Truman worried that if Roosevelt survived his presidency, he (Truman) would be rendered politically insignificant.[100] Yet the vice presidency had also grown into an important office in the twentieth century, especially under the watch of Franklin Roosevelt. As Donald Young has written, "the concept of the *working* Vice President dates only from about 1941. Since then every Vice President has been politically in tune with his President, and has displayed a loyalty to his chief in striking contrast to the circumstances found so often before." Although Wallace fell out of FDR's good graces and was denied renomination, there is no indication that Roosevelt was returning in 1944 to a "pre-Wallace" notion of the vice presidency as an office to be used to control political rivals. Truman was certainly not a presidential rival of FDR's, having been on few but the party leaders' lists of possible presidential or vice presidential candidates. Young concludes of the vice presidential nomination in 1944 that "[n]o one will ever be able to make a great deal of sense out of the President's behavior before this convention." Normally one of the most "astute political statesmen," Roosevelt "allowed himself to be pulled too many ways by too many men."[101]

What seems to unite the biographers of Roosevelt—and what explains their avoidance of more critical perspectives on Roosevelt's decision making in 1944 and 1945—is their assumption, not an unreasonable one, that Roosevelt's probity was beyond question and that he surely would have acted differently had he understood the gravity of his sickness. This is why some biographers reflexively believe that Roosevelt did not know that Bruenn was a cardiologist or that he had heart problems. Hugh Evans, who is critical of FDR's decision making in 1944, suggests why it is easy to accept this perspective on FDR: "It would be logical to note that if Roosevelt had a conscious belief in his impending death he would have been preparing Truman more thoroughly."[102] And because we assume *logical* behavior, we are inclined to the view that FDR and his advisors did not know the extent of his condition.

Yet it seems that we should consider his decision, and that of his advisors and close friends, in precisely a different light, as not merely the result of logical, rational action. The progressive-turned-conservative commentator John T. Flynn was probably the most candid and scathing in his critique of FDR's decision to pursue a fourth term in light of his health.[103] He was also, as it would turn out, largely correct. Despite the status of its messenger, the message does resonate to an important degree. Flynn was especially critical of what he perceived was FDR's lukewarm performance at the Yalta Conference:

> It is, of course, easy to say that Roosevelt, broken on the wheel of service, was with tremendous courage giving the last ounce of his waning strength in the service of his country. But after all, his country in that critical moment of history was entitled to something more in a leader than the *last ineffectual ounces of his strength.*
>
> Yet, this America, so powerful in her economic energies, so tremendous upon the seas, in the air, upon the battlefield, whose might astonished the world, now, in the crucial moment of victory when she would capture or lose the fruits of the victory, put her fortunes into the hands of a drooping, jaded and haggard man, a mere shell, drifting wearily to the grave. But America did not know this.[104]

Whether or not we accept that Roosevelt was outmatched at Yalta, it is nevertheless true that Roosevelt was in serious decline physically for the last year of his life. Flynn estimates that after Roosevelt's schedule was scaled back, in the wake of Bruenn's examination, that Roosevelt worked a four-hour day from thenceforward and that during 1944, Roosevelt "spent 200 days outside the White House in rest or travel which, save in the brief campaign tours, was undertaken for his health." Roosevelt's "doctors were telling him as plainly as words that the only way he could avert death was to go into a form of semi-retirement."[105]

This analysis of Flynn's is not merely the raving of an ideological critic of Roosevelt, although it is partly that. Daisy Suckley's diary recounts the rest regime of Roosevelt during the last year of his life, and it is shocking to read just how much rest—especially napping and sleeping—that President Roosevelt required.[106] Roosevelt himself complained to her in October 1944 that he was suffering from "sleeping sickness" to which Suckley replied that "it was just plain overtiredness." She confided to her diary that the "truth is that he never has the chance to get really rested— It worries me much, as he has no longer the power of 'come-back' which he used to have." In late March of 1945, she similarly confessed that while Roosevelt "looks perhaps a tiny bit better each day . . . he needs 2–3 months off-duty entirely to get back on his feet. He says he can't take the time off, and one wonders just how long he can keep going this way."[107]

And this is where we return to Calvin Coolidge's argument, which opened the chapter, in favor of presidential term limits: "It is difficult for men in high office to avoid the malady of self-delusion. . . . They live in an artificial atmosphere of adulation and exaltation which sooner or later impairs their judgment. They are in grave danger of becoming careless and arrogant."[108] Self-delusion, impaired judgment, carelessness, and arrogance: these all seem to at least partly capture the actions and behaviors of Roosevelt and his circle in 1944–1945. But these are all terms that seem a far cry from "rational" or "logical." This may seem a harsh indictment, but it is not meant to cast aspersions on the sincerity or patriotism of Roosevelt and his advisors. Here there was no sinister motivation to perpetuate a president in office in an act of sheer power consolidation or worse, power accretion. Rather, there was simply a widespread belief—hope is probably more accurate—in the face of increasing evidence to the contrary, that Roosevelt's health would somehow rebound. Roosevelt clearly lived in an "artificial atmosphere" where even his doctors were not about to question his decision making or broach the possibility of his discontinuing service as president. He himself also undoubtedly chose to avoid the serious implications of his declining health.

Daisy Suckley details her (and others') devotion to FDR throughout her diary, at one point writing, in response to Lucy Rutherford's view[109] that FDR looked ill, that "I don't dare acknowledge that I feel the same way about him, for reports spread so rapidly from one person to another."[110] With many such individuals around FDR who thought he was simply indispensable to the nation (or as Suckely put, "the *world* needs him"[111]), it was unlikely that FDR would get the advice that he needed in 1944. Indeed, even "the press of America refrained from publishing alarming stories [of the president's health], altho [*sic*] reporters saw the President whither under their eyes, lose his mellifluous voice, and slow down mentally."[112]

Reporter Robert Nixon astutely observed, "There was a structure built about [Roosevelt] that made people take for granted that he was going to live forever. I'm sure he thought so too. I don't think it ever crossed his mind—the shadow of death. . . . Here was a man that presumably would live forever. Nothing would happen to him."[113] Although death did cross Roosevelt's mind,[114] what is important to note is that this "structure" in all likelihood was held intact by the president's own hand. As we saw, notwithstanding his doctors' attempts to keep information from him, Roosevelt had early on discovered that Bruenn was a cardiologist and that he evidently had heart trouble. Given Roosevelt's legendary reputation for personal interaction and for "reading" people, it is hard to believe that his advisors would have kept the seriousness of his illness from him had he not wanted it that way; and, in fact, the available evidence does not necessarily indicate that Roosevelt did not know the seriousness of his condition. Furthermore, it is unlikely that his advisors "managed" his illness, especially with regard to the press, without Roosevelt's consent, tacit or otherwise. That Roosevelt may have been subject to manipulation by his doctors and advisors—and less directly, party leaders—only *adds to* the testimony of his physical, if not mental, decline in 1944–1945.

Despite FDR's biographers making much of his democratic leadership and connection with the people, in his death we witness a key failure of democracy. Evans has put it well: "Rationalizations aside, the voting public had a right to know that one candidate in the presidential election of 1944 was mortally ill with no realistic expectation of surviving a fourth four-year term."[115] Similarly, Flynn had pointed out the anti-democratic implications of the 1944 election, if a bit heavy-handedly: "He [Roosevelt] was utterly unfit for his high office long before the [1944] election. He was dying slowly at first, rapidly later." Roosevelt had been put into a fourth term "by a carefully arranged deception practiced upon the American people and upon some, at least, of the party leaders."[116] Ferrell takes a somewhat different tack and is more focused in his critique: "And so the months of President Roosevelt's illness passed, with the nation's chief executive keeping his illness a secret, confiding in no one. His physical abilities markedly lessened. A charitable estimate of the time he spent each day doing the public business was four hours, and was closer to one or two. His mind was unaffected; his problem was an inability to concentrate for long periods. . . . He was, and it is saddening to say this for such a great historical figure, in no condition to govern the Republic."[117] And that Roosevelt and his advisors did next to nothing to inform Truman of the problems of the day, not to mention the routine workings of a now-huge federal government, only adds weight to this critical characterization of Roosevelt's leadership in his last year. It is unfortunate that so few have cast a critical eye on the decision making behind Roosevelt's fourth term, as it sheds considerable light on debates over presidential tenure and especially attempts to limit presidential tenure. To return to Jefferson, Roosevelt may not have been a "dotard"[118] in his third and (brief) fourth terms, but "no office . . . less admits the indulgence of age."[119]

We will return to Roosevelt's third and fourth terms in the concluding chapters as Roosevelt is truly a difficult case when considering presidential tenure. His third term undoubtedly provides strong argument for unlimited reeligibility, while his fourth term suggests the problems associated with long tenure in office. The next chapter will consider the debate over and adoption of the Twenty-second Amendment and further treat some of the key questions of long presidential tenure. We will also see the strong connection of the debate in 1947 with the long history of contention over executive tenure in America.

TRADITION RESURGENT

The Twenty-second Amendment

*Yes, the Constitution itself does bind the people in certain
particulars and prevents them from doing certain things
which they might do under stress, prejudice, and emotion.
To argue that the people should never bind themselves so
far as future action is concerned is not in keeping with the
spirit and purpose of our Constitution.*

Earl C. Michener, 1947

The Twenty-second Amendment to the Constitution is among the least discussed of all of our amendments. A simple look at any number of American government or even presidency textbooks reveals little in the way of discussion—or even mention—of the Twenty-second Amendment and its meaning and implications. Occasionally there has been public commentary on the issue, as when President Clinton ignited interest due to his comments in an October 2000 *Rolling Stone* interview. Clinton, of course, was barred by the amendment from seeking a third term; however, he was not barred from registering his dissatisfaction with the amendment and his desire for a third term. Clinton said that he would have run again if not barred by the Twenty-second Amendment and that he believed he would have won a third term. However, he also cautioned that perhaps it is "[b]etter to leave when you're in good shape. I think maybe they should—maybe they should put 'consecutive' there."[1] Clinton would reinforce this position in 2003 with a call to modify the Twenty-second Amendment so that only consecutive third terms would be prohibited.[2] But mostly the amendment is little acknowledged, both by the public and scholars.[3] Interestingly, this characterizes the amendment from its inception in the 80th Congress in 1947. Not only was there relatively little debate in Congress in 1947, but there was scant newspaper coverage or interest group involvement, and public opinion undoubtedly was not keenly attuned to the issue, during the periods of congressional passage and ratification.[4] As Roberta S. Sigel and David J. Butler have put it, the Twenty-second Amendment "was successfully added to the Constitution" in a "quiet, almost unnoticed manner."[5]

"THE TWENTY-SECOND AMENDMENT SHOULD BE STRICKEN FROM THE CONSTITUTION"

Despite this lack of wide study and awareness of the amendment, it has been perceived over the years more unfavorably than not.[6] Although respected sources such as the *New York Times* supported the amendment when it was adopted,[7] a number of scholars at the time saw the amendment as ill-advised at best.[8] This perspective would be ingrained in later generations through the major political science and history texts of the 1950s and 1960s, as a brief look at major texts from the era reveals. *Government by the People*, the venerable Burns and Peltason text, worried in 1957 that "the amendment will probably weaken Presidents during their second term, because powerful leaders in Congress and in the Administration will feel less obliged to support a man who they know will be out of power within a given period of time."[9] Louis Koenig's *The Chief Executive* argued against the "stealthy emasculation" of the presidency wrought by the Twenty-second Amendment, especially "the amendment's potential mischief in a foreign affairs crisis." Not only was the potential for presidents to become "lame ducks" great, but the nation might be deprived of a great leader in a time of crisis. Further, the amendment was "antidemocratic in spirit" and also "posthumous revenge against Franklin Roosevelt for breaking the two-term tradition."[10] Kallenbach was less sharp in his criticisms of the amendment—he preferred the two-term tradition to an "explicit constitutional rule"—but he did note a "substantial majority" of scholars to be against the amendment.[11]

Probably the staunchest criticism of the amendment came in the well-known and influential *The American Presidency*, by the esteemed Clinton Rossiter. For Rossiter, the amendment was an "undisguised slap at the memory of Franklin D. Roosevelt," and he asserted that the Constitution "is not the place to engage in a display of rancor." But, more importantly for Rossiter, the amendment would bring about a weakening of the presidency (especially through the lame duck scenario) and could easily deprive the nation of leadership during a time of crisis. Moreover, he wrote, the amendment "bespeaks a shocking lacking of faith in the common sense and good judgment of the people of the United States." At the end of the day, for Rossiter, "the fact remains that those who take pride and comfort in the amendment are Whigs, men who fear the presidency and put their final trust in Congress, and that those who propose to repeal it are Jacksonians, men who respect Congress but look for leadership to the Presidency. Since this whole book is a salute to the modern Presidency, I doubt that I need to explain further why the Twenty-second Amendment should be stricken from the Constitution."[12]

There would, of course, be some variance. Respected constitutional scholar Edward Corwin, for instance, in *The President*, reveals himself as no supporter of the "indispensable man" theory, the acceptance of which "is next door to despairing of the country." He also upbraids Republicans for the political motivation of their amendment, but with a twist: "In their haste to register disapproval of the late President Roosevelt for seeking a third and then a fourth term, these gentlemen neglected or ignored the really critical issue, which is *whether a President should be permitted to succeed himself at all*."[13] Although seemingly opposed to the Twenty-second Amendment, it is because it did not go far enough in establishing one term with ineligibility. But Corwin is the outlier and Rossiter the norm. Not surprisingly, given the secrecy surrounding FDR's health in 1944 and 1945 (and thereafter), none of these texts questions the dubious pursuit of a fourth term.

There are four main themes in these scholarly criticisms. One is that the amendment was merely or predominantly political (partisan) payback. There is surely something to this characterization. As many observers have pointed out, Republicans in the House and Senate supported the amendment unanimously. And even though they needed Democratic support to cross the two-thirds threshold, most of those Democratic votes were from southern and conservative Democrats who opposed the New Deal and often Roosevelt and his policies.[14] The second main thread is that the amendment, if not merely an act of political punishment, was a spiteful attack on the office of the presidency by a Congress fearful of its diminishing influence. Here the major concern was the "lame duck" nature of a second-term president with no chance of reelection. Third, there is an appeal, sometimes straightforward, often latent, to the idea of an "indispensable" leader who will be needed in a time of emergency or crisis. This can be observed most notably in Rossiter's analysis. Finally, there is a strong assumption that the amendment represents a step backward as it exhibits a distrust of the people not in keeping with American political evolution.

These themes, as we will see, track well with the actual debates over the amendment. As the august assemblage of delegates discovered in 1787, presidential tenure is a complicated and nettlesome issue that does not lend itself to a simple solution. Notwithstanding the dominant caricature that the amendment was the result of spiteful partisanship and institutional jealousy, the congressional debates of 1947 in fact reveal themselves to be subtle and textured and provide a nice summary of the major arguments for and against long presidential tenure. When coupled with what we now know about FDR's pursuit of a fourth term, the Twenty-second Amendment looks less like crass partisanship and more like justifiable—if controversial—statesmanship.

"WE ARE NOT DOING ANYTHING NEW"

Very early in the 80th Congress, with Republicans in control for the first time since 1931, the proposed Twenty-second Amendment to the Constitution came before first the House and then the Senate. As several legislators noted in the debates over the amendment, it was nothing new for presidential tenure to be the subject of proposed reform or amendment. In fact, according to Representative Louis E. Graham (R-PA), "in a period of 139 years 210 attempts have been made to fix the tenure of office of the President of the United States. So we are not doing anything new, unusual, or out of the way at this time."[15] Some of these attempts were to establish a six-year term for the presidency with ineligibility, among other reforms, but there were also numerous attempts to give constitutional sanction to the two-term tradition. As Representative George W. Gillie (R-IN) saw it, "the action of the early Presidents and their writings on the subject make the two-term limitation a virtual postscript to the Constitution."[16] But, of course, Roosevelt's third and fourth terms changed everything and would be the prime motivation for the proposed Twenty-second Amendment. It is not surprising given the context that many at the time perceived the proposed amendment as a personal affront to the memory of Franklin Delano Roosevelt. Representative Adolph J. Sabath (D-IL) summed up this feeling among (mainly) Democrats when he asked, "[c]an we not be fair enough to let rest in peace a man who has done so much for our country and humanity?"[17] But, from the Republican side, something had to be done, regardless of the timing, to ensure that the two-term tradition would be respected by future presidents. For Representative John Jennings Jr. (R-TN), constitutionally sanctioning the two-term tradition was the only way "the people [can] be assured that we shall never have a dictator in this land."[18]

Somewhere in between this talk about allowing FDR to rest in peace and preventing a dictator or despot in our country, the House and Senate engaged in a high-level debate over issues of power, democracy, and constitutional government. There are two categories of argument to be found in the debate. Several of the arguments deal with what might be called "procedural" or formal matters, while the key arguments deal with substantive, theoretical questions of presidential tenure. While the latter are clearly more important than the former, the procedural arguments deserve brief mention.

One key procedural argument was how to contextualize the amendment; that is, was it something radical (as Democrats suggested) or was it a piece with a strong tradition of reform (as Republicans characterized it)? Republicans argued that the amendment would be nothing new, as numerous attempts had been made to reform the tenure of the president since the beginning. Additionally, Republicans appealed to term limits of state governors to support their case. Since many states had restricted the tenure of their governors, restricting presidential tenure was not out of line with mainstream opinion in America. Democrats, of course, disagreed. They retorted that the history of tenure reform had been a failure and that none of the "resolutions [have] ever been able to command sufficient support on the part of the people of the United States," according to Alabama Senator Lister Hill.[19] Moreover, Hill continued, that many governors had term restrictions was beside the point: "The duties, responsibilities, and problems and burdens of the President of the United States . . . cannot be compared with those of the governor of a State."[20] What is more, the people were not clamoring for the amendment: Senator Scott W. Lucas (D-IL), for instance, had "received exactly eight letters from constituents on this question." The people were thereby "not very much excited" about the amendment.[21]

Another key procedural argument was that the amendment was an affront to the memory of FDR. In some ways this is almost a truism, but some Democrats pushed the argument a bit far and characterized it in personal and excessively partisan terms. Putting the argument in maudlin terms was Representative Sabath: "It was a Godsend to the world that we had Franklin D. Roosevelt, whom the people freely chose four times to direct our Government and our destinies, and who served the Nation and all mankind as no other man has ever done before."[22] Although Republicans rejected the idea that the amendment was mean-spirited, they did not—could not—claim that it had nothing to do with FDR. Nevertheless, that it was a response to FDR's seeking third and fourth terms was not important *in and of itself*. It is only when members started addressing what Roosevelt did when in office that a more substantive argument arose.

Relatedly, Republicans and Democrats also argued over whether the people had already decided on the question of the two-term custom when they voted FDR to not only a third term but also a fourth term. Democratic Representative R. Ewing Thomason (TX) bluntly phrased the issue: "I contend the people spoke on this very question in no uncertain terms in 1940 and again in 1944."[23] Republicans responded that the two-term rule was a small part of the debates in the 1940 and 1944 elections and that the question needed to be put as a single issue, absent an actual president or personality: "The issue in 1940 was one as to the relative merits of Franklin Delano Roosevelt and Wendell Willkie. The issue in 1944 was as to the relative merits of Franklin Delano Roosevelt and Thomas E. Dewey,"[24] according to Representative Edward J. Devitt (R-MN).

The last of the procedural arguments was over the method of ratification. The two parties argued mightily over whether state legislatures or state conventions should ratify the amendment should it pass the House and Senate. Republicans favored submitting the question to state legislatures and Democrats favored state conventions. Democrats pointed out that submitting the proposed amendment to the state legislatures, would not constitute a direct expression of the people's will on the question. Senator Claude Pepper of Florida expressed, rather vituperatively, the Democratic concern with legislatures being the repositories of the decision: "What is proposed is to permit the publishers of newspapers who hated Roosevelt, propagandists, and people with money who would like to keep America from having another Roosevelt to influence enough legislatures to keep the people from having the power."[25]

Surely Republicans thought there was more to gain with state legislatures rather than state conventions, especially given that state legislators were likely to sympathize with congressional concerns over executive aggrandizement and a number of state politicians would also sympathize with congressional (especially Republican) concerns about a growing federal government. Nevertheless, all amendments but the Twenty-first had been ratified by state legislatures, and thus tradition was clearly on the side of the Republicans. And after all, as was pointed out in the debates, state legislatures had ratified the Seventeenth Amendment, establishing direct election of senators, even though it represented a curtailment of their power. Whether the convention method would have yielded a more favorable result for opponents of the amendment cannot be known. Public opinion in general, however, did start to turn against a third term in the late 1940s, mirroring the trends within elite Democratic circles. Even by 1943, a majority of the country, according to polls, supported the necessity of a two-term limit, and this would continue throughout the decade.[26] So it is reasonable to conclude that conventions may have achieved a similar unfavorable result for opponents of the amendment. At any rate, while an intriguing part of the congressional debates, this argument was formal rather than substantive.

"LONG PRESIDENTIAL TENURE"

The procedural arguments are an important part of the congressional debate and tell us something of the politicking and jockeying that went on, but they have only tangential bearing on the *substantive* theoretical issues of presidential tenure. And these were surely not neglected. One of the critical arguments was over how to characterize the founders' view of presidential term limits. Opponents of the amendment, of course, made much of the framers' decision not to limit the number of terms a president could serve. Hamilton's *Federalist* contributions were held up as monuments to the founders' thinking on the matter. And other founders, according to Senator Hill, like "James Wilson, Gouverneur Morris, and Roger Sherman, who likewise were members of the constitutional convention—had strong convictions on the subject; they were opposed to any limitation on the people in their right of free election of their president."[27] Moreover, George Washington was claimed as being a strong supporter of the decision of the convention on this front, even though many Republicans also claimed Washington as being the originator of the two-term tradition. In an oft-quoted letter to Lafayette, Washington opined: "Under an extended view of this part of the subject I can see no propriety in precluding ourselves from the service of any man who, in some great emergency, shall be deemed universally most capable of serving the public."[28] As we saw in chapter 3, Washington stepped down after two terms more for personal reasons than for reasons of philosophy.

Republicans, however, correctly adduced Jefferson—if not Washington—as being a major proponent of the two-term tradition; and not only this, his successors had followed his model. Indeed the reeligibility of the president was something early presidents and other framers questioned not long after the ratification of the Constitution—and, as we have seen, the ratifying conventions themselves witnessed key discussions of tenure. From the Republicans' view, then, opponents' appeals to the authority of the framers were limited. There was surely no strong consensus among the founding generation, and any appeal to the "intentions of the framers" to oppose the Twenty-second Amendment would be tendentious. The two-term tradition was indeed in some ways a "virtual postscript" to the Constitution, even if Jefferson was the responsible party, not Washington. While not advancing a positive argument for the two-term tradition on its merits, this position does blunt the appeal to the framers that opponents of the amendment advanced in the debates. As we will see later, some proponents of the amendment even rejected the relevance of the founders' views; the presidency had gained so much in power over the years that their decision not to restrict tenure had been applied to a wholly different office.

The heart of the debate, though, would be over "long presidential tenure" and its implications. According to its proponents, the amendment would do nothing less than secure the liberties of the American people. As Representative John M. Robsion (R-KY) put it, "[i]f long tenure of office of the President was a threat to our republican form of government as stated by President Jefferson nearly 140 years ago, with his limited powers, small disbursements, small Army and Navy and a small number of appointees, how much greater must that threat be to our republican form of government and to the liberties of the American people today."[29] While Robsion was appealing to Jefferson's authority in inaugurating the two-term custom, he went a step further to explain and justify Jefferson's decision, especially within the modern context. Presidents who can maintain themselves in office for a long tenure, according to this argument, could easily end up abridging the rights and liberties of the people, especially in the late 1940s. As Representative Devitt saw it, the "office of President of the United States, especially when held by what is popularly classified as a 'strong President,' presents an opportunity for the exercise of influence all out of proportion to that contemplated by the constitutional founders."[30]

So perhaps it made sense for the founders not to restrict presidential tenure, given the rather modest powers assigned the presidency under the Constitution. But now there was certainly cause for alarm. How, more specifically, could presidents with long tenure jeopardize the liberties of the people? The arguments offered here ranged from subtle treatments of the balance of power in Washington and the American system to general screeds linking FDR to the dictatorships of Europe. For instance, Republican Senator Alexander Wiley (WI) argued that the necessity of the Twenty-second Amendment was supported by the historical record: "Continuance of power in the hands of an individual or party over a considerable period of time made possible a Hitler, a Mussolini, and all the little Fascists. That, Mr. President, is the reason for the proposed constitutional amendment."[31] It is no wonder that some members took exception to the proposed amendment as a vilification of FDR. Most other supporters of the amendment, however, were less heavy-handed in their criticisms of long presidential tenure.

On a very general level, Representative Edwin Arthur Hall (R-NY) worried that "the natural love for power that men in high places often have is increased the longer they remain at the helm. They tend to shape the destiny of a whole people according to their single mind if allowed to go unchecked."[32] The first sentence expresses the age-old fear that men desire power and will be reluctant to give it up. This would be seconded by Connecticut Republican Senator Raymond E. Baldwin's observation that "when the time comes and the opportunity to continue themselves in office and in power is presented, they [politicians] always yield."[33] The second sentence in Representative Hall's statement, though, is perhaps more intriguing and complex. Here he worries of the singular power of a long-serving president and a "single mind" controlling the U.S. political system. Although he does not lay out the argument much more fully, his concern is clearly in keeping with the spirit of the U.S. Constitution. The constitutional structure betrays a strong suspicion of any unilateral action, whether it be from a tyrannical majority or a single individual or small group. It is only with a balancing of groups and interests that the liberties of the people can truly be preserved, according to Madison's justly famous argument in *Federalist* #10.

Representative Jennings more specifically advanced this concern about a consolidation of power in the presidential office: "Without such a limit on the number of terms a man may serve in the Presidency, the time may come when a man of vaulting ambition becomes President.

Such a man, clothed with the vast powers of the Presidency and backed by a subservient Congress, as Commander in Chief of our Army and Navy, could well have in his hands the two mightiest instrumentalities of governmental power, the sword and the purse."[34] From the perspective of 2011, this argument should certainly give one pause. It is clearly prescient in understanding what the future would hold for presidential war power; however, it also suggests the limitations of the Twenty-second Amendment in controlling the rise of presidential power. (Representative Jennings also correctly glimpsed the coming activism of the federal courts.) The office provides considerable power to even first-term presidents to have a large impact on the shape and state of U.S. foreign policy, including decisions of war.

Jennings went on to discuss other ramifications of presidential domination through long tenure. He seized particularly on the long tenure of a president, allowing him to dominate not only Congress but also the federal courts: "Such a President could well name to the Supreme Court of the United States men of his political faith and economic thinking, and these men in passing upon and interpreting acts of Congress, acts of the legislatures of the States, and in construing the Constitution of our country would have the power to substitute their economic philosophy for the law of the land. . . . Such a court could legislate by judicial decision. It could transform our form of government."[35] Given Roosevelt's battles with the Court and the so-called "Court-packing plan," members of Congress, particularly from the Republican side, had some reason to worry about the independent nature of a judiciary with a strong president in the White House and no term limitations. Now, surely, one might claim that this argument is not so much against a *president* continuing in office for long tenure as about one *party* holding the presidency for too long. Senator Francis J. Myers (D-PA) suggested as much: "If the proponents of this resolution desire to cure what they believe is an evil, the limitation might better be placed on political parties, rather than upon individual candidates for the Presidency."[36]

Yet there was a large difference, in many members' views, between the same person holding office for an extended period of time and a party's representatives holding office for a long time. Whereas the same individual would have a largely singular point of view, parties, because of their diversity, would likely elect successors who would inject a new perspective or approach to governing, appointments, and so forth. As Representative Joseph P. O'Hara (R-MN) phrased it, "I have heard my colleagues on the Democratic side of the aisle complain that the test for filling judicial appointments was not whether the individual was a Democrat, but whether he was a particular brand of New Dealer."[37] It was not so much that Democrats retained the presidency but that Roosevelt and his "New Dealers" continued to dominate.

Although O'Hara was specifically worried about presidential appointments to the courts, calling Roosevelt's ability to make administrative appointments for over twelve years "not such a problem,"[38] other members worried deeply about a president's ability to nominate thousands of federal appointees. It was precisely this control over federal offices that allowed Roosevelt to be renominated again by the Democratic conventions of 1940 and 1944. Speaking of the 1940 Democratic Convention, Representative Karl E. Mundt (R-SD) said that "newspaper accounts revealed that well over half of the delegates . . . were on the pay roll of the Federal Government as political appointees or they were the relatives thereof. That made the synthetic draft of 1940 an easy matter."[39] Republican Representative Earl C. Michener (MI) would concur: "The majority of the voters of the party may prefer another man, but the nomination process is controlled by the party machinery."[40]

Thus the voters' free choice was imperiled by a president's ability to appoint federal employees, as these "employees" would be hard-pressed not to renominate their "employer." This argument clearly echoes those made during the Gilded Age, especially with Grant's possible reelection to a third term. In the age of the primary election, this might not seem a big worry, as presidents, to be renominated, must canvass for support within the party. Yet decisions by candidates about whether to challenge an incumbent president are surely influenced by the powers and prerogatives that presidents and their supporters can marshal, especially in terms of money resources and campaign funds. Bill Clinton, given his powers as president, his formidable campaign skills, and his control over the Democratic National Committee—not to mention his popularity—most likely could have secured a nomination for a third term in the absence of the Twenty-second Amendment, even in an era of primary elections.

Long tenure in office, then, would allow a president to dominate the Congress, the courts, the bureaucracy, and the mechanisms for renomination. A "single mind" could dominate the action in Washington and abroad and shape the direction of the country. This would certainly be problematic if in fact it led to presidential domination of war making or judicial interpretation. Moreover, while many might think a president needs like-minded individuals in the bureaucracy, there is surely reason to worry if these individuals' indebtedness to the president helps to assure party renomination. Although Republicans did not have a lot of specifics to adduce in Roosevelt's case beyond the 1940 and 1944 renominations and his attempt to "pack" the Court, it is fair to say that the potential abuses they addressed with the long tenure in office were at least reasonable. Why should we, after all, think that one individual will adequately and selflessly represent and advance the interests of the nation? Even if the individual has the best of intentions, does it not challenge the American constitutional structure, and the ideals underlying that structure, to vest extensive power in not just one branch of government but one person?

"Presidents Have Never Sought to be Dictators"

But Democrats remained relatively untroubled by these claims, trusting not only the American people but leaders themselves: "Presidents have never sought to be dictators," said Senator Harley M. Kilgore (D-WV), "they have been Americans."[41] In the eyes of Senator Pepper, "[o]ur people are to be safely trusted with their own destiny. That is the spirit of democracy and its intent. We do not need to protect the American people with a prohibition against a President whom they do not wish to elect; and if they wanted to elect him, have we the right to deny them the power?"[42] Pepper challenged Republicans to "find in the record of Franklin Roosevelt something which in their opinion justifies the radical deprivation of free franchise from the people of the United States to elect their own President."[43]

Not only were Democrats untroubled by the critique of long tenure, they took the offensive, arguing that FDR was that critical leader who was needed by his country in an emergency. To "have a constitutional limitation on the Presidential tenure of office in 1940 and again in 1944 would have been disastrous," said Democratic Representative Joseph R. Bryson (SC). "[S]uch a change would have thrown our Nation into chaos and jeopardized our security in the face of the gravest military crisis in our Nation's history."[44] Not only was it preposterous to link FDR to the tyrants of Europe, but, in Democrats' view, Roosevelt should be praised for his self-sacrifice and service to his country, as he was the "best man" for the job, in Massachusetts Representative John W. McCormack's view.[45]

Roosevelt, said Representative William T. Byrne (D-NY), "goes down in the pages of history unquestionably as the one man up to date who was absolutely essential and necessary at the time he was nominated and at the time he was elected. The results prove the case."[46] What would have happened to the American political experiment, one member wondered, had Lincoln been prevented from seeking reelection in 1864? As Representative McCormack pointed out, Theodore Roosevelt had already asked this question and answered it thusly: "It would be a veritable calamity if the American people were forbidden to continue to use the services of the one man whom they knew, and did not merely guess, could carry them through the crisis."[47]

Furthermore, opponents of the Twenty-second Amendment argued that limiting the president from pursuing a third term would weaken the presidency and thus deny Americans the necessary leadership that the presidency provides for the political system. Indeed, some members saw the amendment as an example of the "legislative branch pick[ing] on the President," as Democratic Senator W. Lee O'Daniel (TX) put it.[48] Senator Kilgore most effectively laid out this claim: "The Executive's effectiveness will be seriously impaired, as no one will obey and respect him if he knows that the Executive cannot run again because of a constitutional limitation. I may say, Mr. President, that I have had the opportunity in the past 8 years to study the record of governors in States in which there are limitations as to terms, and I have discovered that invariably the last half of the term was a record of failure."[49] This concern over the "lame duck" qualities of a term-limited presidency is a credible and important challenge to the wisdom of the amendment. Although a somewhat subdued issue here in the debates, it would grow in concern among political observers and scholars during the 1950s and thereafter.[50] The next chapter will address the evidence on the lame duck effects of the Twenty-second Amendment.

Most opponents of the amendment, though, did not wish to see presidents routinely serve more than two terms. In fact, most believed that the two-term tradition had served the American people well. It was the problem of enacting a constitutional amendment, very difficult to overturn if necessary, when a "custom" or "tradition" would generally suffice.[51] In fact, some members averred that the constitutional amendment might have the opposite result of its proponents' intentions; that is, because the people might be so constrained in a time of emergency, they might turn to a leader who would actively seek to break constitutional rules and procedures to assume power, thereby rendering the American system subject to dictatorship.[52]

Republicans, naturally, were skeptical of assertions that only Roosevelt could have led the country through World War II and that there are times of crisis when the people will not want to be denied a particular leader's abilities. Supporters of the amendment offered a number of criticisms of what came to be called the "indispensable man" idea. "Much has been made of the argument," said Representative Michener, "that a constitutional limitation on the tenure of the Presidential office would prevent the continuance in office of an experienced President in time of great emergency." However, he continued, this idea "should be completely alien to a democratic society."[53] Representative O'Hara made the point even more provocatively: "If in a country of 140,000,000 people there [arise] occasions where one man, and one man only, is capable of filling the position of the Presidency of the United States, then I say to the advocates of that theory that both democracy and a republican form of government are a failure."[54] Representative Robsion put the matter in more specific and historical terms: "Who can say that some other great American, Democrat or Republican, could not have handled the affairs of this Nation from 1940 to 1945 equally as well as President Roosevelt?"[55]

This issue was perhaps one of the most interesting from the debates. The Republicans can hardly be blamed for their incredulity at some of the extreme Democratic claims that *only* Roosevelt could possibly have led the United States through World War II. But, on the other side, Democrats had a powerful argument—when moderated to say that FDR was certainly among the most qualified in the nation to do the job—as FDR did quite admirably lead the United States through the Pearl Harbor attack and full-scale war with the Axis powers. Perhaps it is a sign of the decorum of the representatives and senators that they did not dwell too much on FDR's death in 1945.[56] Representative Lawrence H. Smith (R-WI) did offer, "[w]e do not accept that theory [indispensability] for it is fallacious and contrary to fact. When Mr. Roosevelt died he was succeeded by Harry S. Truman, yet we have carried on, there has been no cessation of government."[57]

It is unfortunate that more attention was not paid to the presidential transition of 1945, because it speaks to the "indispensable man" issue as well as other concerns of the proponents of the amendment.[58] With FDR dying only three months into his fourth term, an unseasoned and certainly not "indispensable" Harry S. Truman assumed the presidency. Although Truman was not nearly as popular in 1947 as he is today with historians, many senators and representatives had to be at least somewhat surprised at his ability to step into the presidential office and acquit himself commendably. His successes in the postwar negotiations could certainly have been advanced by proponents of the amendment as evidence that there will always be capable and competent leaders, or even that leaders rise to the occasion rather than vice versa. After all, what are the odds that the two indispensable men in the country happened to be on the Democratic ticket in 1944?

There were additional reasons to resist this appeal to crisis leadership, according to the supporters of the amendment. One was that the two-term "custom" or "tradition" would no longer have the power to constrain future presidents, and it would be likely that more and more presidents over time would seek more than two terms. "The custom has been broken," Senator W. Chapman Revercomb (R-WV) argued, "and in the future such an act may have the strength of precedent."[59] Thus it was necessary to give legal weight to the custom or tradition. But more importantly, proponents of the amendment argued, if we admitted that crises required an "indispensable man," or necessitated allowances to the two-term tradition, there would be no end of crises that presidents would see in the future meriting their continuing service in office. Senator Wiley quoted Jefferson accordingly on this matter: "No pretext should ever be permitted to dispense with it [the principle of rotation] because there will never be a time when real difficulties will not exist and furnish a plausible pretext for dispensation."[60] And, in Jefferson's view and that of the proponents of the amendment, presidents could not be trusted to refrain from exploiting "difficulties" and manufacturing or exaggerating crises.

The last substantial thread of the debate was over the Twenty-second Amendment's relationship to democracy. Democrats argued that it would represent a limitation of the democratic rights of the people. This argument has been around since the founding period, being famously advanced—if somewhat tepidly—by Alexander Hamilton, in *The Federalist*. Senator Pepper gave strong voice to this argument: "I think our people are to be safely trusted with their own destiny. That is the spirit of democracy and its intent. We do not need to protect the American people with a prohibition against a President whom they do not wish to elect; and if they wanted to elect him, have we the right to deny them the power?"[61]

And restrictions of democracy have been especially rare over time. While the founders may have restricted democracy, said Representative Sabath, "[w]e have frequently amended our Constitution, as the need arose, to extend the democratic processes on which our Government is solidly built. This amendment goes backward and limits the right of the majority to choose the President."[62] This was a very serious challenge to the amendment, especially in a country that had, in fact, increased the role of the people over time in the political system. The twentieth century had seen primary election reform, the rise of the referendum, and the public opinion poll, not to mention constitutional amendments for the popular election of senators and for a woman's right to vote. Surely it is difficult in the modern era, at least on the face of it, to disagree with Kentucky Democratic Representative Frank L. Chelf's statement that "the man selected and the number of times he is elected or reelected comes under the heading of the people's business. That is their business."[63]

Republicans also appealed to democratic theory, but to support, not oppose, the amendment. According to traditional democratic theory, the strength of democracy resides in its reliance on numerous centers of opinion and perspective. Democracies are dynamic and progressive because there is no dearth of new ideas and visions. Senator Wiley offered this argument most straightforwardly: "When we guarantee that no individual will occupy the Presidential office for more than two terms, we serve to encourage political leadership in other individuals. We assure a constant replacement of new blood into important positions in political parties."[64] Representative Michener pushed this argument even further, asserting that a dominant president not only deprives the nation of other leadership but helps to foster an acquiescent and compliant citizenry, certainly not the citizenry of democratic theory: "Political apathy is a menace to democracy, and blind faith in a leader inevitably means an indifference to great issues and problems. Along with public apathy, there is a stifling of other leaders, so that the capacity for political leadership is weakened."[65] These arguments, especially about public apathy, have received some support in recent years in the field of presidential studies.[66]

Not only that, but while the Constitution may have been democratized in some respects, its spirit was still one of checks and balances. Although we have seen democratic advances, the constitutional setup is still fundamentally "republican" rather than democratic. As Representative Michener saw it, the proposed amendment was not all that out of step with the essence of the Constitution: "Yes, the Constitution itself does bind the people in certain particulars and prevents them from doing certain things which they might do under stress, prejudice, and emotion. To argue that the people should never bind themselves so far as future action is concerned is not in keeping with the spirit and purpose of our Constitution."[67] But this was not just a counter-argument questioning the wisdom of the people and appealing to the republican character of our political system; it was also a reflection on the powers of the modern presidency and a president's ability to prevent the will of the people from being executed. It would be one thing to allow the people to decide on these questions if they were actually making a free decision. However, admonished Michener, they did not have that freedom because "the longer a President remains in office the more difficult it is for the people to remove him."[68]

THE RETURN OF THE WHIGS?

What few observers[69] have noticed about the debate over the Twenty-second Amendment is its strong connection to the historical debates over presidential tenure and power. The proponents of the amendment particularly were harking back to a tradition that had its roots in the colonial period in America. The *Whig* view of executive power, developed in chapters 1 and 2, constituted an important strand of the Republican Party philosophy from the beginning, and that of the Whig Party before it.[70] This model exhibited a strong suspicion of power in general but especially executive power and sought to curb not only what executives could do but how *long* they could do it. Though they may have been motivated in part by partisanship, Republicans in 1947 were also tapping into one of the central threads of their political philosophy. Despite the "stewardship" model of the presidency articulated by Theodore Roosevelt, a Republican, the Republican Party more than the Democratic Party had for many years been the party of weak executive leadership. Even Lincoln has been called by one of his foremost biographers a "Whig in the White House."[71] Surely the Republican presidents of the 1920s—Harding, Coolidge, and Hoover—are not remembered as strong presidents. And Teddy Roosevelt, we must recall, was rejected by his party for renomination in 1912, in part because of his radical reconceptualization of presidential power and the president's role in modern politics.[72] Republicans would ultimately embrace the "stewardship" model of the presidency—or what I have called the plebiscitary model—but it would be long in coming, as Eisenhower's presidency, which embodied traditional Whig deference to Congress in many ways, displayed. Even George W. Bush in some ways—although certainly not in all ways—exhibited Whig tendencies in his actions as president.[73]

Republican supporters of the Twenty-second Amendment, however, also conceded the partial wisdom of the *constitutional* view of executive leadership. As much as they longed for a past with weak executives and dominant legislatures, they realized that the nation would occasionally require strong leadership and that there was clearly something to be gained from experienced leadership. This was, after all, one of the key tenets of Hamilton's philosophy of executive leadership. Yet the constitutional view also contains a strong concern for *balance*, and this is undoubtedly what Republicans believed was missing with a *modern* president serving for a long period of time. This is why some Republicans argued that what the framers had to say on presidential tenure was largely irrelevant: the presidency of the 1940s was far more powerful than that of 1787, and thus was it necessary to restrain it and restore balance to the political system. Also in line with the constitutional view is the mild cynicism regarding the people's abilities that emerges in the Republican arguments.

Democrats, as we saw, appealed at many points in the debates to the wisdom of the framers in failing to adopt term limits for the presidency. One might naturally see them as embodying the constitutional view of executive power. And, to be sure, in some ways they do. Opponents of the amendment were much more likely to look to the presidency as the foundation of the political system and to worry that the amendment might weaken the office. Moreover, Democrats, just like Alexander Hamilton and George Washington before them, worried that term limits might deprive the country of strong and experienced leadership in a time of crisis.

Yet opponents of the amendment were much more in tune with the *plebiscitary* model of executive leadership than the constitutional view. As discussed in chapters 1 and 2, the plebiscitary model sees the presidency as the engine of the U.S. political system, with the president deriving power from a strong connection with the American people. This is obviously in many ways antithetical to the constitutional view, which sought to put distance between the presidency and the people. And when we understand the Democratic Party historically, we realize that "popular" presidential leadership is a key part of its legacy.[74] This legacy dates back to Andrew Jackson, the founder of the modern Democratic Party, and incorporates figures such as Stephen Douglas, Grover Cleveland, William Jennings Bryan, and Woodrow Wilson.[75] FDR's strong popular leadership was more of a culmination than a departure from the Democratic creed on executive leadership. Though the Democratic Party embrace of popular leadership did not bring with it a consistent rejection (or embrace) of term limits,[76] there would seem to be a theoretical affinity between popular presidential leadership and rejection of term limits. Not only does the plebiscitary model postulate a wise public and wise leaders, it places much faith in leadership in general and is more amenable to the "indispensable man" argument, obviously a key tenet of faith among term-limit opponents.

While I reserve judgment on the wisdom and legacy of the Twenty-second Amendment until the next chapter, it should be stressed that the historical objections and characterizations of the amendment are to an important extent misguided. As can be seen throughout this book, there has been from America's colonial beginnings a vigorous theoretical debate over the proper parameters of presidential leadership, especially with regard to the president's tenure in office. The issue became salient again in the 1940s, not just because FDR shattered the two-term tradition but because the power of the presidency grew precipitously in the 1930s and in the 1940s as well. That FDR was unbeatable at the polls surely brought out some vindictiveness in Republicans in 1947, but his long tenure as president also afforded Republicans the opportunity to revisit their theoretical heritage regarding their longstanding concerns with presidential power. It is instructive to note that Republicans themselves consistently prevented—through persuasion or outright opposition—their own members (Grant, Theodore Roosevelt, and Coolidge) from achieving third terms. None of this is to say that the Democratic opponents of the amendment were not at least somewhat principled in the opposition, nor that they had the worse of the arguments. It is to suggest that the drive for the amendment cannot be written off as the product of mean-spiritedness, jealousy, or partisan payback. Rather, it was in keeping with a strong theoretical strain in American political thought and practical party politics. In an important sense, as they said, Republicans were *not* doing anything new.

AMBITION, DEMOCRACY,

AND CONSTITUTIONAL BALANCE

*I know personally from experience that there is a certain
zone which when a man has walked through it, he has
got to be careful. Maybe Time was the scissors that
Delilah used for shearing Samson! . . . I am afraid—
deeply and morally afraid—because I love my country
and want it to go right, that I can hear Delilah's scissors
clicking.*

William Allen White

Since the passage of the Twenty-second Amendment, conventional wisdom has held that presidents become lame ducks in their second terms. This wisdom seemed to hold an especially prominent place during the second term of George W. Bush. For instance, in early 2007 *Newsweek* reported a poll showing that "[w]ith Bush widely viewed as an ineffectual 'lame duck' (by 71 percent of all Americans), over half (53 percent) of . . . respondents now say they believe history will see him as a below-average president." Additionally, "more than half the country (58 percent) say they wish the Bush presidency were simply over."[1] And this with nearly two full years to go in his presidency. The poll and the attitudes conveyed therein raise key questions about presidential tenure in America historically and contemporarily. Can the so-called lame duck phenomenon be empirically verified and grounded? More specifically, did Bush, Clinton, Reagan, and Eisenhower, those presidents ostensibly rendered lame ducks by the Twenty-second Amendment, experience diminished power—and popularity—in their second terms as a direct result of their inability to pursue a third term? Or, alternatively, are second-term failures the result of other factors, such as fatigue, increasing partisan acrimony, or the inevitable clashes of ambitious politicians? Regardless of the cause, do the failures of recent second-term presidents suggest the wisdom of that longstanding reform proposal, the six-year term with no reeligibility?

Beyond questions of reeligibility, what are the American people to do with a president who has lost the confidence of the country but still has half or more of his term remaining? Given that impeachment has traditionally not been used as "vote of no confidence," should Americans consider instituting some form of recall or "no confidence" vote for presidents that may be triggered in the middle of their terms? Although this would obviously run counter to the Hamiltonian perspective, which established the four-year term specifically to insulate the president from the people's immediate judgment, one might wonder whether this perspective is out of touch with a modern democratic nation.

These are all serious questions that follow from the foregoing analysis of presidential tenure, and each is addressed in this concluding chapter. First, the chapter considers the evidence for the lame duck phenomenon. As the previously mentioned poll's suppositions evidence, many today assume the validity of the phenomenon. However, as we will see, there is very little direct evidence to confirm the lame duck theory. This is not to say that the Twenty-second Amendment fails to influence the actions of presidents but rather that the dire predictions of critics have not come to fruition. Nevertheless, if presidential failure in the second term is not directly the result of the two-term limit, it is well to consider the advisability of second terms in general. This is the second main task of the chapter. Presidential historian Lewis Gould—who *does* link second-term failures in part to the Twenty-second Amendment—has recently suggested that because second terms are so rarely successful, modern presidents would be better off serving simply one term.[2] I thereby treat the evidence regarding second-term failures of American presidents in general (not just *modern* presidents) and what might be done to address the problems of second terms. Third, and related, the chapter also examines in some detail the arguments for and against the six-year, non-renewable term, a proposal that has had numerous advocates—including presidents—throughout our history.

Finally, we consider the status quo, our two-term constitutional rule, in light of what has been learned about the lame duck phenomenon as well as second-term failure in general. We also treat arguably the most critical issue of presidential tenure in the twenty-first century: securing adequate leadership in a time of crisis. While concerns with presidents becoming lame ducks seem relatively baseless, the Hamiltonian concern about providing leadership in a time of crisis still resonates, particularly with the development of weapons (nuclear and otherwise) that have the potential for mass destruction. Undoubtedly, it is not fanciful to worry about the country being deprived of an experienced leader in a time of crisis because of the Twenty-second Amendment. Alternatively, considering the great powers at the disposal of modern presidents, the arguments against long presidential tenure remain salient.

"INCONTROVERTIBLY A LAME-DUCK PRESIDENT"

As mentioned briefly in the previous chapter, scholars of political science and history as a general rule were opposed to the Twenty-second Amendment.[3] Many of them predicted that presidential power would wane throughout the second term, with members of Congress and other ambitious politicians increasingly resisting the president (and his policies) as they jockeyed for position in the next presidential election. The lame duck theory suggests that the closer a president comes to the end of a second term—if he or she is barred from seeking reelection—the less relevant the president is to the Washington scene and especially the congressional players who are critical to the passage of many presidential priorities. Despite the conventional wisdom about the lame duck theory, there has been a dearth of analysis, scholarly or otherwise, of the phenomenon.

In the early nineteenth century, the term "lame duck" was used "to describe anyone who was bankrupt or behind on their debt payments. . . . By 1910, newspapers began using the phrase in its current incarnation: a reference to an elected official whose term is nearing an end and, freed from the accountability of voters, could be prone to ineffectiveness or acts of self-interest."[4] Most references prior to the Twenty-second Amendment, however, were to lame duck *Congresses*, not presidents, these being congressional sessions between November elections and the sine die recess in January (or, prior to the Twentieth Amendment, March). After the ratification of the Twenty-second Amendment, the term gained currency in discussions of the presidency, notably second-term presidents. Grossman, Kumar, and Rourke provide perhaps the best, most incisive definition: "[L]ame-duck status has usually not been thought to mean that the president loses all power. The term refers instead to presidents' diminished ability to shape the national policy agenda during their second term or to impose their will on Congress and the rest of the political community in policy disputes."[5]

By the late 1950s, during Eisenhower's second term, popular assessments of the amendment's effect on Eisenhower's power started to appear. Veteran *New York Times* reporter Arthur Krock would write in early 1957, at the beginning of Eisenhower's second term, that the president's "sudden crop of troubles with Congress on domestic and foreign policies" had a number of commentators pointing the finger of blame at the Twenty-second Amendment. Krock, however, dismissed this assessment, saying that of "the President's current troubles, no reasonable relation to the Twenty-Second Amendment can be demonstrated." In fact, among Eisenhower's opponents there was, wrote Krock, "acute appreciation of the power of the Presidential office, and of this particular President, regardless of the fixed limit of his tenure, to appeal successfully to the people to rally to his interest."[6] Later that year, though, journalist Richard Strout would write in a long *Times* magazine piece that "signs are gathering that the real meaning of the enactment [of the Twenty-second Amendment] was not fully understood either by the public, or by the Congress which launched it ten years ago." Strout pointed to a number of "signs" such as Eisenhower's weakening poll numbers and troubles with his congressional agenda, among other things, to suggest that a weakening of presidential power, especially in the second term, had been effected by the Twenty-second Amendment. He also quoted scholar James MacGregor Burns who had written that "virtually all political scientists and students of American history agree" that presidents had been weakened by the amendment.[7]

The "paper of record," then, within the span of five months published two competing viewpoints on the amendment's influence. What is more, *Times* editors would weigh in on the matter themselves in August of 1957 with the editorial "Not Too Lame," calling into question the lame duck effect while also recognizing its possible influence. Although noting that Eisenhower might find his influence weakened if he failed to realize that it is "better to persuade than threaten," he would not be a lame duck, the *Times* said, "if he expresses [the American people's] aspirations and shows the courage to defend those aspirations."[8] This was in line with Strout's prediction that "other less popular second-term Presidents may be hit hard" by the lame duck effect.[9]

Notwithstanding Burns's assessment of unanimity among political scientists in the late 1950s, whether accurate or not, by the late 1970s there would be "no unanimity of scholarly opinion as to whether the Twenty-second Amendment impeded, helped, or had no effect whatsoever on the Administration of Dwight Eisenhower."[10] But despite scholars having viewpoints on the effects of the amendment, very little systematic work on the so-called lame duck effect had appeared by political scientists throughout the 1970s. Part of the reason for this dearth of analysis in the 1960s and 1970s was because only Eisenhower had been affected by the amendment, and generalizing from one case would be tenuous at best. It would not be until Ronald Reagan that a president would again be constrained from a third term by the Twenty-second Amendment.

With the beginning of Reagan's second term, we start to again see serious public discussions of the lame duck hypothesis. In fact, before Reagan even won the second term, Tim Wicker wrote in the *New York Times* that the second term "could be looked at as the first real test" of the lame duck syndrome. He also stated that there was still "controversy" over whether the lame duck syndrome affected Eisenhower's presidency.[11] However, with Reagan facing the Iran-Contra investigation, losing the Senate in the 1986 elections, and then failing in the Senate with the nomination of Robert Bork, it became almost axiomatic that Reagan was affected by the lame duck syndrome. "The cry that President Reagan is now incontrovertibly a lame-duck President grew louder last week as the odds grew longer against the Senate's voting to confirm Judge Robert H. Bork for the Supreme Court," Steven Roberts wrote in the *Times* in October 1987. And even beyond Reagan, the Twenty-second Amendment, Roberts asserted, "guarantees a gradual loss of influence" for presidents.[12] As with Eisenhower, there was some disagreement. According to *Times* writer Anthony Lake, Reagan was "dispelling the myth that a President, especially a lame duck, cannot make foreign policy progress in an election year."[13]

Bill Clinton would face the indignity of lame duck questions in his *first* term, after Republicans won control of the Congress in the 1994 elections, suggesting the occasionally less-than-focused application of the term.[14] By his second term, Clinton's lame duck status would be treated as a truism: "Mr. Clinton is at another dispiriting crossroads, his dwindling tenure *perforce* limiting his power."[15] Although accepting that it was "certainly the case that the inevitable enfeeblement of a second-term, lame-duck president has been made worse by the scandal his reckless adventure with Monica Lewinsky created," even the venerable journalist David Broder treated the lame duck effect on Clinton as self-evident.[16] Despite Clinton and his advisors believing that "talk of lame-duck ennui in the Oval Office was overstated, largely a simplistic analysis driven by the news media,"[17] in a concession to at least the power of the myth, Clinton would parody his own lame duck status at the White House Correspondents' Association dinner in 2000.[18]

Despite all of this public discussion of the lame duck effect on the presidency, there would be very little scholarly examination through the 1980s and 1990s. Not that scholars would refrain from assuming the conventional wisdom. For example, James W. Davis wrote in 1995 that "[t]hough we have the experience of observing only Presidents Eisenhower and Reagan in their second terms, most political experts seem to agree that the long-term effects of the amendment will undermine the effectiveness of most second-term presidents."[19] Gould's recent analysis similarly argues that "when presidents such as Dwight D. Eisenhower, Richard Nixon, Ronald Reagan, and Bill Clinton were safely reelected, the knowledge in Washington that their tenure was limited constricted their ability to push programs forward."[20] Most of these scholarly assessments, however, were rooted more in the conventional public wisdom on lame duck presidents than in rigorous investigation of the phenomenon.

In 2002, a systematic examination of the lame duck syndrome appeared with political scientist James R. Hedtke's volume *Lame Duck Presidents— Myth or Reality*. Hedtke's volume does not definitively answer the question of whether there is a lame duck effect, but it provides considerable insight into the issue. Hedtke examines the presidencies of Eisenhower, Reagan, and Clinton along "persuasion," "command," and "linkage" variables. Persuasion variables are things such as success rates with treaties and domestic policies and confirmation of nominees; command variables are executive orders and agreements and vetoes; and linkage variables include the retention of cabinet officials and presidential approval ratings.[21] What is more, Hedtke also examines two-term presidents who served prior to the Twenty-second Amendment, to provide a point of comparison with the post-amendment presidents Eisenhower, Reagan, and Clinton.

Hedtke's analysis is well conceived and yields several key findings. First, he finds generally that there is no strong evidence to suggest that second-term presidents (before or after the Twenty-second Amendment) experience substantial weakening of power that can be attributed directly to ineligibility.[22] He does find along some variables that presidents lose power in their second terms but argues that "partisan politics and exogenous factors affect presidential power and performance more than the tenure status of the president." For instance, while the nomination failure of Robert Bork might be attributed to Reagan's lame duck status, Hedtke plausibly argues that it was less the result of Reagan's waning tenure and more the party composition of the Senate, which changed hands in the 1986 elections and gave Democrats—who were publicly committed to opposing Reagan's nominees—control.[23]

Second, Hedtke's deft comparison of two-term presidents across time shows the similarities rather than differences among them, suggesting that the Twenty-second Amendment has not added an appreciable burden on second-term presidents that the two-term *tradition* did not already place upon them. This is a critical point, although Hedtke does not develop it. Opponents of the Twenty-second Amendment often argue that by taking away the threat of the third-term pursuit, a president's leverage with Congress, other leaders in his party, and even the country will be substantially attenuated. Although this is questionable in itself, the assumption that second-term presidents prior to the Twenty-second Amendment's passage benefited from this possible threat is quite simply wrong, *except in the case of Franklin Roosevelt*. As supporters of the Twenty-second Amendment argued, in nearly all cases prior to FDR, the two-term tradition operated similarly in the second term of presidents. Before Franklin Roosevelt, it was assumed that a president, upon election to a second term, would not be seeking reelection. It is only with FDR that opponents of the amendment (and scholars) began constructing a narrative of second-term presidents staying quiet about their third-term pursuits so as to conserve power during their second term. In truth, this was a negligible calculation in the minds of most observers and presidents prior to Franklin Roosevelt.[24] This shows how dominant the influence of FDR and his strong presidency is on subsequent scholars and generations. Although some commentators, such as Clinton Rossiter,[25] unabashedly defend the modern presidency of FDR and its break with the past, others seemingly have imbibed the values of the modern presidency so fully that they write them anachronistically over the whole of presidential history.

As noted in chapter 3, once Jefferson stepped down the two-term tradition was officially born, and presidents until FDR, with a few exceptions, neither pursued nor threatened to run for a third term. Indeed, many did not even pursue or threaten to pursue a second term. What is more, two of the more serious third-term pursuits prior to FDR—those of Ulysses S. Grant and Theodore Roosevelt—came after these presidents had been out of the office for a term, and thereby the pursuit could have no effect on their second-term power.[26] Another, more minor pursuit, that of Grover

Cleveland, came after his second nonconsecutive term, and thereby is not readily comparable, as it was unclear to observers whether the two-term tradition applied to consecutive or total terms. Woodrow Wilson would be rendered physically incapacitated before talk of a third term could begin, and Calvin Coolidge in August of 1927 stated his intentions not to seek a third term, undoubtedly failing to preserve his power by withholding his decision until the time of the Republican Convention of 1928. Thus we see that only one president seriously used the threat of a third term to conserve power during the second term, and consequently the dire predictions of opponents of the Twenty-second Amendment that second-term presidents would hereafter be hampered substantially in their second terms is anachronistic or at least normative rather than descriptive.

This is not to say that FDR did not benefit in his second term by keeping his options for a third term open. In fact, it seems obvious in retrospect (and even at the time) that he profited from the uncertainty of his intentions in 1939 and 1940. Not only did Roosevelt preserve his command of the Democratic Party, especially congressional Democrats, during the last two years of his second term, but he also prevented the proliferation of declared candidates for the presidency. By keeping rivals within the party on edge, Roosevelt no doubt preserved his power and staved off the inevitable political stagnation that precedes a potential transfer of power.

Although Hedtke does not find demonstrable empirical evidence of a lame duck effect, he does not discount its qualitative effect. For instance, the lame duck influence may not be measurable because presidents still have similar success rates in second as in first terms, but second-term presidents may scale back their policies and advocate compromise policies rather than bold policies. A quantitative empirical analysis like Hedtke's would not, of course, catch these kinds of variations. What is more, while Hedtke tends to see "partisan" and "exogenous" factors as exclusive from the lame duck status of presidents, he acknowledges that there may be a relationship of influence, so that "a president's lame duck status may enhance the detrimental effects of partisan politics and exogenous factors."[27] It is also conceivable that a president's lame duck status may help to fuel changes in party composition during midterm elections in the second term. Notwithstanding these possible qualitative effects, Hedtke concludes that "for now the lame duck syndrome appears to be more of a political myth than a political reality."[28]

It is worth mentioning briefly two additional scholarly contributions to the study of lame duck presidencies. William Howell and Kenneth Mayer have examined the actions of presidents in their last one hundred days to test the conventional wisdom about the depreciation of power in an outgoing administration. Although their research does not apply only to second-term presidents prohibited from seeking another term— rather, they look at all presidents who are leaving office, whether after one or two terms—it does shed important light on the powers available to second-term presidents. Indeed, their research suggests the very real powers that presidents, including second-term presidents, can and do wield, even when everyone knows that they will be leaving office shortly: "With executive orders, proclamations, executive agreements, national security directives, and memoranda, presidents have ample resources to effectuate policy changes" and "outgoing presidents have every reason to strike out on their own."[29] David Crockett has more directly examined the relationship between presidential term limits and problems in presidents' second terms. Although Crockett does not count himself among the supporters of the Twenty-second Amendment, his analysis suggests that second-term presidents are constrained far more by political factors than they are by the supposed lame duck effects of term limits. Furthermore, he develops some valuable connections between term limitation and Stephen Skowronek's concept of "political time," which will be addressed later in this chapter.[30]

"Watching Him Clean Out His Desk"

The second term of George W. Bush offers further insights into the lame duck phenomenon and also points us to other explanations for second-term failure. As with Eisenhower, Reagan, and Clinton, there is some disagreement over whether Bush was a lame duck and, if he was, to what extent. In keeping with conventional assessments, predictions of Bush's coming lame duck status preceded the midterm congressional elections of 2006. On the eve of the elections, the *Washington Post* breathlessly reported that although clocks in the White House read 825 days left in the Bush presidency, "if the elections go the way pollsters and pundits predict, they might as well read 20 days."[31] With the Republicans losing their majorities in both houses of Congress, the dire analyses would continue. Conservative columnist John Podhoretz would remark the day after the November elections that "[t]he presidency of George W. Bush ended last night."[32]

By the time of Bush's State of the Union message in late January 2007—which the *Washington Post* interpreted as "a message that said he should not be regarded as a lame duck"[33]—it would be standard operating procedure in the world of journalism to dismiss Bush as a lame duck. Indeed, media analyst Howard Kurtz would in early February 2007 observe that "many in the media seem to be writing off President Bush."[34] Typical of this perspective was that of *New York Times* columnist Thomas Friedman: "The American people basically fired George Bush in the last election. We're now just watching him clean out his desk."[35] And it wasn't just the press—whether it is fair to characterize them as "writing off" Bush or not—but Bush's own supporters who began diagnosing him with lame duck syndrome.[36] In fact, like Clinton, Bush himself would acknowledge his own ostensible lame duck status. At a Radio and Television Correspondents' Association dinner in late March 2007, Bush would quip, a "year ago, my approval ratings were in the 30s, my nominee for the Supreme Court had just withdrawn, and my vice president had shot someone. . . . Ah, those were the good old days."[37]

Pronouncements of Bush's lame duck status would grow stronger with his failed battle over immigration reform in June 2007. Although "second term blues are nothing unusual for American presidents," Bush had put himself in "a class all his own" in the battle over immigration reform, according to Anne Davies. While in a parliamentary system "a lame duck leader would quickly find himself facing a challenge in the party room, the US public must instead soldier through until January 2009."[38] The "buzz around D.C. following the 6/28 immigration vote 'is that the proactive phrase of the Bush presidency is over.'" According to "'[s]trategists' of both parties . . . Bush has now moved closer to lame-duck status."[39] And the resignation of key political advisor Karl Rove in mid-August 2007 would be greeted similarly. The *Washington Post* would couch its assessment in a degree of uncertainty: "The White House labored to dismiss the sense that Rove's resignation underscores a lame-duck presidency, even as it felt like an era was coming to an end on the South Lawn yesterday morning."[40] But the *London Times* would see Rove's announcement as "effectively bringing the domestic Bush presidency to a close. . . . His departure signals that on the home front, Mr Bush has truly entered lame-duck status."[41] Former Clinton Chief of Staff John Podesta, employing a clever baseball metaphor, would say of Rove's departure that it was "as if the few remaining fans of the Bush administration [were] headed to the exits after the seventh-inning stretch."[42]

By the end of 2007, that Bush was a lame duck was a truism, and many observers accordingly turned their attention to the 2008 primary and general elections.

But not all commentators saw unquestionable decline in Bush's second term. The *Wall Street Journal*, in an editorial after the immigration debacle, made the seemingly obvious—but often overlooked—point that "[l]ame duck or not, President Bush will retain his veto power to his last day in office."[43] Richard N. Haass, president of the influential Council on Foreign Relations, argued that the "conventional wisdom [that Bush is a lame duck] is wrong. The president retains the ability to do a great deal, especially in foreign policy; the question is whether he has the will and flexibility to use that power wisely."[44] The *National Journal* concurred: "The chief executive can direct—and restrict—the flow of intelligence; when the time comes to reveal it, the president and his surrogates have an unrivaled bully pulpit. Even Congress cannot use its oversight role to direct the president to take specific intelligence actions."[45] And despite then Senator Joseph Biden's evaluation—"Bush is not a lame duck. He's a dead duck"[46]—retired Army Colonel Lee Van Arsdale saw it differently, especially in the context of foreign policy: "Lame duck is a political term. He's more like an 800-pound gorilla, and maybe he has a slight limp."[47]

What is more, beyond the negative action of the veto and the arena of foreign affairs—where presidents are traditionally accorded more leverage than Congress—Bush still retained an exceptional array of powers in his second term, according to Margaret Kritz: "As President Bush begins his final 18 months in office, his clout on Capitol Hill may be diminishing, but he continues to make impressive use of the levers of administrative power that shape governmental policy." Indeed, she noted that as "Bush's second term winds down, the president's critics are bracing for a final outpouring of new regulations, guidance documents, and other executive actions designed to shift federal policy."[48] While the president may have had limited options *legislatively*, it would appear that his powers in foreign affairs and administration were formidable and, in a certain sense, more likely to be wielded considering his putative lame duck status.[49] Even Podesta acknowledged that "the president intend[ed] to exercise executive authority to accomplish his agenda," although he hoped that Bush's "future uses of executive power [would] be carried out with more wisdom."[50] Paradoxically, then, a lame duck president may end up exerting more powers in some ways than a president who is subject to reelection.

This raises an important ambiguity, or even contradiction, in the debates over the lame duck scenario. It is widely assumed—and the term directly implies so—that the lame duck is injured and incapable of acting to his or her full capabilities and abilities. But there is also a sense in which the lame duck, because he is freed from the need for reelection and the potential punishment for unpopular actions, is more powerful than ever—dangerous, in fact. As Howell and Mayer have put it: "Outgoing presidents need no longer concern themselves about the electoral consequences of what they are doing during the transition, or about how a controversial decision will affect the rest of their agendas."[51] Indeed, this was one of Alexander Hamilton's most trenchant criticisms of presidential term limits in *The Federalist*. In *Federalist #72*, Hamilton argued that not only would term limits produce "a diminution of the inducements to good behavior"—for instance, presidents would not undertake "extensive and arduous enterprises" because they would soon have to leave office—but term limits would also encourage *bad* behavior:

> An avaricious man, who might happen to fill the office, looking
> forward to a time when he must at all events yield up the emolu-
> ments he enjoyed, would feel a propensity, not easy to be re-
> sisted by such a man, to make the best use of the opportunity he
> enjoyed while it lasted, and might not scruple to have recourse
> to the most corrupt expedients to make the harvest as abundant
> as it was transitory[.] . . . An ambitious man, too, when he found
> himself seated on the summit of his country's honors, when
> he looked forward to the time at which he must descend from
> the exalted eminence for ever, and reflected that no exertion of
> merit on his part could save him from the unwelcome reverse;
> such a man, in such a situation, would be much more violently
> tempted to embrace a favorable conjuncture for attempting the
> prolongation of his power, at every personal hazard, than if he
> had the probability of answering the same end by doing his
> duty.[52]

Although this tendency on the part of our term-limited presidents has been muted—with the exception perhaps of the infamous "Clinton pardons"—it undoubtedly suggests the limitations of the lame duck concept or at least one of the ironies of presidential term limits.

The foregoing suggests the limitations of the lame duck concept and the need for a broader perspective on the characteristics of second terms in general, whether a president can pursue a third term or not. Even though there is a paucity of scholarly research directly on the concept of the lame duck presidency, scholars have explored, especially recently, the problems of second-term presidents, sometimes referred to as "second-term blues."[53] As John Fortier and Norman Ornstein have put it, "even presidents in office before the adoption of the Twenty-second Amendment found that their second terms did not measure up to their first."[54] It is this literature that helps us to better sift through the applicability of the lame duck concept to the modern presidency.

So, why are second terms—even Franklin Roosevelt's second term—often less successful than first terms? Second terms, after all, would seem to be ideal: a reelected and hence popular president takes the helm after having four years of experience in the office. First, several problems stem, ironically, from the successful reelection effort. According to Grossman, Kumar, and Rourke, reelection efforts are generally "vacuous" and tend to emphasize generalities and "vague promises." The result of this can be "a stalled agenda after the reelection."[55] Presidents often emphasize their previous record and have little of substance with which to "hit the ground running" when the second term begins. Alternatively, despite the lack of policy prescription in reelection bids, some presidents nevertheless tend to interpret their reelections as a "mandate" for action. Here presidents can get themselves into all kinds of trouble—e.g., Roosevelt's "Court-packing" scheme and Bush's Social Security reform—because they have falsely assumed that their *political* support at election time naturally translated into *policy* support.[56] Fortier and Ornstein refer to this problem as being one of "hubris": second-term presidents believe "that their reelection has proven their critics wrong, [and] that their priorities were given a rocket boost."[57] Furthermore, because presidents tend to distance themselves from their political party in reelection bids—appealing to transpartisan themes—"members of Congress feel no obligation to support reelected presidents if they get into trouble during the second term."[58]

A second series of problems can be linked to burnout or fatigue. "The presidency is a big job," Fortier and Ornstein write. "Not only is the president under stress, so is his staff."[59] This can exacerbate the dilemmas of decision making in the second term for a president who, in addition to being hubristic, might be also less mentally and physically sharp. This puts the onus on second-term presidents to surround themselves with quality advisors and administrators. However, the rhythms of the second term make this difficult if not unlikely. As Grossman, Kumar, and Rourke write, "[a]lmost from the beginning of the second term, but accelerating toward the end, many of the most experienced and able presidential appointees reach for lucrative positions in the private sector by trading on their White House connections."[60] And these vacancies can be hard to fill with talented people, especially later in the second term, because the prospect of uprooting one's life for a hectic and demanding Washington career that will be over nearly as soon as it starts is not particularly inviting. Moreover, those political appointees who do stay with a president throughout a second term, while not "going native," will probably come to align themselves more and more with the career civil service and may not be amenable to pursuing major policy changes advocated by the president.[61]

Third, losses in the midterm elections of a presidential second term—almost a truism until the 1998 elections—contribute greatly to a president's possibilities for success. While midterm losses are partly an effect of "second-term blues," they also clearly accelerate the condition. Whether a president loses control of Congress—such as Bush in 2006—or simply faces a smaller majority—like FDR in 1938—the prospects of a president achieving legislative successes are diminished. Not only do a president's own partisans have less faith in the president's leadership and policies, but the opposition party, especially if it has taken control of one or both houses of Congress, will be buoyed by its successes and thus disinclined to cooperate with the president. In fact, if the opposition takes control of even one house of Congress, it is likely to do more than just oppose the president's policies; majority control of the House or Senate gives the opposition party the power to investigate the administration.[62]

This power of investigation leads to another distinct setback for second-term presidents: scandals. While scandals are fueled by the opposition party's ability to investigate a matter of suspected executive malfeasance, they are not merely the product of a changing partisan control of Congress. Indeed, most scandals in a president's second term have their origins in the first term (or even before). However, "generally, scandal needs time to germinate, to be uncovered, and to be regarded by the press and public as timely or relevant."[63] Thus scandals are more prominent in presidential second terms. Scandals perforce bring with them challenges to a president's reputation and public approval but just as importantly consume precious resources and time, and just as time is at a premium.

Finally, a president's political coalition tends to fragment over time.[64] When presidents are newly elected, there is a tendency for supporters to come together and compromise, even if they represent rather different perspectives within the party. And while cracks may show in the president's first term, the immediacy of reelection tends to unify the party around the president. However, during the second term, fissures that have been papered over tend to show themselves again. Most particularly, Fortier and Ornstein write, a president's "supporters know that this may be their last chance to get what they want, so there is often impatience with presidents, which is heightened by unrealistic expectations." Additionally, if a president's public approval dips, which tends to occur over time as well, political supporters will distance themselves to preserve their position for the coming election.[65] Even FDR, famed for holding together a disparate Democratic Party, faced considerable erosion of support in his second term, manifested most strikingly by his failed "purge" of anti–New Deal Democrats in Congress.

What is important to note about these analyses of "second-term blues" is that they generalize about the second terms of presidents *before* the passage of the Twenty-second Amendment as well as after it. Even before the Twenty-second Amendment made two-term presidents "lame ducks," second-term presidents faced considerable problems and setbacks. Indeed, as we noted earlier, before the passage of the Twenty-second Amendment the two-term tradition had the effect of essentially making second-term presidents lame ducks, even though the term "lame duck" was not employed in this period. In nearly all presidential second terms from Jefferson until FDR, it was assumed almost universally that the president would not seek a third term. However much a second-term president is enfeebled by lame duck status—something scholars have yet to sift through systematically—the evidence suggests that the Twenty-second Amendment may not have added much that is new to the dynamics of presidential second terms.

Nevertheless, can we say anything systematic or definitive about the relationship between a president's inability to pursue a third term (whether because of tradition or law) and these analyses of "second-term blues"? Would second-term presidents have experienced less problems had they retained the threat to run for a third term? Let me consider briefly each of the problems I have outlined earlier along this front. First, the problems that follow from "vacuous" and "transpartisan" campaigns for reelection, as well as the hubris that comes from reelection, would seem to be relatively unaffected by the possibility of a third term. Being able to pursue a third or fourth term would seem to have little effect on the dynamics of securing a second term or the manner by which confident presidents view their reelection. It is well to keep in mind that FDR—often "Exhibit A" for term-limit abolitionists—experienced these very same problems that are associated with securing the second term.

Second, several of the problems associated with presidential burnout or fatigue would still be prominent whether or not presidents could seek third terms. Presidents and their staffs would still experience the mental and physical exhaustion that come with the job and the campaign for reelection. And the tendencies of presidential appointees to align with the bureaucracies that they run would seem to be substantially unaffected by a president's ability to pursue a third term—in fact, this dynamic suggests that third terms would present persistent challenges of administration. However, while there would naturally be turnover in staff regardless of the possibility of a third term, it is likely that presidents would be able to attract quality replacements in a second term if the option of continuing in a third term were available.

Third, midterm election losses for the president's party, while undoubtedly complicating a second-term president's leadership, are by no means exclusive to second terms. In fact, first-term presidents' parties nearly always lose seats in the House and also usually in the Senate, just as in second-term midterm elections. And FDR's Democrats experienced substantial losses in the midterm elections of his *third* term, coming during World War II, and after he had been reelected in 1940 in part because of the "emergency" developing in Europe. Indeed, presidential midterm losses are linked more to variables such as the lack of "presidential surge" in turnout and public evaluations of a president's leadership, among other things.[66]

Fourth, presidential scandals would seem to have little relationship to the lame duck phenomenon. That a president could pursue a third term would not stop the presidential behavior that leads to scandal, nor would it stop the midterm losses that allow the opposition party to put the heat on through public criticism and investigation. Rather, it would appear that the best way to prevent presidential scandals is to limit presidents to one term, as it takes considerable time for scandal to percolate and develop. This is why scandals seem to be the provenance of second terms. But there is actually reason to believe that scandal would be just as likely to develop in third or fourth terms, given the passage of time, the range of presidential actions, and the political needs of the opposition party.

Finally, it would seem that a president's inability to pursue a third term clearly does render his political coalition fractious and unstable. This is evident when looking at how partisans will often come together behind first-term presidents at reelection time, even if the president is not riding high in popularity. Incumbent presidents typically will face little in the way of opposition at the primary stage and will find rivals within the party lining up behind them before the general election. Unless a president is so unpopular in the country and with partisans that renomination is questionable—for example, Johnson in 1968—supporters will make a utilitarian calculation that if the president does win reelection, they want to be in line for reward rather than punishment. A president who cannot run again, particularly if unpopular, will face serious tensions within the party, as different factions and rivals seek to assert their control over the party before the next election. FDR's silence on pursuing a third term kept rivals on the sidelines throughout 1939 and 1940 and muted criticisms of his administration from within the party. Bush, on the other hand, could not pursue a third term and faced considerable criticism within the party—and from the many nominees seeking the Republican nomination for 2008.

Even here the inability to pursue a third term explains only so much. The stability of a political coalition is largely related to a president's popularity. For instance, despite setbacks in his second term and being barred from a third term, Ronald Reagan was very popular within his party and the country for most of the term. He faced little in the way of criticism within his party and saw his vice president win not only the Republican nomination in 1988 but also the presidency. A popular president's blessing is in great demand even if that president cannot run for election again. The same could be said for Eisenhower and, to some extent, Clinton. Indeed, some criticized presidential candidate Al Gore for not clinging to Clinton enough in the 2000 campaign. With George W. Bush, however, his popularity in the second term was so anemic that his inability to pursue a third term seemed almost irrelevant. This brings me back to a larger point that needs emphasis: much of a president's success and ability to get things done in a second term (or first term for that matter) is related to popularity. If a president is not popular, whether he can pursue a third term is beside the point. Would Bush have been in a substantially different position in 2007–2008 if he could have pursued a third term? Would his approval numbers suddenly have risen because he could run for a second reelection? The ability to pursue a third term might have had a residual effect on Bush's standing within the party, but not much more.

Ultimately, then, it would appear that the Twenty-second Amendment might have a mildly adverse effect on presidents' success and leadership in a second term. But more than likely this is a rather limited effect— clearly more limited than the conventional wisdom holds—and one that is especially dependent on a president's overall popularity. As was noted previously, in one of the earliest examinations of the lame duck effect, Richard Strout in the *New York Times* perceptively predicted that "other less popular second-term Presidents [than Eisenhower] may be hit hard" by the lame duck effect.[67] Of course, this puts a lot of pressure on second-term presidents to maintain their standing with the public. As the popularity of a president may stave off lame duck effects, the unpopularity of a president may accentuate a president's lame duck status.

Crockett reinforces this idea of the negligible effect of presidential term limitations, but from a slightly different perspective. Building on the work of Skowronek—who identifies a president's place in "political time" by assessing that president's relationship to the underlying political order or ruling coalition[68]—Crockett has argued that a president is more constrained by the political context and the opportunities afforded by it than by the existence of term limits. As Crockett has put it, whether or not there are term limits on the president is "largely irrelevant" because the "long-term parameters of political time have been established, and it is up to the individual presidents to adjust their leadership posture accordingly."[69] If the president's political coalition remains popular or stable, the chances for successful exercise of power are much higher— regardless of term limits—than if the political coalition is fracturing or splintering.

Perhaps the biggest challenge to a second-term president is avoiding the *perception* that he or she is a lame duck.[70] Indeed, the constant drumbeat from media and political elites about a president's lame duck status—which, we will recall, the Clinton folks described as a "simplistic analysis driven by the news media"—may actually have the impact of accentuating that status, giving the phenomenon a bit of a self-fulfilling quality.[71] Despite indications to the contrary, if political observers and especially media and congressional elites accept the lame duck syndrome as axiomatic—and importantly, act upon this assumption—the syndrome is accentuated and intensified and becomes, over time, more and more applicable to second-term presidents. In a perverse way, then, second-term presidents may have more to fear from perceptions of lame duck status than they do from the actual fact of being unable to seek reelection.

THE SIX-YEAR, NON-RENEWABLE TERM

The evidence is far from compelling that recent second-term presidents have experienced second-term troubles as a result of the Twenty-second Amendment. Especially when we take into consideration the influence that the two-term tradition had on presidents prior to the Twenty-second Amendment, it is hard to argue that the amendment added an appreciable burden to presidents *that was not already in effect*. And, further, we have found that the effect of term limits on the second-term troubles of presidents appears limited, constituting one of many potential hazards that have only marginal relationship to term limits. To make the point a bit differently, had all second-term presidents been able to pursue re-election to a third term, there is no reason to believe that their second terms would have ended much differently.

Nonetheless, it is hard to dispute that the second terms of recent presidents have, in Lewis Gould's words, "ended badly." Gould goes so far as to suggest that most modern presidents "would have had a better historical reputation if they had contented themselves with a single elected term and retired at the end of it."[72] Although he does not provide a clear discussion of *why* second terms for modern presidents have been failures, beyond the typical Twenty-second Amendment scapegoating, it is instructive here to consider the arguments for a single term for the presidency. Most often this reform proposal, which has had numerous advocates over the years, has taken the shape of a six-year term with no chance for reeligibility.[73] As we have seen, the one-term principle held particular sway in the nineteenth century with the Whigs and, less consistently, both Republicans and Democrats. Presidents Jackson, W. H. Harrison, Polk, Hayes, and Cleveland all actively promoted the idea in office, and it found its way into party platforms, speeches, and campaigns.

Notwithstanding Gould's ascription of second-term failure to modern presidents, proponents of a single six-year term would point to second-term failures across presidential history and suggest that second terms in general leave something to be desired. And since the inability to pursue reelection does not seem to substantially hamper presidents in their second terms, this inability in a first term would seem to have a similarly limited effect. Surely there are some reasons to recommend this reform proposal.

First, the pursuit of reelection requires extensive politicking and promising that hamstrings a president in the second term. While a president would clearly make promises to gain election in the first place, under this proposal a president, once elected, could do "what is courageous or correct, from a policy standpoint" rather than "what is popular." What is more, a president's actions would not constantly be tainted by "politics" and the pursuit for reelection, even if just the perception thereof.[74] As seen in chapter 3, a major concern of those who have desired second-term ineligibility on the part of the president was the ostensible abuses of party patronage that presidents engaged in to secure reelection. Second, and related, a president would be relieved of the considerable tasks brought about by reelection—giving speeches, raising money, debating, strategizing—and could devote all of his or her time to governing. Indeed, large parts of the fourth year of a first term are devoted to reelection activities,[75] and substantial amounts of the second and third years likely are as well. Third, because of this conservation of time and energy, presidents could use the longer term—six years—to maximum effect and would have "enough time to allow their policies a fair chance to work."[76] Finally, a "president decoupled from public opinion would cast off a dependency which inhibits more than it helps. Such a president would be . . . hampered only by the need to convince other power brokers in the Congress."[77] This is perhaps the most interesting, and yet most peculiar, argument in favor of the six-year, non-renewable term. Because presidents would not depend upon the people for reelection, they would be free to cultivate other sources of support—particularly elite support in Congress and presumably government agencies and, to a lesser extent, the media—to wield their power. This last perspective assumes a certain level of incompetence on the part of the people and sees in the six-year reform a way of reducing their influence on public policy.

One of the most longstanding criticisms of the proposal for a single six-year term is precisely this seeming lack of accountability that presidents would have to the people. While at the time of the founding this was a recommendation for second-term ineligibility, in our day it is clearly a recommendation against it, namely since it is undemocratic.[78] Whether or not the people are capable or competent, it seems fanciful to think that in our democratic age, replete as it is with public opinion polling, there would be any way of "decoupling" a president from public opinion. Indeed, most of the ostensible benefits of the single six-year term seem dependent on a view of politics that is strangely anachronistic, a view that is "pre-polling" in many respects. Just because a president is ineligible for reelection does not mean that media organizations will not incessantly poll to see what the public thinks about the job a president is doing. And because public opinion is the coin of the realm of politics, whether a politician can seek reelection or not is less important than how popular he or she is at any given time. Indeed, even "monarchical" thinkers such as Machiavelli and Thomas Hobbes recognized the key influence of public opinion on princes and sovereign rulers, despite the absence of elections.[79] Furthermore, that "politics" could be removed from a president's tasks or even mitigated is highly questionable. Even presidents with a single six-year term would be concerned about their party's prospects in congressional elections, not to mention their successors' chances of election. So, if not for the polls, then because of upcoming elections—where a president will always have a horse in the race, so to speak—a president will have to be "political."

While the six-year term would perhaps increase the chances of presidential competence by giving presidents the time to learn the office and achieve goals, the reform could also have the perverse effect of "reducing the tenure of relatively effective presidents and increasing the tenure of ineffective presidents."[80] Presidents who would have been punished through denial of reelection after four years would be afforded an extra two years to further alienate supporters and the public through inept policies and actions. It is sobering to imagine, for the sake of argument, if in early 2007 President Bush had just been starting the third year of a six-year presidency. Surely one might argue that if Bush had had four more years, even given his low standing in public opinion polls and with Washington elites, members of Congress would perforce have had to work with him, as pressure would have built on them—and their election prospects—to do something and to "get things done." Yet it is also quite possible, given partisan acrimony, that we would have had not two but four years of relative political stagnation.[81]

Relatedly, the vehicle of "recall" or some type of confidence vote would certainly need to be considered with a six-year term, whether renewable or not. With a four-year term, midterm elections have the effect of pronouncing judgment on presidents and even providing a correction to their policy course. Even though we might have to wait for a president to "clean out his desk," two years is not all that long in political time, given that a full year of the span is consumed with the campaign for the next election. However, with a six-year term—unless the congressional election cycle were altered—the first midterm election in a presidential term would not provide the same sort of corrective power, necessitating or at least raising the prospect of a mechanism for recalling the president or registering the confidence of the public (as in parliamentary systems).

Ultimately, therefore, the single six-year term does not appear to be an improvement on the current electoral setup. Despite the arguments of its supporters, the single six-year term may be just as subject to "politics" and public opinion as the current system. In other words, it might not fundamentally alter political dynamics at the presidential level. What is more, even if it did offer some advantages, they would be slight and would bring with them considerable potential for detrimental effects and "unintended consequences."[82] There especially would be considerable chance of political stagnation or lag in the middle of the six years—a lag that is, under the current system, addressed by the chance for reelection, or, as Bruce Buchanan has nicely put it, "the empowering vitality of re-electability."[83] Surely a preternaturally popular president might be able to stave off lag or stagnation, but this would be highly unusual to sustain over six years—it is hard enough over four. And despite all of the concern about second terms "ending badly," we might easily be faced with quite a few single terms that would end similarly.

Although presidents today lack the "empowering vitality of re-electability" during their second terms, because of it they start off their second terms from a position of strength and generally with substantial public support. As we have seen, they can maintain their strength and influence—even if it inevitably wanes to some degree—by maintaining support in public opinion polls and in the estimation of other Washington actors. For it is especially with public support—rather than the prospect for reelection—that a president can maintain political viability throughout much of the second term. This does not mean that second terms will not always present special challenges to presidents but that these challenges are often only tangentially related to the Twenty-second Amendment and, even when directly attributable to term limitation, are far from insurmountable.

"DELILAH'S SCISSORS CLICKING"

The claims of a lame duck presidency wrought by the Twenty-second Amendment are no doubt exaggerated. The benefits of a single six-year presidential term are chimerical. These conclusions, however, do not constitute, in and of themselves, a defense of our current rules regarding presidential tenure. One might easily grant these conclusions and yet argue that the Twenty-second Amendment nevertheless needs to be repealed, especially because the uncertain modern world may well in the near future demand stable, experienced leadership. This is one of the oldest justifications for reeligibility, as we have seen with Hamilton's deft arguments in *The Federalist* in favor of experienced leadership within the context of an emergency. And this was the decisive factor in FDR's breaking of the two-term tradition in 1940. That we have not experienced crises that demanded the further leadership of Eisenhower or Reagan or Clinton or Bush beyond their second terms does not mean that we will not see a time in the near future when a seasoned president must retire in the midst of a crisis or, to use Lincoln's metaphor, that we will be forced to "swap horses when crossing streams."[84]

Without question, criticisms of presidential term limits seem apposite when considering the election of FDR to a third term. Had the Twenty-second Amendment been in place during FDR's presidency, he would have been unable to serve beyond 1940, and the nation would have been deprived of his wartime leadership, widely regarded as successful. That someone else could have served admirably in FDR's stead is a hypothetical question. The case of Truman's succession does speak to this counterfactual situation, though: Truman was certainly not picked because of his stellar leadership credentials, and yet he ended up (especially in the estimation of historians) being a more than creditable successor. There is reason to believe that a successor in 1940, especially one hand-picked by Roosevelt, would have acquitted himself admirably as well. Nevertheless, it is difficult to argue that Roosevelt's third term was disastrous for the nation, or even on balance undesirable. Alternatively, it is instructive to consider how the young American nation might have fared without George Washington at the helm as the first president.

Yet, as Republicans argued in 1947, it is hard to believe that one man (or woman) could be the *only* person to lead the United States through a crisis, that there would not be numerous other individuals who could assume the mantle of leadership. What is more, a former president might offer informal advice to a successor in a time of emergency or great crisis—there would certainly be no prohibition on this type of arrangement, which Thomas Cronin has described as "the role of national counselor, roving ambassador, or Cabinet member without portfolio."[85] A president might also set an example of humility and public service and accept a formal position in a successor's administration.[86]

The longer presidents stay in office, the more prone they are to insulated, myopic decision making. Chapter 5 brought this point into sharp relief with FDR's problematic pursuit of a fourth term. Given what we have seen in FDR's last year, should we not be wary of presidents—even great presidents—losing focus or sharpness after long tenure in a job that demands perhaps more energy and commitment than any other? In fact, should we not assume that most presidents will, with the passage of time, become fatigued and increasingly prone to poor decision making? This is perhaps one of the most important arguments in favor of presidential term limitations raised by Roosevelt's fourth term. And here we return to the quote that opened the chapter. In 1943, publisher and journalist William Allen White, a shrewd surveyor of the political scene, wrote to then Vice President Henry Wallace regarding Roosevelt: "I have upheld the President probably more often than any other Republican editor in the country. . . . But between you and me, twelve years is going to get him. I mean, get his keen sense of justice, get his quick reaction to evil. I know personally from experience that there is a certain zone which when a man has walked through it, he has got to be careful. Maybe Time was the scissors that Delilah used for shearing Samson! . . . I am afraid—deeply and morally afraid—because I love my country and want it to go right, that I can hear Delilah's scissors clicking."[87] While White was referring particularly to a nasty confrontation between Wallace and Secretary of Commerce Jesse Jones during the third term—which some observers, like White, thought betrayed a singular lack of management skills on the part of Roosevelt—the sense of his insight can easily be applied to the debate over presidential tenure. Through his rich metaphorical language, White articulated a view that many have shared over the years: that tenure in an executive office has a point of diminishing returns. Notwithstanding that different individuals would reach that point at different times, this perspective suggests that, in general, after a certain passage of time, presidential leadership will tend to lose its effectiveness, whether through arrogance and insularity, corruption, or simple fatigue and lack of focus. A corollary to this line of argument suggests the necessity of refreshed leadership after a certain passage of time. As seen in chapter 4, this was ostensibly the reason Postmaster James Farley stood virtually alone in opposition to his boss's pursuit of a third term in 1940.[88]

A key problem in debating presidential tenure is determining how many terms—or how many years—is too long. Naturally, there can be no strict calculus. Jefferson and many others of the founding generation thought that two terms, or eight years, was adequate. In its ratification of the Constitution, for example, North Carolina not only proposed a standard two-term limitation (with the possibility of renewed service—or rotation—after two terms had elapsed) but also provided a key theoretical underpinning of term limits: members of the legislative and executive branches, according to North Carolina, might "be restrained from oppression by feeling and participating in the public burthens, [so] they should at fixed periods be reduced to a private station, return[ed] into the mass of the people."[89] A president would have ample time to pursue his policies and lend stability of administration to government but not enough time to become complacent and removed from the people, or simply distracted or fatigued.

And a by-product would be a reinvigoration of political life every so often with the changeover of leadership. Crockett is right to point out the somewhat limited effect of any reinvigoration brought about by term limits, particularly if we see presidential leadership in terms of Skowronek's concept of political time. Even if a president is forced to vacate office, a successor, especially if from the president's own party, will naturally be limited by the political context. Thus, from this perspective, any revitalization would be muted by the constraints of the president's place in political time and the demands of the dominant political coalition.[90] For instance, when Jefferson stepped down and was replaced by Madison, and when Madison was replaced by Monroe, did these turnovers really revive the political system or the ruling political coalition? Perhaps only to a limited degree, but there will always be differences in perspective and especially personality, even among partisans; and, indeed, a party can use the change of leadership as an opportunity for reexamination and renewal.[91] The reinvigoration is much greater, though, when a forced retirement brings about the victory of the party in opposition to the president. Examples such as Eisenhower's retirement leading to the election of Kennedy or Clinton's retirement allowing for the election of George W. Bush reinforce this view. In the absence of term limits, the advantages of incumbency and the power of the office in general can make it difficult for other leaders, especially from the opposition party, to win office. And, of course, this is what has worried Whigs throughout our history.

Undoubtedly there is a balance to be had here, and there is no perfect solution to the problem of presidential tenure. Although the Twenty-second Amendment has deprived presidents of service *ever again* after two terms, "rotation," or term limitation that sets no limit on the total number of terms served but only *consecutive* terms served, represents a somewhat sophisticated attempt at balancing competing interests. While the nation generally would be spared the problems that accompany long tenure and would benefit from regular renewals of leadership, moderate stability would be ensured, and the possibility would exist for an exceptional leader to return to office after a period of time had elapsed. For instance, had we followed the recommendations of the North Carolina or Virginia ratifying conventions (for no more than two terms in sixteen years), Bill Clinton would have been eligible to run again for the presidency in 2008. Given Clinton's generally high marks with regard to economic management, it is interesting to speculate whether the country would have looked toward the former president had the stock market begun to plummet a year earlier, in September of 2007. Would Clinton's experience and tested leadership in dealing with economic downturns have vaulted him to the forefront of candidates for the presidency? Would the nation have benefited from at least the possibility of an experienced former president's leadership? Indeed, Clinton himself in 2003 called for a modification of the Twenty-second Amendment, to bar only consecutive third terms. As he put it, somewhat presciently, "[t]here may come a time when we elect a president at age 45 or 50, and then 20 years later the country comes up against the same kind of problems the president faced before."[92]

While this idea of the possible return of an experienced leader is critical to the concept of rotation, so is the idea of refreshing the political system periodically. Republicans talked a lot in 1944 about the Roosevelt administration being "tired," and despite the sometimes mean-spirited nature of the attacks, it was a fair characterization. Perhaps this is part and parcel of the modern presidency that FDR himself did so much to create. The job is so demanding that presidents burn out quickly. Indeed, we might look at recent two-term presidencies and suggest that "Delilah's scissors" start "clicking" after five or six years. It is common knowledge that members of a president's administration often cannot serve longer than one term without symptoms of burnout and fatigue, yet we think nothing of presidents serving two terms or even more. None of this is to deny that some mayors and governors, for instance, have served ably for numerous terms with only limited diminution of their abilities and effectiveness. Nonetheless, these individuals are rare, and the demands of the jobs of governor and mayor are not nearly as extensive, nor are the temptations of power and the insulation of the offices as great.

Of course, a powerful retort to any plan for term limitation is that in a democracy, the people should be trusted to decide whether a president can serve three terms, or five terms for that matter. Supporters of FDR often made this argument: the people ultimately decided to give FDR third and fourth terms. Although this argument applies rather nicely to the third term, yet again FDR's fourth term proves nettlesome. Roosevelt biographer James Bishop described FDR's last year, writing that Roosevelt's "achievements seemed to be as inexhaustible as his energy. And that is where the President, and the people, miscalculated."[93] But the people did not miscalculate, because they were not given the information necessary to make a calculation as to the president's ability to continue in the office.

This, ultimately, gets at the major drawback of indefinite reeligibility, or even rotation: ambitious politicians almost never see a conflict between their continued service in office and the promotion of the public good. In fact, they tend to see the two as one and the same. One of the striking features of the tenure debate historically has been how quickly individuals and especially parties have contorted or outright changed their positions on tenure according to political circumstances and calculations of political advantage. Even Franklin Roosevelt, a president widely regarded as one of our greatest, arguably compromised the public good in the belief of his own singularity. It is worthwhile to recall Jefferson's support of term limitation: "If the principle of rotation be a sound one, as I conscientiously believe it to be with respect to this office, no pretext should ever be permitted to dispense with it, because there never will be a time when real difficulties will not exist, and furnish a plausible pretext for dispensation."[94] Jefferson understood as well as anyone that ambitious politicians would never fail to see themselves as indispensable or essential to the nation's continued existence. Particularly after FDR had shattered the tradition, ambition being what it is, it would have been highly unlikely for future presidents to respect the two-term tradition. Subsequent presidents would want to demonstrate their own special qualities and talents, and thereby elevate themselves to FDR's status. And what better way for them to do so but to show that their leadership—like that of Roosevelt's—would be necessary beyond the norm of two terms.

This logic of ambition points to the limitations of rotation, in addition to unlimited reeligibility. Hamilton worried in *Federalist* #72 about term-limited presidents "wandering among the people like discontented ghosts and sighing for a place which they were destined never more to possess."[95] Hamilton's vivid imagery is powerful, but we must consider the alternatives: would we prefer to have "discontented ghosts" merely "wandering" and "sighing" or full-fledged candidates who could pursue the office that they so desire, after the passage of a certain amount of time. It is not hard to envision former presidents—particularly if they would have been relatively young when leaving office—fanning the flames of crisis to encourage a return to their leadership. One only has to consider the lengths—in terms of rhetoric and action—to which Theodore Roosevelt was willing to travel to return to the office of presidency in 1912 in order to see the saliency of this perspective.

Thomas Cronin had it right over two decades ago when he gave "two cheers" for the Twenty-second Amendment.[96] As this book has demonstrated, there is no easy solution to the problem of presidential tenure; indeed, Americans have been debating the subject for several centuries. As we have seen, there are undoubtedly drawbacks to barring our presidents from future service beyond two terms and benefits to be gained from unlimited reeligibility or even plans for rotation. Hence the reason for two and not three cheers. Yet the Twenty-second Amendment strikes key balances: between our trust of leadership and our suspicions of the temptations of power; between the democratic rights of the people and the growing power of the office of the presidency; between demands for stability and the need for renewal. Ultimately, the Twenty-second Amendment—the codification of the two-term tradition—is a fitting compromise or balancing act for a nation with a deeply conflicted history of enabling and alternatively restraining executive power. To paraphrase Jefferson, no pretext should be permitted to dispense with it.

NOTES

CHAPTER 1

The epigraph is from John M. Carey's article, "The Reelection Debate in Latin America," *Latin American Politics and Society*, Spring 2003, 120.

1. See, for instance, the polls discussed in the following stories: Miles Benson, "Clinton Still Strong Draw in Polls," *Cleveland Plain Dealer*, November 12, 2000, and Hilary MacKenzie, "Clinton Looks Good After Lame Debate," *Ottawa Citizen*, October 5, 2000.

2. See Jennifer Steinhauer, "Guiliani Says He Won't Seek a Third Term," *New York Times*, October 4, 2001.

3. David W. Chen and Michael Barbaro, "Council Backs Bloomberg Bid to Run Again," *New York Times*, October 28, 2008.

4. Michael Barbaro and David W. Chen, "A Slim Victory Has Mayor Mending Fences," *New York Times*, November 5, 2009.

5. "Obama's Victory Speech," *New York Times*, November 5, 2008.

6. While Obama's opinion ratings fell significantly throughout his first two years in office—causing some speculation that even a second term might be a difficult achievement—it is important to remember the low points that both Reagan and Clinton experienced in their first terms, prior to their winning second terms.

7. See the Fox News Dynamics poll from 2003, where 75 percent of Americans were opposed to repealing the Twenty-second Amendment and only 20 percent advocated repeal. Dana Blanton, "Most Oppose Allowing President Third Term," June 5, 2003, Fox News, http://www.foxnews.com/story/0,2933,88691,00.html, accessed January 22, 2007.

8. Peter Finn, "Putin Says He'll Retain Influence in Russia After Term Ends in '08," *Washington Post*, October 26, 2006.

9. Craig Timberg, "Bid to Allow Nigerian a Third Term Hits Snag; Lawmakers Lining up Against the Amendment," *Washington Post*, May 13, 2006.

10. "Chad President Inaugurated Amid Opposition Ridicule," Agence France Presse, August 8, 2006. "Uganda's Museveni Sworn in for Third Term," Agence France Presse, May 12, 2006.

11. Carey, "Reelection Debate in Latin America," 119, 124.

12. Hannah Strange, "Emboldened Hugo Chavez to Speed Up His Bolivarian Revolution," *Times Online*, February 16, 2009, http://www.timesonline

.co.uk/tol/news/world/us_and_americas/article5747992.ece, accessed February 16, 2009.

13. John Locke, *Two Treatises of Government*, ed. Peter Laslett (Cambridge: Cambridge University Press, 1988), 368.

14. See, for instance, Locke's discussion of the limits of legislative power, in *Two Treatises*, 355–63.

15. Although prime ministers sometimes offer an important analogue to presidents, given the differences between parliamentary and presidential systems, connections will be made almost exclusively between the U.S. presidency and other presidencies. Parliamentary systems not only draw no strong distinction between legislative and executive branches of government, but prime ministers tend to have less power than presidents. Additionally, prime ministers often have flexible terms (their parties have some control over when to hold elections) and are ultimately dependent on the "confidence" of the legislative body to maintain themselves in office. While this model certainly has something to contribute to debates over executive tenure, the differences are significant enough to make analogizing these models problematic. For an elaboration of these ideas, see Theodore J. Lowi, *The Personal President: Power Invested, Promise Unfulfilled* (Ithaca: Cornell University Press, 1985), 97–99. Notwithstanding these differences, prominent critics of the Twenty-second Amendment pointed to the long-serving Prime Ministers Gladstone (England) and King (Canada) to highlight the presumed flaws of presidential term limits. See, for instance, Henry Steele Commager, "Only Two Terms for a President? *New York Times*, April 27, 1947.

16. The Twenty-second Amendment provides for a president who has assumed the office through vacancy—such as a vice president becoming president due to the death of the president—to run for "reelection" twice if he or she has served less than two years of the previous president's term. Ford, for instance, had he won election on his own in 1976, would have been barred from running for reelection in 1980, given that he served more than two years of Nixon's term after the latter's resignation in the summer of 1974.

17. See "Republican Contract with America," http://www.house.gov/house/Contract/CONTRACT.html, accessed January 20, 2010. Republicans had some internal disagreement with regard to term limits in the House, and an additional proposal in the Contract called for members of the House to be limited to only three, rather than six, terms.

18. For information on governors' term limits, see "Constitutional and Statutory Provisions for Number of Consecutive Terms of Elected Officials," Table 4.9 of *Book of the States* 2007, Council of State Governments, accessed at National Governors Association, http://www.nga.org/Files/pdf/BOS4–9.pdf, January 20, 2010.

19. As described in chapter 2, although the Constitution allows for state

legislatures or the people of the states to select electoral college voters (electors), the framers assumed they would exercise "independent" judgment in their selection of the president rather than merely follow the wishes of their state legislatures or voters.

20. The term "plebiscitary presidency" is used by presidential scholars in sometimes different applications. My usage here is probably closest to that of Jeffrey Tulis, *The Rhetorical Presidency* (Princeton: Princeton University Press, 1987). Tulis sees a major change in the presidency coming in the early twentieth century. Similarly, I see the rhetoric and actions of Theodore Roosevelt—especially in the 1912 election—as emblematic of the plebiscitary changes that come in the twentieth-century presidency. For related arguments, but with a slightly different timeline, see Lowi, *Personal President*.

21. Roosevelt discussed this theory of the presidency in *The Autobiography of Theodore Roosevelt*, ed. Wayne Andrews (New York: Charles Scribner's Sons, 1958).

22. Chapter 3 also addresses the third-term rumblings that surrounded the presidencies of Grover Cleveland and Woodrow Wilson.

CHAPTER 2

1. John Locke, *Two Treatises of Government*, ed. Peter Laslett (Cambridge: Cambridge University Press, 1988).

2. *The Portable Thomas Jefferson*, ed. Merrill D. Peterson (New York: Penguin, 1975), 430.

3. *Federalist #72*, in *The Federalist*, ed. Henry Cabot Lodge (New York: G. P. Putnam's Sons, 1888), 453–54.

4. As I will discuss, although considered the classic statement of legislative supremacy, Locke's view of executive power was actually rather nuanced and included considerable flexibility for the executive, on the condition that any discretion be used to support the public interest and be publicly legitimated, not unlike Hamilton's view. Both the Whig and constitutional views, then, owe an intellectual debt to John Locke.

5. See Bernard Bailyn, *The Ideological Origins of the American Revolution* (Cambridge: Belknap of Harvard University Press, 1967); Gordon Wood, *The Creation of the American Republic, 1776–1787* (Chapel Hill, University of North Carolina Press, 1969); Forrest McDonald, *Novus Ordo Seclorum: The Intellectual Origins of the Constitution* (Lawrence: University Press of Kansas, 1986); and Jack N. Rakove, *Original Meanings: Politics and Ideas in the Making of the Constitution* (New York: Alfred A. Knopf, 1996).

6. See Charles C. Thach, *The Creation of the Presidency 1775–1789* (Baltimore: Johns Hopkins University Press, 1922); *Inventing the American Presidency*, ed. Thomas E. Cronin (Lawrence: University Press of Kansas, 1989);

Forrest McDonald, *The American Presidency: An Intellectual History* (Lawrence: University Press of Kansas, 1994); Evarts Boutell Greene, *The Provincial Governor in the English Colonies of North America* (New York: Russell & Russell, 1966 [1898]); and Harvey C. Mansfield Jr., *Taming the Prince: The Ambivalence of Modern Executive Power* (Baltimore: Johns Hopkins University Press, 1993 [1989]).

7. Greene, *The Provincial Governor*, 1, emphasis added.

8. "Massachusetts Agreement on the Legislature, May 9, 1632," in *Colonial Origins of the American Constitution: A Documentary History*, ed. Donald S. Lutz (Indianapolis: Liberty Fund, 1998), 43.

9. "Massachusetts Body of Liberties, December 1641," in *Colonial Origins*, 79.

10. "Organization of the Government of Rhode Island, March 16–19, 1642," in *Colonial Origins*, 172. It is also worth noting that the document later (p. 173) states that Rhode Island is "a DEMOCRACIE, or Popular Government; that is to say, It is in the Powre of the Body of Freemen orderly assembled, or the major part of them, to make or constitue Just Lawes."

11. "Fundamental Orders of Connecticut, January 14, 1639," in *Colonial Origins*, 211–12.

12. "Charter of Liberties and Privileges, October 30, 1683," in *Colonial Origins*, 256.

13. Ibid., 257.

14. See, for instance, "Constitution for the Council and Assembly in Virginia, July 24, 1621," in *Colonial Origins*, 336–38.

15. Greene, *The Provincial Governor*, 10.

16. Ibid., 6.

17. Ibid., 48.

18. Ibid., 49–51.

19. Ibid., 51–52.

20. A recent treatment of the influence of Locke on the American founding generation can be found in Jerome Huyler, *Locke in America: The Moral Philosophy of the Founding Era* (Lawrence: University Press of Kansas, 1995).

21. All information on state constitutions in the following section, with the exception of the Massachusetts constitution, comes from the Avalon Project, Yale Law School, http://avalon.law.yale.edu/default.asp, accessed October 16, 2008.

22. Rakove, *Original Meanings*, 250.

23. The executive council idea will not receive extensive treatment here given space constraints. However, it should be noted that the idea of a council was critical to revolutionary thought and even held sway to an important extent at the Constitutional Convention.

24. Thach, *Creation of the Presidency*, 28.

25. John A. Fairlie, "The Veto Power of the State Governor," *American Political Science Review* 11, no. 3 (August 1917), 474–75. See also "Constitution of South Carolina, March 19, 1778," Avalon Project.

26. Hamilton in *Federalist #70* would argue that even though there was a "council" to advise the governor of New Jersey, its advice was only that and not binding, unlike the other states' councils (excluding New York, which did not provision a council).

27. Wood, *Creation of the American Republic*, 226, 227.

28. Ibid., 137.

29. Rakove, *Original Meanings*, 252.

30. Donald M. Roper, "The Governorship in History," *Proceedings of the Academy of Political Science* 31 (May 1974), 19.

31. This means postponing the assembly, but no more than sixty days in a year in this case.

32. For Adams's influence on the Massachusetts constitution, see George C. Homans, "John Adams and the Massachusetts Constitution," *Proceedings of the American Philosophical Society* 125 (August 1981).

33. "Massachusetts Constitution," *The Founders' Constitution*, Volume 1, Chapter 1, Document 6, University of Chicago Press, at http://press-pubs.uchicago.edu/founders/documents/v1ch1s6.html, accessed March 21, 2006. "Counsellors and Senators" is a somewhat confusing term: it refers merely to one group of persons, those elected to the Senate, who also have the possibility of serving as members of the council.

34. Wood, *Creation of the American Republic*, 435.

35. "Articles of Confederation," in *Colonial Origins*, 382.

36. Ibid., 378.

37. Wood, *Creation of the American Republic*, 394.

38. See Wood, *Creation of the American Republic*, 404–5. A common perception of state legislatures at the time was that they were incompetent and ill-equipped to respond to economic developments and problems.

39. *Federalist #6*, 26. Of course, with regard to domestic "factions," Hamilton and others had such events in mind as Shays' Rebellion in Massachusetts.

40. *Federalist #3*, 13.

41. Wood, *Creation of the American Republic*, 394.

42. Ibid., 395.

43. For an extended discussion of the growing animus toward legislatures in the 1780s, see Wood, *Creation of the American Republic*, 403–13.

44. It should be remarked that the Convention, given the high proportion of men supportive of constitutional reform, was in some ways unrepresentative of opinion in America. As would be seen at ratification, many still harbored deep concerns about strong executive leadership. Many delegates

to the Convention and also Hamilton in *The Federalist* referred to the necessity of making the executive or president "independent" of the legislature.

45. This is how Richard J. Ellis, ed., *Founding the American Presidency* (Lanham, Md.: Rowman & Littlefield, 1999), 63–66, describes the debate over presidential selection, which, as suggested, is intimately related to the debate over presidential tenure.

46. Quoted in James Madison, *Notes of Debates in the Federal Convention of 1787*, introduction by Adrienne Koch (New York: W. W. Norton, 1966), 31.

47. Ibid., 119–120.

48. Ibid., 116.

49. Ibid., 307.

50. Ibid., 306.

51. Ibid., 308.

52. Ibid., 310.

53. Ibid., 311.

54. Ibid., 312.

55. Ibid., 325.

56. Ibid., 326.

57. Ibid., 358.

58. Ibid., 359.

59. Ibid., 366.

60. See Ibid., 366–67, for the full debate.

61. Ibid., 372.

62. Ibid., 577.

63. Ibid., 589.

64. Ibid., 592, emphasis in the original.

65. Ibid., 578.

66. Ellis, *Founding the American Presidency*, 97.

67. *Federalist* #68, 423–24.

68. For instance, those supportive of legislative selection could take heart from the House of Representatives selecting the candidate if no one received a majority of electoral votes. And indeed, several members of the Convention believed this would be the norm; the electoral college would effectively produce legislative selection, in their eyes. Those opposed to legislative selection, though, could embrace the popular nature of the election system. Supporters of states' rights, similarly, could hardly object to the House of Representatives voting as states to select the president, nor could they object to the allocation of electoral votes, which gave states qua states a not-so-insignificant boost. Yet, "nationalists" could also point to the predominance of larger states in the electoral vote tally.

69. For a fuller discussion of the Anti-Federalist take on presidential ten-

ure, see Thomas E. Cronin, "Presidential Term, Tenure, and Reeligibility," in Cronin, *Inventing the American Presidency*, 72–76.

70. Cato, "No. 4, November 8, 1787," in *The Complete Anti-Federalist*, 7 vols., ed. Herbert J. Storing (Chicago: University of Chicago Press, 1981), accessed through "The Founders' Constitution," University of Chicago Press, http://press-pubs.uchicago.edu/founders/documents/a2_1_1s6.html, August 12, 2006, emphasis in the original.

71. The authorship of the Federal Farmer papers are more in dispute, scholarly opinion suggesting initially the Virginian Richard Henry Lee and then later New York's Melancton Smith.

72. Federal Farmer, "No. 14, January 17, 1788," in Storing, *The Complete Anti-Federalist*, accessed through "The Founders' Constitution," University of Chicago Press, http://press-pubs.uchicago.edu/founders/documents/a2_1_1s10.html, August 12, 2006.

73. Federal Farmer, "No. 14."

74. George Mason, "Debate in Virginia Ratifying Convention," in Jonathan Elliot, ed., *The Debates in the Several State Conventions on the Adoption of the Federal Constitution. . . .* , 5 vols., 2nd ed. (New York: Burt Franklin, n.d. [1888]), accessed through "The Founders' Constitution," University of Chicago Press, http://press-pubs.uchicago.edu/founders/documents/a1_4_1s16.html, August 12, 2006.

75. Ibid.

76. Ibid.

77. Ibid.

78. "Ratification of the Constitution by the State of Virginia, June 26, 1788," Avalon Project.

79. "Ratification of the Constitution by the State of New York, July 26, 1788," Avalon Project.

80. "Ratification of the Constitution by the State of North Carolina, November 21, 1789," Avalon Project.

81. "Ratification of the Constitution by the State of Rhode Island, May 29, 1790," Avalon Project.

82. *Federalist #70*, 436.

83. Ibid., 437.

84. Some Anti-Federalists argued for a "plural" executive, not unlike the "council" that composed Pennsylvania's executive.

85. Ibid., 446.

86. Ibid., 448.

87. Ibid., 449.

88. Ibid.

89. *Federalist #72*, 451.

90. Ibid.

91. Ibid., 454–55.

92. Ibid., 455.

93. Ibid., 451–54.

94. *Federalist* #71, 447.

95. See, for instance, the analysis of Wilson's view of the presidency in David Nichols, *The Myth of the Modern Presidency* (University Park: Penn State University Press, 1994), 36, 47, 56.

96. See, for example, Bruce Miroff, "Monopolizing the Public Space: The President as a Problem for Democratic Politics," in *Rethinking the Presidency*, ed. Thomas Cronin (Boston: Little, Brown, 1982).

97. Surely Hamilton saw the electoral college and the wisdom of the independent electors as somewhat of a safety valve. Nevertheless, the constitutional view requires some theoretical contortions to bring its disparate views together.

98. Mansfield, *Taming the Prince*, 200.

99. See Locke, *Two Treatises of Government*, 374–80.

100. This "postscript" concept is more fully explored in chapter 6.

CHAPTER 3

The epigraph is from Joseph Hawley, editor of the *Hartford Courant*, quoted in "Editorial Article 5—No Title," *New York Times*, March 15, 1875.

1. "Thomas Jefferson to the Legislature of Vermont, December 10, 1807," in *The Writings of Thomas Jefferson*, vol. 16, ed. Andrew A. Lipscomb and Albert Ellery Bergh (Washington, D.C.: Thomas Jefferson Memorial Association, 1905), 293.

2. See Bruce Peabody, "George Washington, Presidential Term Limits, and the Problem of Reluctant Political Leadership," *Presidential Studies Quarterly* 31, no. 3 (2001), for an excellent analysis of Washington's role in the development of the two-term tradition.

3. Quoted in Peabody, "George Washington, Presidential Term Limits, and the Problem of Reluctant Political Leadership," 442.

4. George Washington, "Farewell Address," Avalon Project, Yale Law School, http://www.yale.edu/lawweb/avalon/washing.htm, accessed July 23, 2008.

5. Washington, "Farewell Address," emphasis added.

6. Peabody, "George Washington, Presidential Term Limits, and the Problem of Reluctant Political Leadership," 443.

7. "Thomas Jefferson to James Madison, December 20, 1787," in *The Portable Thomas Jefferson*, ed. Merrill D. Peterson (New York: Penguin, 1975), 430–31.

8. "Thomas Jefferson to William Short, September 20, 1788," in *The Writings of Thomas Jefferson*, vol. 7, 145–46.

9. "Thomas Jefferson to John Taylor, January 6, 1805," in *The Writings of Thomas Jefferson*, vol. 11, 56–57.

10. Additionally, on the subject of possible political opportunism, although Jefferson faced increasing political opposition in his second term—especially because of the failure of his embargo policy—it is unlikely that that political situation influenced his decision not to seek a third term. We have seen that by 1805 he had already resolved to serve only two terms. Moreover, his handpicked successor, James Madison, won comfortably, suggesting the continuing popularity of Jefferson in the face of his embargo policy.

11. "Thomas Jefferson to Messrs. Abner Watkins and Bernard Todd, December 21, 1807," in *The Writings of Thomas Jefferson*, vol. 16, 298.

12. "Thomas Jefferson to the Legislature of Vermont, December 10, 1807," in *The Writings of Thomas Jefferson*, vol. 16, 294.

13. "Thomas Jefferson to John Taylor," 57.

14. "Thomas Jefferson to Citizens of Philadelphia, February 3, 1809," in *The Writings of Thomas Jefferson*, vol. 16, 329, emphasis added.

15. Even Madison, who was notably young as a participant at the Constitutional Convention, was nearly sixty-six years old when he left the presidency at the end of his second term.

16. See, for instance, "Thomas Jefferson to James Madison, January 30, 1787," in *Portable Jefferson*, 417: "I hold it that a little rebellion, now and then, is a good thing, and as necessary in the political world as storms in the physical."

17. See "Thomas Jefferson to William Smith, November 13, 1787," in *The Writings of Thomas Jefferson*, vol. 6, 373: "What signify a few lives lost in a century or two? The tree of liberty must be refreshed from time to time with the blood of patriots and tyrants. It is its natural manure."

18. "Thomas Jefferson to Joseph C. Cabell, October 24, 1817," in *The Writings of Thomas Jefferson*, vol. 19, 251. Jefferson seems to use the term "bark" to mean a "ship" or "vessel."

19. "Thomas Jefferson to Henry Guest, January 4, 1809," in *The Writings of Thomas Jefferson*, vol. 12, 224.

20. "Thomas Jefferson to John Taylor," 57.

21. Thomas Jefferson, "Autobiography," in *The Writings of Thomas Jefferson*, vol. 1, 119.

22. Although Theodore Roosevelt lost in 1912, it is not evident that his pursuit of a third term played a significant role in that loss. The split in the Republican Party was far more important.

23. "Thomas Jefferson to John Taylor," 57.

24. Ralph Ketcham, *James Madison: A Biography* (New York: Macmillan, 1971), 606.

25. As Cunningham has said, "Monroe let it be known early on that he would follow the example of his predecessors and decline reelection to a third term." Noble E. Cunningham Jr., *The Presidency of James Monroe* (Lawrence: University Press of Kansas, 1996), 167.

26. Charles W. Stein, *The Third-Term Tradition: Its Rise and Collapse in American Politics* (Westport, Conn.: Greenwood Press, 1972 [1943]), 47.

27. Stein, *Third-Term Tradition*, 48.

28. Andrew Jackson, "First Annual Message, December 8, 1829," in John T. Woolley and Gerhard Peters, *The American Presidency Project*, University of California, Santa Barbara, http://www.presidency.ucsb.edu/ws/?pid=29471, accessed August 24, 2008.

29. Andrew Jackson, "Fourth Annual Message, December 4, 1832," *American Presidency Project*, http://www.presidency.ucsb.edu/ws/index.php?pid=29474, accessed August 24, 2008.

30. Andrew Jackson, "Second Annual Message, December 6, 1830," American Presidency Project, http://www.presidency.ucsb.edu/ws/index.php?pid=29472, accessed August 24, 2008.

31. See Stein, *Third-Term Tradition*, 46–58, for an explanation of Jackson's motivations.

32. Ibid., 58, emphasis added.

33. See Michael F. Holt, *The Rise and Fall of the American Whig Party* (New York: Oxford University Press, 1999), 17–18, for a discussion of Jackson's influence on the development of Whig Party philosophy.

34. See ibid., 110, for Harrison's role advancing the anti-executive ethos during the campaign of 1840.

35. William Henry Harrison, "Inaugural Address, March 4, 1841," *American Presidency Project*, http://www.presidency.ucsb.edu/ws/?pid=25813, accessed August 25, 2008.

36. "Theophilus Fisk to James K. Polk, May 31, 1844," in *Correspondence of James K. Polk*, vol. 7, ed. Wayne Cutler (Nashville: Vanderbilt University Press, 1989), 171, emphasis in the original. See also "Aaron V. Brown to James K. Polk, May 30, 1844": "In your acceptance you must some way or other express your self in favor of the one term system. This is important. I might say all important & you will know exactly *how* it will be highly useful" (266).

37. "Samuel H. Laughlin to James K. Polk, May 31, 1844," *Correspondence of James K. Polk*, 174.

38. "Jacob Thompson to James K. Polk, June 7, 1844," *Correspondence of James K. Polk*, 212.

39. Paul H. Bergeron, *The Presidency of James K. Polk* (Lawrence: University Press of Kansas, 1987), 17.

40. James K. Polk to Henry Hubbard et al., June 12, 1844," *Correspondence of James K. Polk*, 241.

41. James K. Polk to Cave Johnson, June 24, 1844," *Correspondence of James K. Polk*, 276, emphasis in the original.

42. *Polk: The Diary of a President, 1845–1849*, ed. Allan Nevins (New York: Longmans, Green and Co., 1952), 298.

43. David Herbert Donald, *Lincoln* (London: Jonathan Cape, 1995), 476.

44. John C. Waugh, *Reelecting Lincoln: The Battle for the 1864 Presidency* (New York: Crown Publishers, Inc., 1997), 18.

45. Donald, *Lincoln*, 124.

46. Ibid., 491.

47. Quoted in ibid., 474.

48. *The National Conventions and Platforms of All Political Parties*, ed. Thomas Hudson McKee (Baltimore, Md.: Friedenwald Company, 1906), 127.

49. Ibid., 126.

50. Quoted in Donald, *Lincoln*, 507.

51. "The One-Term Principle," *New York Times*, April 16, 1864.

52. See the recent work by Alvin S. Felzenberg, *The Leaders We Deserved (and a Few We Didn't): Rethinking the Presidential Rating Game* (New York: Basic, 2008), for a much more charitable view of Grant's presidency.

53. "Congress: The Presidential One-Term Question in the Senate," *New York Times*, January 12, 1872.

54. "The One-Term Principle," *New York Times*, December 15, 1871.

55. *National Conventions and Platforms*, 146, emphasis added.

56. "The One-Term Principle," *New York Times*, September 20, 1871.

57. "A Converted Politician," *New York Times*, June 20, 1874.

58. "Third Term," *New York Times*, October 16, 1874, emphasis in the original.

59. "Editorial Article 5—No Title," *New York Times*, March 15, 1875.

60. Stein, *Third-Term Tradition*, 77.

61. "Washington: President Grant on the Third Term Question," *New York Times*, May 31, 1875.

62. Stein, *Third-Term Tradition*, 79.

63. "Forty-Fourth Congress," *New York Times*, December 16, 1875.

64. Rutherford B. Hayes, "Inaugural Address, March 5, 1877," *American Presidency Project*, http://www.presidency.ucsb.edu/ws/index.php?pid=25822, accessed August 30, 2008.

65. Stein, *Third-Term Tradition*, 84.

66. Herbert J. Clancy, *The Presidential Election of 1880* (Chicago: Loyola University Press, 1958), 27.

67. For much more on the election of 1880, see, among others, Clancy, *Election of 1880*, and Stein, *Third-Term Tradition*.

68. "Third Term Discussions," *New York Times*, February 23, 1880.

69. He did not. See "The Democratic Nominees," *New York Times*, July 31, 1880, for the full text of Hancock's acceptance letter. He mentions nothing of the sort in his letter, nor did the Democratic Party place a one-term plank in their 1880 platform.

70. "The One-Term Principle," *New York Times*, July 15, 1880.

71. See "What the Machine is Doing," *New York Times*, May 9, 1880, and "States in the National Convention, *New York Times*, May 29, 1880, for discussions of the party leaders and "machines" that were opposed to Grant in 1880.

72. "Accepting a Great Trust," *New York Times*, August 20, 1884.

73. In fact, after the successive failures of William Jennings Bryan in 1896 and 1900, there was a drive within the party to nominate Cleveland in 1904. See Stein, *Third-Term Tradition*, 134–42.

74. Stephen Skowronek, *The Politics Presidents Make* (Cambridge, Mass.: Belknap Press of Harvard University Press, 1993), 45–49.

75. There were, of course, some voices that opposed Cleveland's election in 1888 on one-term grounds. See, for instance, "The Second Term," *New York Times*, April 26, 1887.

76. Cleveland's nomination in 1892 provoked an intriguing, if weak, reaction on the part of some who thought that three *nominations* as the party's presidential candidate were somehow a violation of the two-term tradition. The *New York Times* said of the position, leveled mainly by anti-Cleveland newspapers, that nothing could be "sillier and more irrelevant than to represent the opposition to a third term as opposition to the third nomination of a man who served but one term." What is more, in 1892, Cleveland had been out of office for four years, thereby dismissing the danger, which the *Times* allowed was very real, of an incumbent president using the machinery of power to perpetuate himself in office. "Cleveland and the 'Third Term,'" *New York Times*, May 3, 1892.

77. *National Conventions and Platforms*, 297.

78. Jeff Taylor, *Where Did the Party Go? William Jennings Bryan, Hubert Humphrey, and the Jeffersonian Legacy* (Columbia: University of Missouri Press, 2006), 167.

79. See "Mr. Bryan Speaks at Canton," *New York Times*, October 16, 1900, for an example of Bryan's advocacy of one term for the presidency.

80. See "Talks of a Third Term," *New York Times*, June 10, 1901.

81. "President Does Not Want a Third Term," *New York Times*, June 12, 1901.

82. "Enjoys His Triumph," *New York Times*, November 9, 1904.

83. "League Is Organized to Re-elect Roosevelt," *New York Times*, December 28, 1906.

84. "Editors Still for Roosevelt," *New York Times*, April 9, 1907.

85. See, for instance, "Roosevelt for Third Term," *New York Times*, April 10, 1907, and "Objects to Third Term," *New York Times*, April 23, 1907.

86. "Roosevelt Warns Official Boomers," *New York Times*, November 24, 1907.

87. "Third Term Resolution," *New York Times*, December 10, 1907.

88. "No Third Term for Roosevelt," *New York Times*, December 12, 1907. And yet some would still parse Roosevelt's words. See "3d Term 'Shall' and 'Will,'" *New York Times*, December 15, 1907.

89. "Convention's Second Day," *New York Times*, June 18, 1908.

90. "Lodge Denounces Third Term Talk," *New York Times*, June 18, 1908.

91. Stein, *Third-Term Tradition*, 144–221, is nearly exhaustive on Roosevelt's pursuit of the third term. See also James Chace, *1912: Wilson, Roosevelt, Taft and Debs—The Election That Changed the Country* (New York: Simon & Schuster, 2005), and Sidney M. Milkis, *Theodore Roosevelt, the Progressive Party, and the Transformation of American Democracy* (Lawrence: University Press of Kansas, 2009), for fresh examinations of the 1912 election and Roosevelt's role therein.

92. "I Will," *New York Times*, August 27, 1910.

93. See also, for instance, "The President's State of Mind," *New York Times*, September 17, 1910, where Theodore Roosevelt's "vociferous and obstreperous campaign for the nomination" is further discussed.

94. Stein, *Third-Term Tradition*, 184–85.

95. "Roosevelt Says He Will Accept Nomination," *New York Times*, February 26, 1912.

96. Roosevelt Won't Bolt," *New York Times*, February 27, 1912.

97. "Of Course," *New York Times*, February 28, 1912.

98. "The Third-Term Pledge," *New York Times*, February 18, 1912. Among the more amusing parodies was one that referred to Roosevelt's "candidacy for the third Non-consecutive Cup of Coffee Term." See "Political Poets in the Campaign," *New York Times*, March 17, 1912.

99. Quoted in Stein, *Third-Term Tradition*, 181.

100. "Roosevelt Speaks to a Great Throng," *New York Times*, June 18, 1912.

101. "Mr. Roosevelt's Speech," *New York Times*, June 18, 1912.

102. William Howard Taft, "Acceptance Speech by President William Howard Taft, Washington, August 2, 1912," in *History of American Presidential Elections, 1789–1968*, vol. 3, ed. Arthur Schlesinger (New York: Chelsea House Publishers, 1971), 2204.

103. Ibid., 2219, emphasis added.

104. Woodrow Wilson, "Acceptance Speech by Governor Woodrow Wilson, Baltimore, August 7, 1912," in ibid., 2236.

105. "Democratic Party Platform of 1912," *American Presidency Project*, http://www.presidency.ucsb.edu/ws/index.php?pid=29590, accessed September 10, 2008. Wilson would not explicitly pledge himself to this plank, even though the platform writers did.

106. "Third-Term Fight Shelved By House," *New York Times*, February 6, 1912.

107. "Favors 6-Year Term for the Presidency," *New York Times*, May 14, 1912.

108. "Wrangle on Six-Year Term," *New York Times*, August 20, 1912.

109. "Oppose Single-Term Plan," *New York Times*, February 9, 1913.

110. "Wilson Blocked One-Term Bill," *New York Times*, October 13, 1914.

111. "Limiting Temptation," *New York Times*, February 3, 1913.

112. Stein, *Third-Term Tradition*, 226.

113. "The One-Term Plank," *New York Times*, October 16, 1914.

114. "Wilson in 1916, His Party's Slogan," *New York Times*, February 16, 1914.

115. Ibid.

116. The Democratic Party had not held the presidency for two consecutive terms since before the Civil War: Pierce and Buchanan.

117. See "Bryan Put Wilson in Two-Term Class," *New York Times*, February 17, 1916, and "Bryan Pledged to Wilson," *New York Times*, June 15, 1916.

118. "Third-Term Boom for Wilson Wins Cheers in Indiana," *New York Times*, June 20, 1918.

119. "Wilson Not a Candidate," *New York Times*, March 1, 1919.

120. See, for instance, "Senator Advised Nominating Wilson," *New York Times*, December 4, 1919, and "Gerard Won't Run If Wilson Wants To," *New York Times*, December 17, 1919.

121. "Some Think M'Adoo Opens Way for Wilson," *New York Times*, June 19, 1920. See also Stein, *Third-Term Tradition*, 246.

122. "The Third Term," *New York Times*, January 2, 1920.

123. Even with Franklin Roosevelt on the Democratic ticket as vice presidential nominee in 1920, Democrats lost the election by a wide margin, with Republicans Warren Harding and Calvin Coolidge receiving more than 60 percent of the popular vote.

124. The amendment reads: "No person shall be elected to the office of the President more than twice, and no person *who has held the office of President, or acted as President, for more than two years of a term to which some other person was elected President* shall be elected to the office of the President more than once" (emphasis added). One of the key arguments in Coolidge's case was that he had only served a brief part of Harding's term, and thus he should have been eligible—even per the two-term tradition—to serve two more terms. Had the Twenty-second Amendment been in

place in the 1920s, Coolidge would have been able to run for reelection in 1928.

125. "Republicans Look to 1928 Candidates," *New York Times*, March 30, 1925.

126. "Coolidge's Success to Fix 1928 Plans," *New York Times*, August 24, 1925. See also "Third-Term Doctors Disagree," *New York Times*, April 18, 1927, "Public Attitudes Helping Coolidge," *New York Times*, May 23, 1927, and "Republican Group Fights Third Term," *New York Times*, May 30, 1927.

127. "Coolidge Forces Are Lining Up for 1928," *New York Times*, August 15, 1926.

128. See "Plan Congress Vote on the Third Term," *New York Times*, February 10, 1927, and "Moves to Prohibit Third Term By Law," *New York Times*, February 22, 1927.

129. "The New Third-Term Strategy," *New York Times*, April 21, 1927. The *Times* reported incredulously that many visitors came to see Coolidge, and all of them talked about the third term afterward—but then they insisted that Coolidge did not speak about it.

130. "Not To Be Forced," *New York Times*, May 1, 1927.

131. The *Times* interpreted it as such, for instance. See "Now Six Presidents against Third Term," *New York Times*, August 3, 1927.

132. See "Callers Still Cling to Coolidge Hope," *New York Times*, September 18, 1927.

133. Quoted in Cyril Clemens and Athern P. Daggett, "Coolidge's 'I Do Not Choose to Run': Granite or Putty?" *New England Quarterly* 18, no. 2 (June 1945), 149.

134. "Coolidge Insists He Is Out of Race," *New York Times*, September 25, 1927.

135. "Compromising the President," *New York Times*, April 23, 1928.

136. Richard V. Oulahan, "Hoover Strength Grows: Convention Chiefs Wait More Definite Word from President," *New York Times*, June 10, 1928.

137. "The Sense of the Senate," *New York Times*, February 11, 1928.

138. Calvin Coolidge, *Autobiography of Calvin Coolidge* (New York: Cosmopolitan, 1929), 241.

139. As the *Times* put it, commenting on one of Coolidge's clarifications, this was one of "Mr. Coolidge's latest attempt[s] to stop the movement of self-seeking politicians to 'draft' him for another nomination." See "Compromising the President."

140. Clemens and Daggett, "Coolidge's 'I Do Not Choose to Run,'" 163. See pages 161–163 for more detail on the argument that Coolidge did desire a third term.

141. Stein, *Third-Term Tradition*, 344.

CHAPTER 4

The epigraph quotes Turner Catledge, "All-Absorbing Political Riddle," *New York Times*, June 18, 1939.

1. Had Theodore Roosevelt won the Republican nomination, the election between Roosevelt and the Democratic candidate, had it been Woodrow Wilson or not, may still have been a tight one. But given that Roosevelt and Republican standard-bearer William Howard Taft between them gained more than 50 percent of the popular vote nationally and in many of the key electoral states—Wilson did not clear 42 percent of the national vote and won the electoral votes of many key states by a similar or even smaller percentage—it is reasonable to conclude that with the Republican nomination, Franklin Roosevelt's cousin might well have been the first successful challenger to the tradition.

2. Charles W. Stein, *The Third-Term Tradition: Its Rise and Collapse in American Politics* (Westport, Conn.: Greenwood Press, 1972 [1943]), 317.

3. See "More Now Expect a Third-Term Race," *New York Times*, June 18, 1939, where polls on the third-term issue from 1937, 1938, and 1939 are discussed.

4. Delbert Clark, "The Third-Term Issue Revives the Old Debate," *New York Times*, July 11, 1937.

5. See Chesly Manly, "Purge Attempt Considered Bid for Third Term," *Chicago Tribune*, September 7, 1938.

6. "Mr. Roosevelt's Third Term," *Chicago Tribune*, December 11, 1938.

7. See, for example, "Roosevelt Urged by Union to Run," *New York Times*, May 28, 1939, and "Hague is '100%' for Roosevelt Third Term," *New York Times*, August 5, 1939.

8. See "Ickes Keeps Silent on the Third-Term Idea," *New York Times*, July 29, 1938, and "Third Term Move Possible, Ickes Says," *New York Times*, October 20, 1938.

9. Ickes's defense of the third term as presented here is from a press statement he released discussing the article. See "Michelson Joins Third-Term Talk," *New York Times*, June 11, 1939.

10. Although John Garner was not named in the *Look* article, Ickes was in part making a critique of then vice president Garner and his (and others') suitability to carry on the reform-minded policies of the New Deal.

11. "Murphy Declares He Is for Third Term," *New York Times*, July 14, 1939.

12. "Lightning rod" is how Jeane Nienaber Clarke describes Ickes's service to Roosevelt in *Roosevelt's Warrior: Harold Ickes and the New Deal* (Baltimore: Johns Hopkins University Press, 1996), 369.

13. "Roosevelt Shuns 3D-Term Comment," *New York Times*, June 7, 1939.

14. Catledge, "All-Absorbing Political Riddle."

15. See, for instance, "Hague Is '100%' for Roosevelt Third Term," and Felix Belair Jr., "President Silent on Kelly Speech," *New York Times*, August 15, 1939.

16. "3d Term Sentiment Increased by War," *New York Times*, October 1, 1939.

17. "Third-Term Victory Is Called Doubtful," *New York Times*, March 13, 1940.

18. "Sentiment for a Third Term Up Sharply Since Nazi Invasion, Gallup Survey Finds," *New York Times*, June 5, 1940.

19. "Third-Term Trend Still Held Strong," *New York Times*, June 28, 1940.

20. "Harrison Now Says a 3D Term Is Vital," *New York Times*, January 6, 1940.

21. "M'Nutt Comes Out for Third Term," *New York Times*, May 31, 1940.

22. "Hillman Supports Roosevelt 3D Term," *New York Times*, January 7, 1940.

23. "Third Term Vital, Ickes Tells Labor," *New York Times*, May 19, 1940.

24. "Mr. Roosevelt Confesses," *Chicago Tribune*, July 20, 1940. Pushing things to the absurd would be Bert Stand, secretary of the Tammany organization of New York City, who argued for a fourth term because the third was "already in the bag," and then further suggested that civil service be extended to the presidency so that Roosevelt could continue indefinitely. See "Tammany Proposes a 'Fourth Term' Move, and Even Civil Service for the Presidency," *New York Times*, July 10, 1940.

25. Only Vice President Garner, in December 1939, and Postmaster Farley, in March 1940, would officially declare for the nomination; unofficial candidates included the likes of Roosevelt confidante Harry Hopkins, Montana Senator Burton Wheeler, Federal Security Administrator Paul McNutt, Attorney General Robert Jackson, and Secretary of State Cordell Hull, among others.

26. "Michelson Joins Third-Term Talk," *New York Times*, June 11, 1939.

27. Arthur Krock, "Democrats' Dilemma Deepens as Days Pass," *New York Times*, February 11, 1940.

28. Herbert S. Parmet and Marie B. Hecht, *Never Again: A President Runs for a Third Term* (New York: MacMillan, 1968), 172–73.

29. "Discounts Effect of Farley's Stand," *New York Times*, March 22, 1940.

30. "Democrats Reach California Accord," *New York Times*, March 15, 1940.

31. Parmet and Hecht, *Never Again*, 35.

32. James MacGregor Burns, *Roosevelt: The Lion and the Fox* (New York: Harcourt, Brace & World, 1956), 411–12.

33. Turner Catledge, "'If Not Roosevelt, Who?' Party Asking," *New York Times*, March 10, 1940.

34. Parmet and Hecht, *Never Again*, 33–34.

35. Truman Presidential Library and Museum, Samuel Rosenman Interview, http://www.trumanlibrary.org/oralhist/rosenmn.htm#oh1, accessed August 2, 2007.

36. Parmet and Hecht, *Never Again*, 34.

37. Arthur Krock, "'Draft' of Roosevelt Is Traced to Inner Circle of the New Deal," *New York Times*, July 18, 1940.

38. See, for instance, Parmet and Hecht's discussion of a meeting between Roosevelt and Farley in July 1939 in which they discussed possible successors (*Never Again*, 19–20). The *Chicago Tribune* had as early as 1938 identified the White House failure to find favor with possible successors. See "Mr. Roosevelt's Third Term," *Chicago Tribune*, December 11, 1938.

39. Parmet and Hecht, *Never Again*, 35–36.

40. Burns, *Roosevelt: The Lion and the Fox*, 409.

41. Quoted in Parmet and Hecht, *Never Again*, 173. Roosevelt had apparently told Farley that he (Roosevelt) would make up his mind on a third term no later than February 1940.

42. Clark, "Third Term Issue."

43. Catledge, "All-Absorbing Political Riddle."

44. Turner Catledge, "Third Term Showdown Expected to Come Soon," *New York Times*, July 30, 1939. Incidentally, this is one of the earliest references in the *Times* to the "lame duck" phenomenon as applied to the presidency.

45. "New Dealers Say Roosevelt Must Run for Third Term to Meet Willkie Challenge," *New York Times*, June 29, 1940. The officials, interestingly, seemed more concerned with Roosevelt's reelection preserving the New Deal than they did with meeting the challenges of World War II.

46. Parmet and Hecht, *Never Again*, 168.

47. Burns, *Roosevelt: The Lion and the Fox*, 424–25.

48. Ibid., 425.

49. Truman Presidential Library and Museum, Walter Trohan interview, http://www.trumanlibrary.org/oralhist/trohan.htm, accessed August 2, 2007. Trohan was a reporter for the *Chicago Tribune*.

50. "Choice Left Open," *New York Times*, July 17, 1940.

51. "Invitation to a Draft," *New York Times*, July 17, 1940.

52. For a detailed discussion of the convention politics, see Parmet and Hecht, *Never Again*, 181–89.

53. Burns, *Roosevelt: Lion and the Fox*, 428.

54. Ted Morgan, *FDR: A Biography* (New York: Simon and Schuster, 1985), 530.

55. See Arthur Krock, "Democrats End a Task with Little Happiness," *New York Times*, July 21, 1940, for a detailed discussion of the ill will within the party after the nomination of Wallace.

56. Burns, *Lion and the Fox*, 432.

57. Turner Catledge, "Will Try to Rally All 3D Term Foes," *New York Times*, July 25, 1940.

58. "A. E. Smith Calls Third Term a Peril," *New York Times*, October 27, 1940.

59. "Mr. Roosevelt Renominated," *New York Times*, July 18, 1940. The *Tribune*, not surprisingly, had been skeptical of the "draft" from the beginning. See Arthur Sears Henning, "3D Term Clique Puts Roosevelt 'Draft' in Gear," *Chicago Tribune*, January 18, 1940.

60. Krock, "'Draft' of Roosevelt."

61. "Mr. Roosevelt Renominated."

62. "Burke Challenges Third Term Group," *New York Times*, September 6, 1940.

63. "Senate Declares against Third Term by 56 to 26 Vote," *New York Times*, February 11, 1928.

64. Henry N. Dorris, "Roosevelt's Lead Low in Maryland," *New York Times*, November 3, 1940. Although Tydings did not actively campaign for President Roosevelt, he also did not actively oppose him.

65. "2 Reverse Stand Against 3D Term," *New York Times*, July 24, 1940.

66. See chapter 2 for a full discussion of these debates over presidential tenure between the Federalists and Anti-Federalists.

67. Of course, just because no record remains of such a conversation or discussion does not mean that one or more did not occur. If close advisors did discuss such matters with FDR, though, these discussions were held in confidence and likely will remain unknown.

68. "Text of Willkie's Address at Rally in Convention Hall in Camden, N.J.," *New York Times*, November 1, 1940.

69. "Text of the Address of Wendell Willkie in Accepting the Presidential Nomination," *New York Times*, August 18, 1940.

70. Two good examples are "Text of Willkie Speech on Defense," *New York Times*, October 5, 1940, and "Text of Willkie's Speech before 25,000 in Chicago," *New York Times*, October 20, 1940.

71. "The Text of Willkie's First Major Speech in the Presidential Campaign," *New York Times*, September 17, 1940. Willkie tempers the remark a bit in the following statement: "[Roosevelt] may not want dictatorship and I do not think he does. But in his hands our traditions are not safe."

72. "Text of the Willkie Speech Warning of State Socialism," *New York Times*, October 19, 1940.

73. "Text of Willkie's Address at Rally in Syracuse," *New York Times*, October 15, 1940.

74. "Text of Willkie Speech at Louisville," *New York Times*, October 29, 1940.

75. "Text of Willkie's Address at Rally in Syracuse."

76. "Text of Willkie Speech at Louisville."

77. Ibid.

78. "Text of Wendell Willkie's Address before Women's Clubs at Detroit," *New York Times*, October 1, 1940.

79. "Text of Willkie's Speech before 25,000 in Chicago."

80. "Text of Willkie Speech at Louisville."

81. "Text of Wendell Willkie's Address at Minneapolis on the Farm Problem," *New York Times*, October 20, 1940.

82. The following references are to "Text of President's Speech Accepting 3d Nomination," *New York Times*, July 19, 1940.

83. Congress would in September of 1940 pass the Selective Service and Training Act, providing for a widespread "draft" of Americans.

84. The *Chicago Tribune*, for instance, was stinging in its criticism. As it saw it, "the third term," which Roosevelt wanted all along, "needed a war." The speech clearly showed "the duplicity of a man given to histrionics, a man obsessed with visions of extraordinary grandeur, and a man who craftily seeks his way into the sympathies and illusions of a people who may be deluded by such craftiness. He has a low opinion of the sound judgment of the people of the United States." See "Mr. Roosevelt Confesses."

85. The term comes from the title of Clarke's book on Ickes, *Roosevelt's Warrior*.

86. See James C. Hagerty, "Reaction to Speech Pleases Willkie; He May Tour West," *New York Times*, August 19, 1940, where Hagerty reports that Ickes was "named by President Roosevelt to present the New Deal retort." Fittingly, Willkie would designate a surrogate, New Hampshire Senator H. Styles Bridges, to respond to Ickes.

87. "Text of Secretary Ickes's Address in Reply to Wendell Willkie's Acceptance Speech," *New York Times*, August 20, 1940.

88. "Democrats to Spur Tempo of Campaign," *New York Times*, October 13, 1940.

89. "The Text of Mayor La Guardia's Speech Backing Roosevelt," *New York Times*, September 13, 1940.

90. "Text of Wallace Speech at Madison Square Garden Labor Rally," *New York Times*, November 1, 1940.

91. "Text of Secretary Hull's Address," *New York Times*, November 2, 1940.

92. The following passages are from "Text of President Roosevelt's Final Major Campaign Address Asking for a Vote of Confidence," *New York Times*, November 3, 1940.

93. There is enough ambiguity, though, that he could also be referring self-righteously to anti–New Deal Democrats and the Court that he finally prevailed against, at least in terms of policy.

94. See "Text of Wallace Speech at Madison Square Garden Labor Rally."

95. The other two points made by Hamilton—that term limits discourage "good behavior" and encourage bad behavior—really find no counterpart in the arguments in favor of Roosevelt's third term. This is in part because the other three were so much more prominent, but also because defending the third term was so rarely, if at all, the centerpiece of the speeches of Roosevelt and his supporters.

96. For more discussion on these points, see *Federalist #70*, in *The Federalist*, ed. Henry Cabot Lodge (New York: G. P. Putnam's Sons, 1888).

97. As we will see in the concluding chapter, the concept of "lame duck" did not really even assume a place in public discourse on the presidency until FDR's second term.

CHAPTER 5

Epigraph quote is from *Autobiography of Calvin Coolidge* (New York: Cosmopolitan, 1929), 241.

1. George Gallup, "Roosevelt's Fate Is Linked to War," *New York Times*, June 6, 1943.

2. Charles Hurd, "Third Term 'Last,'" *New York Times*, November 3, 1940.

3. Bertram D. Hulen, "4th Term Is Urged on the President," *New York Times*, March 4, 1943.

4. "Insists Democrats Bar a Fourth Term," *New York Times*, April 12, 1943.

5. Turner Catledge, "Fourth-Term Race Taken for Granted," *New York Times*, July 11, 1943.

6. See "Nye, Smith Doubt Roosevelt '44 Run," *New York Times*, July 18, 1943, and "Fourth Term Race Likely, Says Hatch," *New York Times*, July 25, 1943.

7. William Allen White, "Thinks Roosevelt May Not Run Again," *New York Times*, October 11, 1943.

8. Roosevelt explained basically that he would now have to be Dr. Win the War rather than Dr. New Deal, as he had been previously.

9. John H. Crider, "Roosevelt Uses Allegory to Explain 'Win the War,'" *New York Times*, December 29, 1943.

10. Charles Hurd, "Midwest Leaders Back Roosevelt," *New York Times*, January 22, 1944.

11. John H. Crider, "No News on That, Says President to Reporter's Fourth-Term Query," *New York Times*, February 9, 1944.

12. See "Truman for Fourth Term," *New York Times*, February 23, 1944, and "Truman Declares for a Fourth Term," *New York Times*, March 27, 1944. Although in hindsight the speeches would appear to show a senator jockeying for the vice presidential nomination, this does not appear to be the case. Even up to the last moment—the actual nomination—Truman seems to have had no real interest in the vice presidential nod.

13. "Wagner Comes Out for Fourth Term," *New York Times*, April 2, 1944.

14. "President Not to Run, Wheeler Believes," *New York Times*, April 19, 1944.

15. Warren Moscow, "Roosevelt Drive Is Started Here," *New York Times*, May 9, 1944.

16. Turner Catledge, "President Hints of Stay in Office," *New York Times*, May 27, 1944.

17. "The President's Letter," *New York Times*, July 12, 1944. See also Charles Hurd, "President's Stand," *New York Times*, July 12, 1944. Not surprisingly, Republicans would be nearly apoplectic in their criticisms of Roosevelt's "soldier" comment. See Warren Moscow, "President Chided on 'Soldier' Role," *New York Times*, July 13, 1944.

18. Warren Moscow," Rickenbacker Hits at a 4th Term; Calls for War Sacrifice by Labor," *New York Times*, February 23, 1943.

19. "Insists Democrats Bar a Fourth Term," *New York Times*, April 12, 1943.

20. "Spangler Demands Roosevelt Say 'No,'" *New York Times*, May 8, 1943.

21. "Taft Says Roosevelt Exalts Federal Power and Makes 'Mere Shell' of Our Institutions," *New York Times*, March 12, 1944.

22. "Text of Governor Dewey's Formal Acceptance of the Presidential Nomination," *New York Times*, June 29, 1944. See also, for instance, "Text of Dewey Speech Arraigning New Deal in Home and Foreign Fields," *New York Times*, October 17, 1944.

23. "Text of Gov. Dewey's Address at Portland, Ore.," *New York Times*, September 20, 1994. See also Warren Moscow, "Dewey Attacks Roosevelt's Role as Indispensable," *New York Times*, September 20, 1944.

24. "Text of Dewey's 'Point-by-Point' Denunciation of the Speech Made by the President," *New York Times*, September 26, 1944.

25. Turner Catledge, "Vote Is 1,086 to 90," *New York Times*, July 21, 1944.

26. "Truman for Fourth Term."

27. "Wagner Comes Out for Fourth Term."

28. Catledge, "Vote Is 1,086 to 90."

29. Arthur Krock, "Roosevelt Aides Now Appear Less Certain," *New York Times*, October 8, 1944.

30. See, for instance, the following: "Text of Governor Dewey's Speech on Foreign Policy before Republican Women at Louisville," *New York Times*, September 9, 1944, "Text of Dewey's Speech at Los Angeles Stressing Security," *New York Times*, September 23, 1944, and "Text of Governor Dewey's Address on 'This Must Be the Last War' at Forum Here," *New York Times*, October 19, 1944.

31. Arthur Krock, "1940 Lead Slashed," *New York Times*, November 9, 1944.

32. See Ross T. McIntire, *White House Physician* (New York: Putnam and Sons, 1946), and John T. Flynn, *The Roosevelt Myth* (New York: Doubleday, 1948).

33. Herman E. Bateman, "Observations on President Roosevelt's Health during World War II," *Mississippi Valley Historical Review* 43, no. 1 (June 1956), 102.

34. Howard G. Bruenn, "Clinical Notes on the Illness and Death of President Franklin D. Roosevelt," *Annals of Internal Medicine* 72 (1970).

35. Geoffrey C. Ward, ed., *Closest Companion: The Unknown Story of the Intimate Friendship between Franklin Roosevelt and Margaret Suckley* (Boston: Houghton Mifflin, 1995).

36. All oral histories are taken from the Truman Presidential Library and Museum website, http://www.trumanlibrary.org/oralhist/oral_his.htm, accessed August 2, 2007.

37. The charge of nostalgia is leveled at Doris Kearns Goodwin's *No Ordinary Time: Franklin and Eleanor, the Home Front in World War II* (New York: Simon and Schuster, 1994) by Robert H. Ferrell in his *The Dying President: Franklin D. Roosevelt, 1944–1945* (Columbia: University of Missouri Press, 1998), 2. See also Hugh E. Evans, *The Hidden Campaign: FDR's Health and the 1944 Election* (Armonk, N.Y.: M. E. Sharpe, 2002); Robert E. Gilbert, *The Mortal Presidency: Illness and Anguish in the White House* (New York: Fordham University Press, 1998); and Kenneth R. Crispell and Carlos F. Gomez, *Hidden Illness in the White House* (Durham: Duke University Press, 1988). James Bishop's *FDR's Last Year, April 1944–April 1945* (New York: William Morrow, 1974) deals with Roosevelt's illnesses during his last year but is clearly more inclined to hagiography than the more recent work, Bishop's aim being "to draw a highly personal—yes intimate—portrait of a great leader in his time of trial" (2).

38. Gilbert, *Mortal Presidency*, 52–53.

39. See chart of FDR's blood pressure readings in Ferrell, *Dying President*, 153–56.

40. With the possibility of Roosevelt pursuing a fourth term in 1944 a very real one, press stories might tend to focus more on FDR's health in 1944 than, say, in 1942 or 1943. And, indeed, *New York Times* accounts of FDR's health are significantly fewer in those years. Still, it was also the case that Roosevelt's physical condition was deteriorating significantly in late 1943 and early 1944, and thus questions were raised by reporters and others about Roosevelt's health. See Table 4.2 in Evans, *Hidden Campaign*, 51.

41. Gilbert, *Mortal Presidency*, 54.

42. Bruenn, "Clinical Notes," 580.

43. Bishop, *FDR's Last Year*, 6.

44. Bruenn, "Clinical Notes," 580–84.

45. Ibid., 583.

46. James MacGregor Burns, *Roosevelt: The Soldier of Freedom* (New York: Harcourt, Brace, Jovanovich, 1970), 449. Although dated, this is a "classic" and award-winner in the annals of Roosevelt biography.

47. *Closest Companion*, 295, 296 emphasis in the original. Burns, *Roosevelt: Soldier of Freedom*, suggests as much in his retelling of Bruenn's examination and later developments; see 449–51. See also Goodwin, *No Ordinary Time*, 496–97.

48. See Ferrell, *Dying President*, 72. See also *Closest Companion*, 372, for one of the several entries depicting Fox's role in blood pressure readings.

49. Quoted in Ferrell, *Dying President*, 108.

50. Evans, *Hidden Campaign*, 60. Evans especially does a nice job of showing the disconnection between McIntire's statements to the press and the reality of FDR's health.

51. Walter Trohan, "Disclose Heart Specialist Is with Roosevelt," *Chicago Tribune*, August 6, 1944.

52. John C. Crider, "President's Health 'Satisfactory'; Unique Report Made by McIntire," *New York Times*, April 5, 1944. Roosevelt himself had engaged in similar duplicity a few days earlier—perhaps unwittingly, for we cannot say with certainty when Roosevelt found out about his heart condition—telling the press that he had been suffering from a mild case of bronchitis. See John H. Crider, "Roosevelt Was Ill of Bronchitis, but Says That He Is Feeling Fine," *New York Times*, March 29, 1944.

53. Charles Hurd, "President's Health 'Excellent,' Admiral McIntire Reports," *New York Times*, June 9, 1944.

54. "Says President Is Fit," *New York Times*, September 26, 1944.

55. "Roosevelt Is Well, His Physician Says," *New York Times*, October 13, 1944.

56. Robert Ferrell details interesting evidence to suggest that officials in the White House—perhaps even with Roosevelt's knowledge—called in J. Edgar Hoover and the FBI in the fall of 1944 to silence doctors at the Bethesda Naval Hospital, who had begun to gossip about President Roosevelt's condition, word of it having leaked out among the hospital staff. *Dying President*, 87–88.

57. "Whispering Drive Seen by Hannegan," *New York Times*, October 14, 1944. The *Chicago Tribune* would challenge that there was a "whispering" campaign, observing that "[t]here is no need to whisper. That [Roosevelt's health] is one of the principal issues of this campaign and cannot be evaded by false appeals to delicacy." See "Mr. Roosevelt's Health," *Chicago Tribune*, October 17, 1944.

58. Truman Presidential Library and Museum, Robert G. Nixon interview, October 16, 1970, http://www.trumanlibrary.org/oralhist/nixon2.htm, accessed August 2, 2007, emphasis in the original.

59. Truman Presidential Library and Museum, Joseph A. Fox interview, http://www.trumanlibrary.org/oralhist/foxja.htm, accessed August 2, 2007.

60. Walter Trohan, "F.D.R. Switches 1945 Inaugural to White House," *Chicago Tribune*, November 15, 1944. Robert Nixon would similarly characterize the inaugural: "He [Roosevelt] was failing. Perhaps that was the main reason why he didn't go through this agonizing public inaugural on the steps of the Capitol." Truman Presidential Library and Museum, Robert G. Nixon interview, October 16, 1970, http://www.trumanlibrary.org/oralhist/nixon2.htm, accessed August 2, 2007. See also Gilbert, *Mortal Presidency*, 60.

61. Truman Presidential Library and Museum, Harry Easley interview, http://www.trumanlibrary.org/oralhist/easleyh.htm, accessed August 2, 2007. Many of Roosevelt's aides and visitors in December and January had indeed noticed his poor appearance, loss of weight, and overall haggardness. See Gilbert, *Mortal Presidency*, 59–60, and Evans, *Hidden Campaign*, 84–86, for further discussion of Roosevelt's health at this time.

62. Truman Presidential Library and Museum, Joseph A. Fox interview, http://www.trumanlibrary.org/oralhist/foxja.htm, accessed August 2, 2007.

63. "Roosevelt Health Fine, Says Doctor," *New York Times*, January 21, 1945.

64. Flynn, *Roosevelt Myth*, 397.

65. See Gilbert, *Mortal Presidency*, 60–69; Ferrell, *Dying President*, 98–110; Crispell and Gomez, *Hidden Illness*, 125–33, 146; and Burns, *Roosevelt: Soldier of Freedom*, 564–80.

66. Gilbert, *Mortal Presidency*, 61.

67. Ibid., 62.

68. "President Returns Home in 'Great' Health; 'He Is in Grand Spirits,' Secretary Reports," *New York Times*, March 1, 1945.

69. Truman Presidential Library and Museum, Robert K. Walsh interview, http://www.trumanlibrary.org/oralhist/walshr.htm, accessed August 2, 2007.

70. Truman Presidential Library and Museum, Carleton Kent interview, http://www.trumanlibrary.org/oralhist/kentc.htm#oh1, accessed August 2, 2007.

71. Truman Presidential Library and Museum, Robert L. Riggs interview, http://www.trumanlibrary.org/oralhist/riggsrl.htm, accessed August 2, 2007.

72. Truman Presidential Library and Museum, Samuel Rosenman interview, http://www.trumanlibrary.org/oralhist/rosenmn.htm#oh1, accessed August 2, 2007.

73. Arthur Krock, "End Comes Suddenly at Warm Springs," New York *Times*, April 13, 1945. See also McIntire's *White House Physician* for similar arguments.

74. "Roosevelt Health Long Under Doubt," *New York Times*, April 13, 1945.

75. "Roosevelt's Health Failed Steadily Since Late in '43," *Chicago Tribune*, April 13, 1945.

76. David McCullough, "I Hardly Know Truman," *American Heritage* 43, no. 4 (July/August 1992).

77. See, for instance, Evans, *Hidden Campaign*, 62–66; Gilbert, *Mortal Presidency*, 57–58; and David McCullough, *Truman* (New York: Simon & Schuster, 1992), 295–96, 308. Burns, on the other hand, downplays the whispering about Roosevelt's health and says only that "whether the President completed another term or not, the next Vice President would be in a commanding position in 1948." See *Roosevelt: Soldier of Freedom*, 503.

78. Truman Presidential Library and Museum, Edwin W. Pauley interview, March 3, 1971, http://www.trumanlibrary.org/oralhist/pauleye.htm#oh1, accessed August 2, 2007.

79. Robert H. Ferrell, *Choosing Truman: The Democratic Convention of 1944* (Columbia: University of Missouri Press, 1994), 3.

80. See ibid., 14–26, for a discussion of the leaders' and Roosevelt's handling of Wallace.

81. Ferrell, *Dying President*, 78.

82. See, for instance, Edwin Pauley's discussion of the letter, Truman Presidential Library and Museum, Edwin W. Pauley interview, March 3, 1971, http://www.trumanlibrary.org/oralhist/pauleye.htm#oh1, accessed August 2, 2007.

83. Burns, *Roosevelt: Soldier of Freedom*, 509.

84. *Closest Companion*, 318, emphasis in the original.

85. Truman Presidential Library and Museum, Robert G. Nixon interview, October 9, 1970, http://www.trumanlibrary.org/oralhist/nixon1.htm, accessed August 2, 2007. See also Ferrell, *Choosing Truman*, 6–7, for the politics of the nomination.

86. Alonzo L. Hamby, *Man of the People: A Life of Harry S. Truman* (New York: Oxford University Press, 1995), 280.

87. Donald Young, *American Roulette: The History and Dilemma of the Vice Presidency* (New York: Holt, Rinehart and Winston, 1965), 203.

88. McCullough, *Truman*, 320–21.

89. Ferrell, *Dying President*, 88. Truman would later suggest that he and Roosevelt had a much closer relationship, but this is considered to be an exaggeration on Truman's part. See Ferrell, *Choosing Truman*, 8.

90. As McCullough recounts (*Truman*, 333, 339): "Vice President Truman had been told only that if it was 'absolutely urgent,' he could make contact with the President through the White House." In his eighty-five days as vice president, outside of cabinet meetings, Truman met with Roosevelt *twice* and at "neither time was anything of consequence discussed."

91. Truman Presidential Library and Museum, Gould Lincoln interview, http://www.trumanlibrary.org/oralhist/lincolng.htm, accessed August 2, 2007.

92. Quoted in McCullough, *Truman*, 355.

93. Edwin Pauley, however, disputed this widely accepted account, saying, "[p]eople kept referring things to Truman that would ordinarily have gone to Roosevelt, except for his health; and Truman's visiting pouch to the White House I'll guarantee you was very large with important things to be done by the President. More and more you found Roosevelt relying on Truman's advice and he was actually putting Truman forward toward the last." See Truman Presidential Library and Museum, Edwin W. Pauley interview, March 4, 1971, http://www.trumanlibrary.org/oralhist/pauleye.htm#oh2, accessed August 2, 2007.

94. Goodwin, *No Ordinary Time*, 496.

95. Conrad Black, *Franklin Delano Roosevelt* (New York: Public Affairs, 2003), 1093. Black is an interesting biographer of Roosevelt, to say the least: a political conservative, yet a great admirer of Roosevelt.

96. See Ferrell, *Dying President*, 76.

97. Goodwin, *No Ordinary Time*, 495–97.

98. Ted Morgan, *FDR: A Biography* (New York: Simon & Schuster, 1985), 737.

99. See Black, *Franklin*, 1111, and Evans, *Hidden Campaign*, 66–70.

100. Hamby, *Man of the People*, 284.

101. Young, *American Roulette*, 174, 237, emphasis on the original.

102. Evans, *Hidden Campaign*, 83.

103. Flynn had been a columnist for the progressive *New Republic* during the 1930s and an early supporter of Roosevelt. However, he increasingly turned against Roosevelt and his policies and particularly involvement in World War II. He would go on to work with the American First movement, a conservative anti-interventionist group. He would obviously have an ideological grudge against Roosevelt, and this clearly emerges in his book. For more on Flynn, see John E. Moser, *Right Turn: John T. Flynn and the Transformation of American Liberalism* (New York: New York University Press, 2005).

104. Flynn, *Roosevelt Myth*, 396–97, emphasis on the original.

105. Ibid., 369, 371.

106. See *Closest Companion*, 344–66, where Suckely describes Roosevelt's routine at Warm Springs in November–December 1944.

107. *Closest Companion*, 330, 401.

108. Coolidge, *Autobiography*, 241.

109. Lucy Mercer Rutherford was in all likelihood the mistress of FDR at some point between 1913, when she came to work for the Roosevelts, and 1920, when she married. There is some evidence that their affair continued in some form in the years thereafter. Rutherford was with Roosevelt in Warm Springs when he died. See Resa Willis, *FDR and Lucy* (New York: Routledge, 2004), for a recent treatment of the relationship.

110. *Closest Companion*, 351.

111. Ibid., 309, emphasis added.

112. "Roosevelt's Health Failed Steadily," *Chicago Tribune*.

113. Truman Presidential Library and Museum, Robert G. Nixon interview, October 9, 1970, http://www.trumanlibrary.org/oralhist/nixon1.htm, accessed August 2, 2007.

114. Roosevelt specifically outlined this possibility to Daisy Suckley in May 1944: "If I know I am not going to be able to carry on for another four years, it wouldn't be fair to the American people to run for another term." He said he would wait to see how he felt. He allowed, though, that he had his own candidate for president if he decided to step down. Cautioning Daisy, "don't breathe it to a soul," he said that he had in mind the industrialist Henry J. Kaiser, a man with almost no political experience. Roosevelt thought Kaiser would deal well with Stalin and Churchill and that he would ask his (Roosevelt's) advice when needed. See *Closest Companion*, 302. Of course, nothing came of this fleeting notion, but it does suggest that Roosevelt worried he might not be able to continue in the office, and just as importantly, it manifests a certain singularity of self that undoubtedly comes with being president, especially a third-term president.

115. Evans, *Hidden Campaign*, xiv.

116. Flynn, *Roosevelt Myth*, 409. Flynn says that "two dying men" were pushed on the country in 1944: Roosevelt and Harry Hopkins, his key advisor. The quote is still accurately rendered, though, when applied singularly to Roosevelt.

117. Ferrell, *Dying President*, 4.

118. "Thomas Jefferson to John Taylor, January 6, 1805," in *The Writings of Thomas Jefferson*, vol. 11, ed. Andrew A. Lipscomb and Albert Ellery Bergh (Washington, D.C.: Thomas Jefferson Memorial Association, 1905), 57.

119. "Thomas Jefferson to Citizens of Philadelphia, February 3, 1809," in *The Writings of Thomas Jefferson*, vol. 16, 329.

CHAPTER 6

Representative Michener, a Republican supporter of the amendment, is quoted in the epigraph from his speech during the House debates over the Twenty-second Amendment (*Congressional Record*, 80th Congress, 1st Session, 1947, 863).

1. William J. Clinton, *Weekly Compilation of Presidential Documents* 36, no. 49 (2000), 2992–93.

2. "Clinton Calls for Third Term," BBC News, May 29, 2003, http://news .bbc.co.uk/2/hi/americas/2946802.stm, accessed February 18, 2009.

3. A recent exception to this rule is James R. Hedtke, *Lame Duck Presidents—Myth or Reality* (Lewiston, N.Y.: Edwin Mellen Press, 2002). Among other things, the book looks at the Twenty-second Amendment's effect on the second-term successes of Presidents Eisenhower, Reagan, and Clinton.

4. See Fredrick D. Zucker, "The Adoption of the Twenty-Second Amendment," PhD diss., Pennsylvania State University, 1958, 120–29. As Zucker's study is exhaustive on many fronts, the reader is directed to it for additional texture and details.

5. Roberta S. Sigel and David J. Butler, "The Public and the No Third Term Tradition: Inquiry into Attitudes Toward Power," *Midwest Journal of Political Science* 8, no. 1 (February 1964), 39.

6. But see, for instance, Thomas E. Cronin, "Two Cheers for the Twenty-second Amendment," *Christian Science Monitor*, February 23, 1987.

7. See "The 22d Amendment," *New York Times*, February 28, 1951.

8. One of the most searching of these analyses was Henry Steele Commager, "Only Two Terms for a President," *New York Times*, April 27, 1947. Among the major early scholarly statements was Paul G. Willis and George L. Willis, "The Politics of the Twenty-second Amendment," *Western Political Quarterly* 5 (September 1952).

9. James MacGregor Burns and Jack Walter Peltason, *Government by the People*, 3rd edition (Englewood Cliffs, N.J.: Prentice-Hall, 1957), 471.

10. Louis W. Koenig, *The Chief Executive* (New York: Harcourt, Brace, & World, 1964), 65–66.

11. Joseph E. Kallenbach, *The American Chief Executive* (New York: Harper & Row, 1966), 194, 195. Kallenbach refers to a "survey of scholarly opinion made by Senator Kefauver," who was launching a movement to repeal the amendment in 1957. See also Paul B. Davis, "The Results and Implications of the Enactment of the Twenty-Second Amendment," *Presidential Studies Quarterly* 9, no. 3 (Summer 1979), 297–300, where Davis discusses in detail Estes Kefauver's survey.

12. Clinton Rossiter, *The American Presidency*, 2nd ed. (New York: Mentor, 1960), 222–24, 226–27.

13. Edward S. Corwin, *The President: Office and Powers*, 1787–1957, 4th ed. (New York: New York University Press, 1957), 37–38, emphasis in the original.

14. See Zucker, "Adoption of Twenty-Second Amendment," chapters 7 and 8, for a detailed look at the congressional voting on the amendment, with an emphasis on partisan breakdown.

15. *Congressional Record*, 80th Congress, 1st Session, 1947, 847.

16. Ibid., 860.

17. Ibid., 842.

18. Ibid., 852.

19. Ibid., 1771.

20. Ibid., 1778.

21. Ibid., 1773.

22. Ibid., 842.

23. Ibid., 866. See also the similar characterization by Representative John E. Lyle (D-TX), ibid., 854.

24. Ibid., 859.

25. Ibid., 1972.

26. Reported in Joseph E. Kallenbach, "Constitutional Limitations on Reeligibility of National and State Chief Executives," *American Political Science Review* 46 (1952), 450.

27. *Congressional Record*, 80th Congress, 1st Session, 1947, 1772.

28. Quoted by Senator Hill in ibid., 1771.

29. Ibid., 850.

30. Ibid., 859–60.

31. Ibid., 1995.

32. Ibid., 868.

33. Ibid., 1778.

34. Ibid., 852.

35. Ibid.

36. Ibid., 1866.

37. Ibid., 856.

38. Ibid.

39. Ibid., 858.

40. Ibid., 862.

41. Ibid., 1948.

42. Ibid., 1971.

43. Ibid., 1965.

44. Ibid., 848.

45. See ibid., 843.

46. Ibid., 852.

47. Theodore Roosevelt quoted by Representative McCormack in ibid., 843.

48. Ibid., 1799.

49. Ibid., 1949.

50. For two prominent commentaries from the 1950s, see Richard L. Strout, "The 22d Amendment: A Second Look," *New York Times*, July 28, 1957, and Arthur Krock, "Two-Term Amendment in Eisenhower's Case," *New York Times*, March 3, 1957. The former sees waning influence in the presidency because of the amendment, whereas the latter takes the opposite position.

51. See, for instance, Senator Hill in *Congressional Record*, 80th Congress, 1st Session, 1947, 1771.

52. *Congressional Record*, 80th Congress, 1st Session, 1947, 843.

53. Ibid., 862.

54. Ibid., 856.

55. Ibid., 850.

56. See John D. Morris, "Limit of Two Terms for Any President Approved by House," *New York Times*, February 7, 1947, where Morris notes that members at least tried to keep politics out of the debates.

57. *Congressional Record*, 80th Congress, 1st Session, 1947, 869.

58. It is unfortunate but not surprising. Republicans were in a difficult position. To praise Truman's leadership might have helped to advance their cause in supporting the Twenty-second Amendment, but politically it would have been unwise, especially with the 1948 election upcoming.

59. *Congressional Record*, 80th Congress, 1st Session, 1947, 1946.

60. Ibid., 1681.

61. Ibid., 1971.

62. Ibid., 842.

63. Ibid., 851.

64. Ibid., 1681.

65. Ibid., 862.

66. See particularly Bruce Miroff's concept of the president "monopolizing the public space." Bruce Miroff, "Monopolizing the Public Space: The President as a Problem for Democratic Politics," in *Rethinking the Presidency*, ed. Thomas Cronin (Boston: Little, Brown, 1982). Yet again, however, we see that the Twenty-second Amendment, while it might help somewhat to encourage "multiple leadership," is rather limited in effectively curtailing presidential domination of the "public space" and the political system.

67. *Congressional Record*, 80th Congress, 1st Session, 1947, 863.

68. Ibid., 862.

69. Rossiter is a notable exception.

70. See John Gerring, *Party Ideologies in America*, 1828–1996 (New York: Cambridge University Press, 1998), for a discussion of the evolution of party ideologies. Most scholars assume, as does Gerring, a philosophical and political connection between the Whig and Republican parties.

71. See chapter 10, "A Whig in the White House," in David Donald, *Lincoln Reconsidered: Essays on the Civil War Era* (New York: Vintage Books, 1961).

72. The incumbent Republican president, Taft, especially, would make this one of his central criticisms of Roosevelt. For more on the debates between Taft and Roosevelt in the 1912 election, see Michael J. Korzi, "Our Chief Magistrate and His Powers: A Reconsideration of William Howard Taft's 'Whig' Theory of Presidential Leadership," *Presidential Studies Quarterly* 33, no. 2 (June 2003).

73. Bush showed considerable deference to Congress in domestic affairs,

wielding the veto only once through 2006, for instance. On the other hand, he clearly pushed presidential authority in matters of war and foreign policy.

74. For a skillful analysis of the emergence of "presidential populism," see Terri Bimes, "The Metamorphosis of Presidential Populism," PhD diss., Yale University, 1999.

75. Obviously, neither Douglas nor Bryan attained the presidency, but their *campaigns* for the presidency established benchmarks for the growing popularization of the presidency in the nineteenth and early twentieth centuries.

76. Jackson, for instance, at numerous points during his presidency advocated a single term for presidents but served two terms. See Hedtke, *Lame Duck Presidents*, 39. Grover Cleveland, had he been more popular with Democrats in 1896, more than likely would have accepted renomination and run for a third term. Woodrow Wilson was also on record supporting term limits (the Democratic platform in 1912 recommended one term for the president), but in "neither word nor act did Wilson discourage the third-term nomination he was destined not to get." See Fred Rodell, *Democracy and the Third Term* (New York: Howell, Soskin, 1940), 74–74, 82.

CHAPTER 7

The epigraph quotes White (speaking about FDR) and is taken from Donald Young, *American Roulette: The History and Dilemma of the Vice Presidency* (New York: Holt, Rinehart and Winston, 1965), 194.

1. Brian Braiker, "A Sorry State: A Web Exclusive," *Newsweek*, http://www.msnbc.msn.com/id/16840614/site/newsweek, accessed January 29, 2007.

2. Lewis L. Gould, *The Modern American Presidency* (Lawrence: University Press of Kansas, 2003), xiii.

3. A searching early analysis is Henry Steele Commager, "Only Two Terms for a President," *New York Times*, April 27, 1947. Among the major early scholarly statements was Paul G. Willis and George L. Willis, "The Politics of the Twenty-second Amendment," *Western Political Quarterly* 5 (September 1952). See also Joseph E. Kallenbach, *The American Chief Executive* (New York: Harper & Row, 1966), 194, 195. Kallenbach refers to a "survey of scholarly opinion made by Senator [Estes] Kefauver," who was launching a movement to repeal the amendment in 1957.

4. David Kocieniewski, "The Lame Duck's Waddle to Oblivion," *New York Times*, November 19, 2006.

5. Michael B. Grossman, Martha Joynt Kumar, and Francis E. Rourke, "Second-Term Presidencies: The Aging of Administrations," in *The Presidency and the Political System*, 6th ed., Michael Nelson (Washington, D.C.: CQ Press, 2000), 236.

6. Arthur Krock, "Two-Term Amendment in Eisenhower's Case," *New York Times*, March 3, 1957.

7. Richard L. Strout, "The 22d Amendment: A Second Look," *New York Times*, July 28, 1957.

8. "Not Too Lame," *New York Times*, August 8, 1957.

9. Strout, "The 22d Amendment."

10. Paul B. Davis, "The Results and Implications of the Enactment of the Twenty-Second Amendment," *Presidential Studies Quarterly* 9, no. 3 (Summer 1979), 295.

11. Tom Wicker, "A 'Lame Duck' Test," *New York Times*, October 28, 1984.

12. Steven V. Roberts, "Battered but Still Swinging, Reagan Enters Final Rounds," *New York Times*, October 11, 1987.

13. Anthony Lake, "Reagan Disproves A Lame-Duck Myth," *New York Times*, April 24, 1988. It is instructive to note that Lake served as a national security advisor in the Nixon administration but also later in the Clinton administration.

14. Todd S. Purdum, "A Wounded President Strives Not to Become a Lame Duck," *New York Times*, December 8, 1994.

15. Todd S. Purdum, "Is Clinton's Legacy Clouded?" *New York Times*, August 23, 1998, emphasis added.

16. David S. Broder, "Clinton's Not the Only One with Legacy Problems," *Washington Post*, November 7, 1999.

17. Peter Baker and John F. Harris, "To Boost His Presidency and Party, Clinton Leaps into the Policy Void," *Washington Post*, January 11, 1998.

18. Marc Lacey, "Clinton Spoofs Himself as Lame Duck Leader," *New York Times*, May 1, 2000.

19. James W. Davis, *The American Presidency*, 2nd ed. (Westport, Conn.: Praeger, 1995), 406. It is worth noting that Davis provides no citation for this claim about "experts."

20. Gould, *Modern American Presidency*, 98.

21. James R. Hedtke, *Lame Duck Presidents—Myth or Reality* (Lewiston, N.Y.: Edwin Mellen Press, 2002), 70.

22. Hedtke is also careful to make sure that he focuses especially on the last two years of the second term, as they would seem, according to the lame duck theory, to evidence more signs of weakening, since the term is drawing to a close.

23. Hedtke, *Lame Duck Presidents*, 152.

24. As seen in chapter 3, however, one could argue that Coolidge's silence on the third term until August of 1927 was partly a matter of preserving his power in Washington. The *New York Times* suggested as much. See "Not To Be Forced," *New York Times*, May 1, 1927.

25. Rossiter declares in no uncertain terms his support of the modern presidency. See Clinton Rossiter, *The American Presidency*, 2nd ed. (New York: Mentor, 1960), 226–27.

26. As seen in chapter 3, there was obviously a movement for a third term for Grant in 1876, but it did not even reach the nomination stage, whereas in 1880 Grant would be a serious candidate at the Republican National Convention. Even if we acknowledge that Grant was, at least for a time, a serious candidate in 1876, it is simply not the case, given Grant's model of leadership, that he used that threat to secure persuasive powers and advantages for himself to stave off his lame duck status. Some might even conclude that Grant's model of presidential leadership was lame duck through and through.

27. Hedtke, *Lame Duck Presidents*, 152.

28. Ibid., 214.

29. William G. Howell and Kenneth R. Mayer, "The Last One Hundred Days," *Presidential Studies Quarterly* 35, no. 3 (September 2005), 534.

30. David A. Crockett, "The Contemporary Presidency: 'An Excess of Refinement': Lame Duck Presidents in Constitutional and Historical Context," *Presidential Studies Quarterly* 38, no. 4 (December 2008). Crockett also addresses the literature on "second-term blues," as I do. Additionally, see Stephen Skowronek, *The Politics Presidents Make* (Cambridge, Mass.: Belknap Press of Harvard University Press, 1993).

31. Peter Baker and Michael A. Fletcher, "Elections May Leave Bush an Early Lame Duck," *Washington Post*, October 18, 2006.

32. John Podhoretz, "Lame Duck Bush Is Left Crippled by a Crushing Vote of No Confidence," *New York Post*, November 8, 2006.

33. Dan Balz, "The State of the President: Beleaguered," *Washington Post*, January 24, 2007.

34. Howard Kurtz, "The Press, Turning Up Its Nose at Lame Duck," *Washington Post*, February 5, 2007.

35. Thomas Friedman, "Running on Empty: The Democrats Must Take the Lead on Iraq and Energy," *New York Times*, January 30, 2007. This column is also highlighted and quoted in Kurtz, "The Press."

36. See Tim Shipman, "Allies Desert Lame Duck President," *Sunday Telegraph*, April 8, 2007.

37. Marsha Mercer, "Bush Makes Threats by Day, Jokes by Night," *Seattle-Post Intelligencer*, April 4, 2007.

38. Anne Davies, "Taking Aim at a Lame Duck," *The Age*, June 16, 2007.

39. "Bush: Together, at Last, at Twilight Time," *The Hotline*, July 2, 2007. The article is a compilation of U.S. news reports following the failure of immigration reform.

40. Peter Baker and Michael A. Fletcher, "Rove to Leave White House

Post; Transition Continues among Bush Aides," *Washington Post*, August 14, 2007.

41. Tim Reid, "End of 'Bush's Brain' Will Bring Down the Curtain on Lame-Duck President," *Times* (London), August 14, 2007.

42. John Podesta, "Last Guys Standing," *Washington Post*, August 16, 2007.

43. "Veto Victory," *Wall Street Journal*, July 18, 2007.

44. Richard N. Haass, "Don't Count Him Out Yet," *Newsweek International*, July 23, 2007.

45. Shane Harris, "Slight Limp, Not Lame," *National Journal*, July 28 2007.

46. James Kitfield, "Options Fewer in Iraq," *National Journal*, July 28 2007.

47. Harris, "Slight Limp, Not Lame."

48. Margaret Kritz, "Thumbing His Nose," *National Journal*, July 28, 2007.

49. This conclusion is consistent with that of Howell and Mayer, "Last One Hundred Days."

50. Podesta, "Last Guys Standing."

51. Howell and Mayer, "Last One Hundred Days," 550.

52. Alexander Hamilton, *Federalist #72*, in *The Federalist*, ed. Henry Cabot Lodge (New York: G. P. Putnam's Sons, 1888), 452–53.

53. The term comes from *Second-Term Blues: How George W. Bush Has Governed*, ed. John C. Fortier and Norman J. Ornstein (Washington, D.C.: Brookings Institution Press, 2007).

54. Fortier and Ornstein, *Second-Term Blues*, 1.

55. Grossman, Kumar, and Rourke, "Second-Term Presidencies," 225–26.

56. Ibid., 232.

57. Fortier and Ornstein, *Second-Term Blues*, 2.

58. Grossman, Kumar, and Rourke, "Second-Term Presidencies," 226.

59. Fortier and Ornstein, *Second-Term Blues*, 2–3.

60. Grossman, Kumar, and Rourke, "Second-Term Presidencies," 230.

61. Ibid., 229.

62. Fortier and Ornstein, *Second-Term Blues*, 4.

63. Ibid.

64. See Colleen J. Shogan, "The Contemporary Presidency: The Sixth Year Curse," *Presidential Studies Quarterly* 36, no. 1 (March 2006), for an in-depth discussion of weakening political coalitions.

65. Fortier and Ornstein, *Second-Term Blues*, 5.

66. See James E. Campbell, "The Presidential Surge and Its Midterm Decline in Congressional Elections, 1868–1988," *Journal of Politics* 53, no. 2 (May 1991), for a more detailed analysis.

67. Strout, "The 22d Amendment."

68. Skowronek identifies four types of presidents in his model: reconstructive (opponents of a vulnerable regime or political coalition), articula-

tive (affiliated with a resilient regime), preemptive (opponents of a resilient regime), and disjunctive (those affiliated with a vulnerable regime). Skowronek's overall point is that historically a president's relationship to the underlying political coalition (or where a president falls in "political time") has been critical to his leadership possibilities. See Skowronek, *Politics Presidents Make*, for a fuller discussion.

69. Crockett, "The Contemporary Presidency: 'An Excess of Refinement,'" 719.

70. Fortier and Ornstein, *Second-Term Blues*, 1, make the quite important point that a president's success or failure is related to the perspectives of "other Washington institutions."

71. It is something like the repeated mispronunciation or misapplication of a word: if enough people consistently mispronounce or misapply a word, it will over time become accepted usage.

72. Gould, *Modern American Presidency*, xiii, 237.

73. Bruce Buchanan, "The Six-Year One Term Presidency: A New Look at an Old Proposal," *Presidential Studies Quarterly* 18, no. 1 (Winter 1988), 129–30.

74. Ibid., 131, 133.

75. David C. Nice, "In Retreat from Excellence: The Single Six-Year Presidential Term," *Congress & the Presidency* 13, no. 2 (Autumn 1986), 210.

76. Buchanan, "Six-Year One Term Presidency," 132.

77. Ibid., 134.

78. Nice, "In Retreat from Excellence," 210.

79. For instance, Machiavelli speaks famously in *The Prince* about the need for a prince to avoid the "hatred" of his people. Although fear should be chosen above love, hatred, or "unpopularity" is to be avoided at all costs. See Niccolo Machiavelli, *The Prince*, introduction by Harvey Mansfield (Chicago: University of Chicago Press, 1985), chapter 19. Hobbes, similarly, says that a good ruler, among other things, treats citizens equally in terms of the administration of the laws and especially taxation, avoids the passage of laws "not Necessary for the People," and endeavors to be "reverenced and beloved of his People." And this in a monarchy, no less. See Thomas Hobbes, *Leviathan*, ed. C. B. Macpherson (Penguin, 1968), 385–86, 388, 390–91.

80. Nice, "In Retreat from Excellence," 218.

81. From some perspectives, a government that is hamstrung and unable to do much would not necessarily be a bad thing. To most observers, though, political stagnation is considered detrimental.

82. Buchanan, "Six-Year One Term Presidency," 138–40.

83. Ibid., 129.

84. As mentioned in chapter 3, Lincoln said his reelection in 1864 reminded him of "a story of an old Dutch farmer, who remarked to a companion

once that 'it was not best to swap horses when crossing streams.'" Quoted in David Herbert Donald, *Lincoln* (London: Jonathan Cape, 1995), 507.

85. Thomas E. Cronin, "Two Cheers for the Twenty-second Amendment," *Christian Science Monitor*, February 23, 1987.

86. The case of Vladimir Putin accepting the position of prime minister in his successor Dmitry Medvedev's administration arguably fits this model, but surely some would ascribe less than virtuous motivations to Putin's course of action.

87. White quoted in Young, *American Roulette*, 194.

88. According to *Chicago Tribune* reporter Walter Trohan, a close friend of Farley's, Farley thought that "taking a third term would stop younger men from coming up in the party and wreck the whole structure." Truman Presidential Library and Museum, http://www.trumanlibrary.org/oralhist/trohan.htm, accessed August 2, 2007.

89. "Ratification of the Constitution by the State of North Carolina, November 21, 1789," Avalon Project, Yale Law School, http://www.yale.edu/lawweb/avalon/avalon.htm, accessed March 21, 2006.

90. See Crockett, "The Contemporary Presidency: 'An Excess of Refinement," 718–20.

91. George H. W. Bush, for instance, was clearly less ideological than his predecessor Reagan, and this played a role in how his presidency and its possibilities came together. Although succeeding JFK because of death, not retirement, Lyndon Johnson clearly had a different agenda than Kennedy and did indeed revitalize the political system during his time in office. Of course, in the case of the transition from JFK to LBJ, the influence of Kennedy's assassination on the subsequent political context should not be underestimated. However, the point is merely that the personality of Johnson played a big role in the politics of his time, even though he and Kennedy were both Democrats presiding over a relatively stable (to use Skowronek's language) political coalition or regime.

92. "Clinton Calls for Third Term," BBC News, May 29, 2003, http://news.bbc.co.uk/2/hi/americas/2946802.stm, accessed February 18, 2009. Clinton had also floated this reform in an interview with *Rolling Stone* in October 2000. See William J. Clinton, *Weekly Compilation of Presidential Documents* 36, no. 49 (2000), 2992–93.

93. James Bishop, *FDR's Last Year, April 1944–April 1945* (New York: William Morrow, 1974), ix.

94. "Thomas Jefferson to Henry Guest, January 4, 1809," in *The Writings of Thomas Jefferson*, vol. 12, ed. Andrew A. Lipscomb and Albert Ellery Bergh (Washington, D.C.: Thomas Jefferson Memorial Association, 1905), 224.

95. Hamilton, *Federalist #72*, 453.

96. Cronin, "Two Cheers for the Twenty-second Amendment."

INDEX

Ferrell, Robert, 115, 122–23
Flynn, John T., 108, 113, 120, 122, 197n103
Fortier, John, 155, 157
Fox, George, 110–11
Fox, Joseph, 112
Fremont, John, 57
Friedman, Thomas, 152

Gallup, George, 81, 83
Gallup poll, 83, 103
Garfield, James, 59, 62
Garner, John, 84–85, 88–89, 186n10
Georgia constitution, 22
Gerry, Elbridge, 29
Gillie, George W., 127
Giuliani, Rudy; and pursuit of third term, 1–2
Goodwin, Doris Kearns, 118
Gould, Lewis; and critique of Twenty-second Amendment, 144, 148, 161–62
Graham, Louis E., 127
Grant, Ulysses S., 56; and lame duck effect, 204n26; and political party corruption, 58–59, 134; and third term, 10, 44, 58–64, 134, 142, 149; world tour of, 61
Greeley, Horace; nomination of, 58–59; and one-term presidency, 58–60
Grossman, Michael B., 145, 155–56

Haass, Richard N., 153
Hall, Edwin Arthur, 132
Hamby, Alonzo, 116
Hamilton, Alexander; on crisis leadership, 8–10, 14, 36, 96–97, 99, 144–45, 165, 175n26; and debate over Twenty-second Amendment, 130; and distrust of the people, 40, 81, 99, 138; on electoral college, 30, 33–34, 178n97; on energy in the executive, 33–34; on executive reeligibility, 35–36, 40, 154, 191n95; on executive tenure, 8, 14, 99, 170; on four-year term, 34–36, 40; and plebiscitary model, 38, 99–100; on state disunity, 25; and Whig model, 33–34; views at Constitutional Convention of, 29–30
Hancock, Winfield Scott, 63
Hannegan, Robert, 105, 108, 112
Hanson, John, 24–25
Harding, Warren, 75, 140
Harrison, Byron, 84
Harrison, William Henry; and support of one-term presidency, 53–54
Hawley, Joseph, 60
Hayes, Rutherford B.; and one-term presidency, 59, 61, 63, 65
Hedtke, James R.; on lame duck effect, 148–50
Hill, Lister, 128
Hillman, Sidney, 84
Hobbes, Thomas, 163, 206n79
Hopkins, Harry, 82, 85, 89, 106
Hoover, Herbert, 140
Howell, William, 151, 154
Hull, Cordell, 85, 87–88, 97–98

Ickes, Harold, 106; and promotion of Roosevelt (Franklin) third term, 82, 85 86, 89, 97, 186n10
indispensable man theory; Dewey critique of, 106; and Jefferson, 169–70; and Roosevelt (Franklin), 92, 94–95, 106, 135–38; and Truman, 137–38; and Twenty-second Amendment debate, 135–38, 142, 166; Willkie critique of, 92, 94–95
Iran-Contra investigation, 147

Jackson, Andrew, 141–42; and one-term presidency, 52–53; and two-term tradition, 51–53
Jackson, Robert, 85
Jackson, Samuel, 107

Jefferson, Thomas, 51, 54, 63, 82, 93, 179n10; and debate over Twenty-second Amendment, 131; on executive tenure, 13, 48–50, 123, 169–70; and indispensable man theory, 169–70; on rotation, 47–51; and two-term tradition, 9–10, 41, 43, 45–46; view of the people of, 50, 138; and Whig model, 13–14, 39
Jennings, John Jr., 128, 132–33
Johnson, Lyndon B., 207n91
Jones, Jesse, 166

Kaiser, Henry J., 198n114
Kallenbach, Joseph, 125
Kelly, Edward Joseph, 86
Kennedy, John F., 207n91
Kent, Carleton, 114
Ketcham, Ralph, 51
Kilgore, Harley M., 135–36
Koenig, Louis, 125
Kritz, Margaret, 153
Krock, Arthur, 84, 90, 146
Kumar, Martha Joynt, 145, 155–56
Kurtz, Howard, 152

Lafayette, Marquis de, 46
La Follette, Robert, 74
La Guardia, Fiorello, 97
Lake, Anthony, 147
lame duck effect; and Bush (George W.), 143, 151–54, 159–60; and Clinton (William), 143, 147–48, 159; definition of, 145; and Eisenhower, 143, 146–48; and Grant, 204n26; Hedtke on, 148–50; *New York Times* on, 86, 146; and Nixon, 148; origins and development of, 145–48, 188n44; and presidential popularity, 146, 159–60, 164–65; and Reagan, 143, 147–49, 159; and Roosevelt (Franklin), 80, 86, 95, 100, 149–50, 159; scholarly analysis of, 145–51; and

Twenty-second Amendment, 11, 125–26, 136, 143–55, 160–61; and two-term tradition, 149–50, 157, 161
Landon, Alf, 89
Lewinsky, Monica, 147
Liberal Republican Party, 54; and nomination of Greeley, 58–59; and one-term presidency, 59
Lincoln, Abraham; and crisis leadership, 57, 136, 165; and one-term presidency, 56–57; and Whig beliefs, 140
Lincoln, Gould, 117
London Times, 152
Look magazine, 82
Locke, John, 3; and constitutional model, 173n4; and prerogative, 40, 173n4; and Whig model, 13, 40, 173n4
Lodge, Henry Cabot, 67
Lowi, Theodore J., 172; and plebiscitary model, 173n20
Lucas, Scott W., 128

Machiavelli, Niccolo, 163, 206n79
Madison, James, 13, 47, 132; on executive reeligibility, 28; and two-term tradition, 51
Mansfield, Harvey; on Locke, 40
Maryland constitution, 21
Mason, George; on executive reeligibility, 28; opposition to presidency, 28; and rotation, 31
Massachusetts constitution, 23; and veto power, 23
Mayer, Kenneth, 151, 154
McClurg, James, 28
McCollough, David, 117
McCormack, John W., 135–36
McIntire, Ross; and health of Roosevelt (Franklin), 108–14, 118
McKellar, Kenneth, 90
McKinley, William, 44, 75; and rejection of third term, 66

McNutt, Paul, 84
Michelson, Charles, 84
Michener, Earl C., 134, 137, 139–40
Miroff, Bruce, 201n66
modern presidency. *See* plebiscitary model of executive
monarchy, 37–38; and tenure restrictions, 6, 37–38; Whig view of, 8
Monroe, James, 50; and two-term tradition, 51, 180n25
Montesquieu; on executive tenure, 31
Morgan, Ted, 118
Morris, Gouvernour; on legislative selection of executive, 28
Morris, Lewis, 17
Mundt, Karl E., 134
Murphy, Frank, 82
Myers, Francis, J., 133

National Journal, 153
New Deal, 82–84, 87–88, 90–91, 94, 97–99, 106
New Hampshire constitution, 18
New Jersey constitution, 20
New Jersey plan, 27
New Nationalism, 68, 70
New York constitution; influence on presidency of, 22; and veto power, 22
New York Times, 11, 57, 58, 72–73, 104, 109; on Grant third term, 60, 62–63; on lame duck effect, 86, 146; on one-term presidency, 60, 73; on Roosevelt (Franklin) health, 114; on Roosevelt (Franklin) third term, 81, 83, 88–90; on Roosevelt (Theodore) third term, 68–70; and support of Twenty-second Amendment, 125
Newsweek, 143
Nixon, Richard M.; and lame duck effect, 148
Nixon, Robert, 112, 116, 122
North Carolina constitution, 21–22

Obama, Barack, 2, 171n6
Obasanjo, Olusegun, 2
O'Daniel, W. Lee, 136
O'Hara, Joseph P., 133–34, 137
one-term presidency, 10, 43, 63, 77, 161; and Bryan, 65–66, 71; and Cleveland, 64–65; Democratic Party and, 54–55, 65–66, 71–74; and Greeley, 58–60; and Harrison, 53–54; and Hayes, 59, 61, 63, 65; and Jackson, 52–53; and Liberal Republican Party platform, 59; and Lincoln, 56–57; *New York Times* on, 60, 73; and political party corruption, 58–61, 64–65; and Polk, 54–55, 180n36; and Republican Party, 56–60; and Whig Party, 10, 53–54; and Wilson (Woodrow), 65, 72–73. *See also* six-year term reform
Ornstein, Norman, 155, 157
Outlook magazine, 69

Pauley, Edwin, 115, 197n93
Peabody, Bruce, 47
Peltason, Jack Walter, 125
Pendleton Act, 59
Penn, William, 17
Pepper, Claude, 129, 135, 138
Perkins, Frances, 85, 106
Pennsylvania constitution; and plural executive, 20–21; and rotation, 21; and Whig model, 20–21
Pinckney, Charles, 27, 29
plebiscitary model of executive, 8–9, 81; and Anti-Federalists, 38; critique of, 39; and Democratic Party, 141–42; and executive tenure, 38–42; and Hamilton, 38, 99–100; and Lowi, 173n20; and Roosevelt (Franklin), 9, 99–100; and Roosevelt (Theodore), 8–9, 38–39, 42, 68, 173n20; and Tulis, 173n20; and Twenty-second Amendment, 140–42; view of the

plebiscitary model of executive (*cont.*)
people of, 39; and Wilson (Woodrow), 38, 71
Podesta, John, 152–53
Podhoretz, John, 151
political party corruption; and Grant, 58–59, 134; and one-term presidency, 58–61, 64–65; and Roosevelt (Franklin) third term, 94; and rotation, 62–64, 69–71, 162
political scandals; and second terms, 156–59
Polk, James; one-term presidency and, 54–55, 180n36; and pressure for reelection, 55
prime ministers; and executive tenure, 172n15
privy councils. *See* executive councils
Progressive Party. *See* Bull Moose Party
Putin, Vladamir, 2, 207n86

Ralston, Samuel, 74
ratifying conventions. *See* state ratifying conventions
Reagan, Ronald, 171n6, 207n91; and lame duck effect, 143, 147–49, 159; and third term, 2
Reid, Whitelaw, 60
Republican Party; and Coolidge third term, 75–77, 142; and Grant third term, 60, 62–64, 142; and one-term presidency, 56–60; and Roosevelt (Theodore) third term, 71–72, 79, 140–42; and Whig model, 9, 11, 140–42
Revercomb, W. Chapman, 138
Rickenbacker, Edward V., 105–6
Riggs, Robert, 112, 114
Roberts, Steven, 147
Robsion, John M., 131, 137
Rolling Stone magazine, 124
Roosevelt, Anna, 111

Roosevelt, Franklin, 50; address to Congress of, 113–14; and attempted "purge" of anti-New Deal Democrats, 81, 90, 93, 157; campaign tour of, 112; and constitutional model, 99–100; Court-packing plan of, 93, 133, 135, 155; and crisis leadership, 10, 36, 39, 79–80, 83, 95–99, 135–38, 165; death of, 114; Democratic Party support of, 80–91, 94, 97, 104–8, 115–18; Farley opposition to, 85–86, 88–89, 167; fourth inauguration of, 112–13, 195n60; and fourth term, 10–11, 101–23, 166, 168–69, 198n114; health problems of, 10, 49, 102–14, 118–23, 193n40, 194n52, 194nn56–57, 196n77; and indispensable man theory, 92, 94–95, 106, 135–38; and lame duck effect, 80, 86, 95, 100, 149–50, 159; and plebiscitary model, 9, 99–100; and relationship with Truman, 10–11, 102–3, 117–18, 123, 196nn89–90, 197n93; Rutherford and, 197n109; and second-term setbacks, 157–58; and third term, 79–100, 191n95, 159; and third-term setbacks, 158; and Truman nomination, 10, 102–3, 115–17, 119; and Twenty-second Amendment, 125–30, 132–38, 142; and two-term tradition, 80–81, 91, 93, 96–97, 170; and Wallace nomination, 89; and Yalta Conference, 113–14
Roosevelt, James (Jimmy), 116
Roosevelt, Theodore, 50, 7, 186n1; on crisis leadership, 136; and plebiscitary model, 8–9, 38–39, 42, 68, 173n20; and Republican Party opposition, 71–72, 79, 140–42; and rotation, 44, 64, 67–72; Taft opposition to third term of,

44, 67, 69–72; and third term, 10, 42, 44, 62, 64, 66–73, 149, 170; world tour of, 68
Roper, Donald, 22
Rosenman, Samuel, 85, 114
Rossiter, Clinton, 125–26, 149
rotation, 6; Anti-Federalist support of, 32–33 and Articles of Confederation, 25; Clinton (William) on, 168; and Constitutional Convention, 29; and crisis leadership, 168–69; and Grant third term, 62–64; Jefferson on, 47–51; Mason on, 31; in Pennsylvania constitution, 21; and political party corruption, 62–64, 69–71, 162; and Roosevelt (Theodore), 44, 64, 67–72; and state ratifying conventions, 32, 63, 167–68; and two-term tradition 63; in Virginia constitution, 20
Rourke, Francis E., 145, 155–56
Rove, Karl, 152
royal governors. *See* colonial governors
Rutherford, Lucy Mercer; relationship with Roosevelt (Franklin), 197n109

Sabath, Adolph J., 127–29, 139
scandals. *See* political scandals
second-term blues, 155–161
Seventeenth Amendment, 130
Sherman, William Tecumseh, 76
Sigel, Roberta S., 125
six-year term reform, 6, 72, 144, 161–65; and public opinion, 161–62. *See also* one-term presidency
Skowronek, Stephen, 65, 151, 160, 167, 205–6n68
Smith, Al, 89
Smith, Lawrence H., 137
South Carolina constitution, 18–19; and veto power, 19
Spangler, Harrison, 104, 106

Springer Resolution, 61, 67
Springer, William, 61
Stalin, Joseph, 113
Stand, Bert, 187n24
state constitutions; and executive councils, 18–25, 174n23, 175n26; influence of colonial governorships, 17–18; and tenure limits, 18–25; and veto power, 19, 22–23; and weak executives, 18, 24. *See also constitutions of individual states*
state governors, 7; influence on presidency of, 15; and tenure limits, 4–6, 18–25, 128
state ratifying conventions; and rotation, 32, 63, 167–68
Stein, Charles, 77
stewardship theory of the presidency. *See* plebiscitary model of executive
Strout, Richard, 146, 160
Suckley, Margaret (Daisy), 109–11, 116, 121–22, 198n114
Sumner, Charles, 58

Taft, Robert, 87, 106
Taft, William Howard, 68, 186n1; and opposition to Roosevelt third term, 44, 67, 69–72; and two-term tradition, 70
Tammany Hall; on Roosevelt (Franklin) fourth term, 187n24
term limit proposals. *See* one-term presidency, rotation, six-year term reform, *and* Twenty-second Amendment
Thach, Charles, 18
Thomason, R. Ewing, 129
Thompson, Jacob, 55
Tilden, Samuel, 63
Trohan, Walter, 88
Truman, Harry, 112, 165; and indispensable man theory, 137–38; lobbies for Roosevelt (Franklin)

Anti-Federalists, 30–33, 36, 38, 94–95; and Articles of Confederation, 25–26; and executive restraint, 24; and Hamilton, 33–34; and Jefferson, 13–14, 39; and Locke, 13, 40, 173n4; and Pennsylvania constitution, 20–21; and presidency, 33–34; and Republican Party, 9, 11, 140–42; and Roosevelt (Franklin) fourth term, 10–11; and tenure restrictions, 36–42, 168; and Twenty-second Amendment, 9, 11, 140–42; view of the people of, 38–39; and Virginia constitution, 19–20; and Willkie, 94–95

Whig Party, 56; and one-term presidency, 10, 53–54; and veto power, 53

White, William Allen, 104, 166

Wicker, Tim, 147

Wiley, Alexander, 132, 138–39

Williamson, Hugh, 30

Willkie, Wendell; and critique of Roosevelt (Franklin) third term, 91–94; and indispensable man theory, 92, 94–95; nomination of, 87–88; and Whig model, 94–95

Wilson, James, 30; on popular election of president, 28

Wilson, Woodrow; 119, 142, 186n1; and one-term presidency, 65, 72–73; and plebiscitary model, 38, 71; and third term, 74, 150

Wood, Gordon, 20, 25–26

Yalta Conference, 113–14, 120

Young, Donald, 116, 119

Other Titles in the Joseph V. Hughes Jr. and Holly O. Hughes Series on the Presidency and Leadership:

continued next page